Modern Essays

RPH Editorial Board

and

H.S. BHATIA

M.A. (English)
Formerly Sr. Lecturer in English (Reader's Grade)
A.S. College, Khanna (Punjab)

RAMESH PUBLISHING HOUSE, New Delhi

Published by:

O.P. Gupta *for* Ramesh Publishing House

Admin. Office:

12-H, New Daryaganj Road, Opp. Officers' Mess,
New Delhi-110002 ☏ 23261567, 23275224, 23275124

E-mail: info@rameshpublishinghouse.com
Website: www.rameshpublishinghouse.com

Showroom:

● Balaji Market, Nai Sarak, Delhi-6 ☏ 23253720, 23282525
● 4457, Nai Sarak, Delhi-6, ☏ 23918938

32nd Edition: 1911

Book Code: R-468

HSN Code: 49011010

ISBN: 978-93-89480-22-1

Contents

(iv)

(v)

Modern Essays

Article 370 Scrapped

A Preview

- End of Jammu and Kashmir Special Status
- Two Union Territories
- Other Provisions
- Article 370
- Can Article 370 Be Revoked?
- Article 35A

Ending Jammu and Kashmir's special status in the Indian Union, the BJP government extended all provisions of the Constitution to the State in one go, downsized the State into two Union Territories and allowed all citizens to vote and buy property in the State. The Union Territory (UT) of Jammu and Kashmir will have a Lieutenant Governor and the maximum strength of its Assembly will be of 107 seats, which will be further enhanced to 114 after a delimitation exercise according to the act passed by Parliament on August 6, 2019. The current effective strength of the Jammu and Kashmir Assembly is 87, including four seats in the Ladakh region, which will now be a separate UT without a legislature. Twenty-four seats of the Assembly continue to remain vacant as they fall under Pakistan-occupied Kashmir (PoK).

The UT of Ladakh will have Kargil and Leh districts. There shall be a Council of Ministers in the successor UT of J&K consisting of not more than 10 per cent of the total number of members in the Legislative Assembly, with the Chief Minister as the head to aid and advise the Lieutenant Governor in the exercise of his functions in relation to matters with respect to which the Legislative Assembly has power to make laws. The new UT would have reservation in the Assembly seats. "The number of seats to be reserved for the Scheduled Castes and the Scheduled Tribes in the Legislative Assembly, having regard to the relevant provisions of the Constitution...," the act said.

> **WHAT IT MEANS**
> - J&K will now have no separate flag or Constitution. Tenure of assembly will be for 5 years, not 6; Indian Penal Code will replace Ranbir Penal Code.
> - People from other states are now eligible to purchase land and properties. Non-permanent residents can permanently settle in state.
> - Outsiders can now be employed in state govt and companies and be eligible for scholarships in state-run educational institutions.
> - RTI Act will be applicable in J&K.

As per the Act the Lieutenant Governor of the successor UT of J&K may nominate two members to the Legislative Assembly to give representation to women, if in his opinion women are not adequately represented in the Legislative Assembly. The Act said the Lok Sabha would have five seats from the UT of J&K, while Ladakh would have one seat. Jammu and Kashmir will be the largest union territory (UT) in the country in terms of area once it is carved out, following the Centre's move to bifurcate the state. Ladakh will be the second largest UT after it comes into force. With this, the total number of UTs in the country will go up to nine—J&K, Ladakh, Delhi, Puducherry, Daman and Diu, Dadra and Nagar Haveli, Chandigarh, Lakshadweep and Andaman and Nicobar Islands. Currently, only two UTs—Delhi and Puducherry—have Legislative Assemblies. With addition of J&K, the number will go up to three. UTs with Legislative Assemblies have Lt Governors.

Article 370: ● Article 370 grants special status to Jammu & Kashmir. ● It specifies that except for defence, foreign affairs, communications and ancillary matters (specified in the Instrument of Accession), the Indian Parliament needs the state government's concurrence for applying all other laws. ● This means that J&K's

residents live under a separate set of laws, including those related to citizenship, ownership of property, and fundamental rights. ● It also means that J&K has its own flag and constitution; Jammu & Kashmir has its own criminal code (Ranbir Penal Code).

> **FIRST TIME A STATE HAS BECOME A UT**
>
> There have been earlier instances of a category C state (as former chief commissioners' territories were classified at the time of adoption of the Constitution) becoming a UT. But this is the first time after the 1956 states' reorganisation that a full-fledged state has been relegated to a UT (or two).

Can Article 370 Be Revoked?: ● Clause 3 of Article 370 states that the President may, by public notification, declare that this article shall cease to be operative but only on the recommendation of the Constituent Assembly of the state. ● But many legal experts are of the view that abrogating the provision would put the accession of the state to India in jeopardy because the nature of the accession of J&K into the Union of India was totally different from the merger of all other states, whether small or big.

Article 35A: ● While Article 370 details ties J&K will have with India, Article 35A grants residents some special rights. ● 35A enables the J&K Assembly to define permanent residents and allows it to issue PRCs to people in J&K.

Chandrayaan-2

A Preview

- ❖ Mission Launch
- ❖ Objective
- ❖ Orbiter
- ❖ Pragyan Rover
- ❖ Lander Deviated from its Path
- ❖ Design
- ❖ Vikram Lander

Chandrayaan-2 is the second lunar exploration mission developed by the Indian Space Research Organisation (ISRO), after Chandrayaan-1. It consists of a lunar orbiter, the Vikram lander, and the Pragyan lunar rover, all of which were developed in India. The main scientific objective is to map the location and abundance of lunar water via Pragyan, and ongoing analysis from the orbiter circling at a lunar polar orbit of 100 × 100 km.

The mission was launched on its course to the Moon from the second launch pad at Satish Dhawan Space Centre on 22 July 2019 at 2.43 PM IST by a Geosynchronous Satellite Launch Vehicle Mark III (GSLV Mk III). The craft reached the Moon's orbit on 20 August 2019 and began orbital positioning manoeuvres for the landing of the Vikram lander. Vikram and the rover were scheduled to land on the near side of the Moon, in the south polar region at a latitude of about 70° south at approximately 1:50 am on 7 September 2019 and conduct scientific experiments for one lunar day.

However, the lander deviated from its intended trajectory starting at 2.1 kilometres (1.3 mi) altitude, and had lost communication when touchdown confirmation was expected. Initial reports suggesting a crash have been confirmed by ISRO chairman K. Sivan, stating that the lander location had been found, and "it must have been a hard landing".

As of 8 September 2019, on-going efforts are being made by ISRO in hopes of restoring communications with Vikram. Communication attempts will likely cease on 21 September 2019, fourteen days after Vikram's landing attempt. The orbiter, part of the mission with eight scientific instruments, remains operational and is expected to continue its seven-year mission to study the Moon.

Objectives

The primary objectives of the Chandrayaan-2 lander were to demonstrate the ability to soft-land on the lunar surface and operate a robotic rover on the surface. Scientific goals include orbital studies of lunar topography, mineralogy, elemental abundance, the lunar exosphere, and signatures of hydroxyl and water ice. The orbiter will map the lunar surface and help to prepare 3D maps of it. The onboard radar will also map the surface while studying the water ice in the south polar region and thickness of the lunar regolith on the surface.

Design

The mission was launched on a Geosynchronous Satellite Launch Vehicle Mark III (GSLV Mk III) with an approximate lift-off mass of 3,850 kg (8,490 lb) from Satish Dhawan Space Centre on Sriharikota Island. As of June 2019, the mission has an allocated cost of ₹ 978 crore which includes ₹ 603 crore for space segment and ₹ 375 crore as launch costs on GSLV Mk III. Chandrayaan-2 stack was initially put in an Earth parking orbit of 170 km perigee and 40,400 km apogee by the launch vehicle.

Orbiter: As of September 2019, the Chandrayaan-2 orbiter is orbiting the Moon on a polar orbit at an altitude of 100 km (62 mi). The orbiter carries eight scientific instruments; two of them are improved versions of those flown on Chandrayaan-1. The approximate launch mass was 2,379 kg (5,245 lb). The Orbiter High Resolution Camera (OHRC) will conduct high-resolution observations of the landing site prior to separation of the lander from the orbiter. The orbiter's structure was manufactured by Hindustan Aeronautics Limited and delivered to ISRO Satellite Centre on 22 June 2015.

Vikram Lander: The mission's lander is called Vikram, named after Vikram Sarabhai (1919–1971), who is widely regarded as the founder of the Indian space programme.

The Vikram lander detached from the orbiter and descended to a low lunar orbit of 30 km × 100 km (19 mi × 62 mi) using its 800 N (180 lbf) liquid main engines. It then performed a comprehensive check of all its on-board systems before attempting a soft landing that would have deployed the rover, and perform scientific activities for approximately 14 Earth days. Vikram spacecraft apparently crash-landed. The lander's location has been spotted on the surface via thermal imaging, but its condition is unknown. The approximate combined mass of the lander and rover is 1,471 kg (3,243 lb).

Pragyan Rover: The mission's rover is called Pragyan. The rover's mass was about 27 kg (60 lb) and would operate on solar power. The rover would move on 6 wheels traversing 500 meters on the lunar surface at the rate of 1 cm per second, performing on-site chemical analysis and sending the data to the lander, which would relay it to the Mission Control on the Earth.

Gaganyaan Mission

A Preview

- ❖ Human Spaceflight
- ❖ Design
- ❖ Landing in Arabian Sea
- ❖ Developments
- ❖ Will be Placed in Low Earth Orbit

Gaganyaan or Sky Vehicle, an orbital spacecraft with crew members, is one giant step in the development of the Indian Human Spaceflight Programme. Gaganyaan is being designed to carry three people which will be equipped with rendezvous and docking capability. In its maiden crewed mission, Indian Space Research Organisation (ISRO) has built an autonomous 3.7-tonne spacecraft which is going to orbit the Earth at 400 km altitude for up to seven days with a three-person crew on board. India has planned to launch this crewed spacecraft on ISRO's GSLV Mk III in December 2021. However, Gaganyaan, which is being manufactured by Hindustan Aeronautics Limited (HAL), had its first un-crewed experimental flight on 18 December 2014. The design of the crew module has been completed in May 2019.

However, ISRO continued to develop the Gaganyaan orbital vehicle on the tests performed with their scaled 550 kg Space Capsule Recovery Experiment (SRE), which was launched and recovered in January 2007. After a gap of ten years, the latest effort for the Indian Human Spaceflight Programme took a new life in 2017. It was Prime Minister Narendra Modi who announced in his 15 August 2018 speech that Gaganyaan project will take shape and the latest design will have a crew of three. There was an estimate that a crewed spacecraft would require about ₹ 124 billion over a period of seven years, including the ₹ 50 billion for the initial work. Finally in December 2018, the government approved further ₹ 100 billion for a 7-days crewed flight of 3 astronauts to take place by 2021.

Gaganyaan is being designed and built indigenously which will carry a 3-member crew to orbit and safely return to the Earth after the mission duration of few orbits and up to seven days. Its service module is powered by two liquid propellant engines. The crew module is mated to the service module, and together they are called the orbital module. Based on the payload capability of the GSLV-III booster, the service module would have a mass of about 3 tonnes. The space capsule is built keeping in mind the life support and environmental control systems. There will be technological equipment and system equipped with emergency mission abort and emergency escape that can be done at the first stage or second stage of the rocket burn.

The Gaganyaan or India's human spaceflight will take 16 minutes to reach the orbit where it will stay for five to seven days. The spacecraft will be placed in a low earth orbit of 300-400 km. ISRO claimed that the Gaganyaan crew model and orange space suits at the Bengaluru Space Expo's 6th edition. The space suits were developed at Vikram Sarabhai Space Centre, Thiruvananthapuram. With the ability to hold one oxygen cylinder, the suit will allow the astronaut to breathe in space for 60 minutes. The capsule will rotate around the Earth every 90 minutes, and astronauts will be able to witness sunrise and sunset. The three astronauts will be able to see India from space every 24 hours, while they conduct experiments on micro-gravity. For its return, the capsule will take 36 hours, and will land in the Arabian Sea near the Gujarat coast.

National Register of Citizens (NRC)

A Preview

- ❖ What is NRC
- ❖ Large Scale Migration
- ❖ Supreme Court Verdict
- ❖ Eligibility for NRC

The National Register of Citizens (NRC) is a register list which contains names of all genuine Indian citizens. The register was first prepared after the 1951 Census of India. Now the NRC is being updated in Assam to include the names of those persons (or their descendants) who appear in the NRC, 1951 or in any of the Electoral Roll up to the midnight of 24 March 1971 or in any one of the other admissible documents issued up to midnight of 24 March 1971, which would prove their presence in Assam or in any part of India on or before 24 March 1971.

In the year 2013, the current update process was started when the Supreme Court of India passed orders for its updation. The entire NRC project is headed by the State Coordinator of National Registration, Assam under the strict monitoring of Supreme Court of India. The main objective of NRC update is to identify Indian citizens from amongst all the residents of Assam to determine their identification of legal citizens or illegal migrants in the state, who entered Indian territories after the midnight of 24 March 1971. It also aimed at determining the citizenship of the applicants who have applied for inclusion of their names in the updated NRC.

Between 1948 and 1971, there were large scale migrations from Bangladesh (then East Pakistan) to Assam. Given this continuing influx of illegal migrants from Bangladesh into Assam, student leaders of Assam in 1979 came out in fierce protest demanding detention, disenfranchisement and deportation of illegal immigrants from Assam. The historic movement which came to be known as Assam Agitation or Assam Movement was initiated by All Assam Students' Union (AASU) and All Assam Gana Sangram Parishad (AAGSP) and lasted a span of 6 years. The movement, however, culminated in the signing of the landmark Memorandum of Settlement (MoS) - the Assam Accord. It was signed by the All Assam Students' Union (AASU), Central and State Governments on 15 August 1985, at the behest of then Prime Minister Rajiv Gandhi in New Delhi.

Under the NRC, person who are eligible for inclusion are:

- Persons whose names appear in NRC, 1951.
- Persons whose names appear in any of the Electoral Rolls up to 24 March (midnight), 1971.
- Descendants of the above persons.
- Persons who came to Assam on or after 1 January 1966 but before 25 March 1971 and registered themselves in accordance with the rules made by the Central Government.
- People who are original inhabitants of Assam and their children and descendants who are citizens of India provided their citizenship is ascertained by authority.
- Inclusion of names as voters who can apply to be updated in NRC. However, their names will be finally included only when the appropriate Foreigner Tribunal declares them as non-foreigners.
- Persons who can provide any one of the documents issued up to midnight of 24 March 1971 as mentioned in the list of documents admissible for citizenship.
- All Indian Citizens including their children and descendants who have moved to Assam post 24 March 1971 would be eligible for inclusion in the updated NRC on adducing satisfactory proof of residence in any part of the country (outside Assam) as on 24 March 1971.

A Promise of $5 Trillion Economy

A Preview

- ❖ PM's Announcement
- ❖ Lesson from Asian Tigers
- ❖ Population Challenges
- ❖ The Primary Focus
- ❖ Unequal Progress

In July 2019, the Prime Minister Narendra Modi, while addressing chief ministers, announced that he dreamed India to be a $5 trillion economy by 2024, the year when he would once again seek faces re-election. The very project seems highly ambitious as the Prime Minister himself admitted that the task would be challenging but achievable. Getting India's GDP from $2.8 trillion economy to $5 trillion in five years is something the country would want to achieve. This mean reaching $5 trillion mark by 2024 the economy would have to grow at over 12 per cent a year, which is almost double since in the first quarter of 2019 Indian economy grew at slower than 6 per cent.

The primary focus is: India must aspire to achieve a sustained double-digit growth without which the country would not hope to employ almost one million young people who join its workforce every month. In order for India to emerge as $5 trillion economy, the country must find ways to speed up economic growth having an upper-middle-income economy with a prosperous and thriving middle class.

The country here needs to learn from thriving economies particularly the Asian tigers and China; while the prerequisites for the kind of growth that could transform the fortunes of China and of the Asian tigers (Hong Kong, Singapore, South Korea and Taiwan) are still well below the expected results. Though energy supply and infrastructure are far better at the moment to build a world-class manufacturing sector, supportive markets for land and labour simply are two areas where India has to work very hard. On the human resources front, successive governments in the past failed to educate young Indians and provide them with the vocational skills they need to succeed in a modern economy. Modi government faces the same conundrum, and how will he address the issue is going to affect the outcome of the $5 trillion economy outcomes.

First of all we need not be pessimistic. What is required is the very change in 'business-as-usual; perception or the pace with which Indian economy has been growing for the last ten years. More so, India must adopt standard much higher which stands between 5 per cent to 8 per cent on an average, and if India continues to grow at 6 per cent a year, our economy will hit $5 trillion in output in ten years or by 2029, which is five years more than what the Prime Minister has declared.

No doubt, the Indian economy in 2029 will be much different of what it is now if it is still growing at 6 per cent there will be vastly unequal results not just in terms of personal income and wealth, but development scenarios between regions. Here, the Prime Minister's ambitious plan seems futuristic since he knows the current pace, even if it continues, would fail to offer what India needs in the year 2024 or 2029. We can be sure that unequal progress will be a major issue: some parts of India, for example, the southern peninsula, the national capital of Delhi, and the coastal regions of Gujarat and Maharashtra are surely going to achieve relatively well-off, middle-income status, other regions like Madhya Pradesh, Bihar, Rajasthan and North East states may lag behind. In addition, the vast hinterland of India where population growth is highest will remain poor and under-developed. Hence, the focus of the current government must be to generate economic upheaval in these regions so that a collective growth would see India through to a formidable economy. Attitudes and priorities need comprehensive planning and implementation in addition to the genuine efforts to achieve targeted results.

Reservation for EWS

A Preview

- ❖ Aims of Reservation
- ❖ Reservation for EWS
- ❖ Reservation After Independence
- ❖ Eligibility Criteria

Reservation policy in India has been aimed at uplifting the socio-economic status of people from backward class and those with poor economic conditions. Hence, reservation for Schedule Caste (SC) and Schedule Tribe (ST), and later for Other Backward Caste (OBC) was promulgated. It was Dr. B R Ambedkar who, while framing the Constitution, framed the reservation policy of India inserting many Articles in the Indian Constitution. For example, Article 15, which grants reservation to these two sections of people; the Article 15 was amended by the Constitution (Amendment) Act, 1951 under which the state is empowered to make provisions for the advancement of any socially and educationally backward classes of citizens or for the SCs and STs.

Since Independence these categories like SCs, STs and OBCs enjoyed the fruit of reservation; however, a section of upper caste people who remained unemployed or slipped to the bottom of socio-economic rung which was felt by the Modi government. The Government of India under the Prime Minister Narendra Modi introduced 10 per cent reservation quota for the Economically Weaker Section (EWS) among General Category candidates in government jobs and educational institutions. The Union Government of India tabled the Constitution (One Hundred and Twenty-Fourth Amendment) Bill, 2019 which provided 10 per cent additional quota for the EWS students amongst the erstwhile unreserved category or General category students.

The eligibility to get the EWS certificate is not only purely based on annual family income but also based on the held property. The income limit has been set by the central government for admission to central government-owned colleges and jobs offered by the central government. A state government is authorized to extend the income limit further for candidates seeking reservation under EWS category in the state-owned colleges and state government's jobs.

In India, there are two kinds of seats—merit seats and reserved seats. Merit seats are open to all while reserved seats are quotas provided to separate categories with a view to uplift them. There are different kinds of reservations quotas in India—OBC quota, SC quota, ST quota etc. EWS quota is the latest reservation quota introduced. Persons who are not covered under the scheme of reservation for SCs, STs, and OBCs and whose family has a gross annual income below ₹ 8 lakh are only identified as EWSs for benefit of reservation.

Who can take the benefit from EWS reservations:
- Those having annual household income below ₹ 8 lakh.
- Those having agriculture land below 5 acres.
- They should not have a flat of 1,000 square feet or more.
- They should not possess land of 100 sq yards in notified municipality areas and 200 yards in non-notified areas.

Annual household include the income of all family members and will cover all sources like salary, agriculture, business etc.

Statue of Unity

A Preview

- ❖ Inauguration
- ❖ Statue of Unity Movement
- ❖ A Tribute to Patel
- ❖ Its Features

Paying tributes to great leaders of our nation, government, from time to time, build statues to keep the memory live in the heart of the people. On 31 October 2018, the 143rd anniversary of Sardar Vallabhbhai Patel, the Prime Minister Narendra Modi inaugurated the Statue of Unity and dedicated it to the nation. It was the Prime Minister (then Gujarat Chief Minister) who had announced the project to commemorate Sardar Vallabhbhai Patel in 2010. At that time, the project was named Gujarat's tribute to the nation. Designed by Indian sculptor Ram V Sutar and with a budget of ₹ 2,989 crore, the construction of the Statue of Unity began on 31 October 2014 by Larsen & Toubro.

The Statue of Unity is a colossal statue of Sardar Vallabhbhai Patel, the first Home Minister of independent India and the iron man who was born in 1875 and died in 1950. One of the stalwarts of India's struggle for freedom, a close aide of Mahatma Gandhi and the man who unified 552 princely states into India after independence, Sardar Patel's contribution to the nation building is unprecedented. With 182 metres height, the Statue of Unity is the world's tallest statue, which is located on a river island facing the Sardar Sarovar Dam on river Narmada, about 100 kilometres southeast of Vadodara. The statue depicts Sardar Patel as one of the most prominent leaders of the Indian independence movement, the first Deputy Prime Minister of India, and responsible for the integration of hundreds of princely states into the modern Republic of India.

Before the construction work began, an awareness drive named the Statue of Unity Movement was started to support the construction of the statue. In support of the project by 2016, a total of 135 metric tonnes of scrap iron had been collected and about 109 tonnes of it was used to make the foundation of the statue after processing. The Statue of Unity is a replica of Patel's statue in the Ahmedabad International Airport. The design is explained as "the expression, posture and pose justify the dignity, confidence, iron will as well as kindness that his persona exudes. The head is up, a shawl flung from shoulders and hands are on the side as if he is set to walk".

The Statue of Unity, as it appears, depicts Patel's dhoti-clad legs and the use of sandals for footwear, the serious and contemplating face. It is built to withstand winds of up to 180 kilometres per hour and earthquakes measuring 6.5 on the Richter scale which are at a depth of 10 km and within a radius of 12 km of the statue. This is aided by the use of two 250-tonne tuned mass dampers which ensure maximum stability. The total height of the Statue of Unity is 240 m (790 ft), with a base of 58 m (190 ft) and the actual statue of 182 m (597 ft). The height of 182 m was specifically chosen to match the number of seats in the Gujarat Legislative Assembly.

E-commerce

A Preview

- ❖ What is E-commerce
- ❖ Disadvantages
- ❖ Importance
- ❖ Impact

E-Commerce, also known as e-Business, or electronic business, is simply the sale and purchase of services and goods over an electronic medium, like the Internet. It also involves electronically transferring data and funds between two or more parties. Simply put, it is online shopping as we commonly know it.

e-Commerce started way back in the 1960s when organizations began to use Electronic Data Interchange (EDI) to transfer documents of their business back and forth. The 1990s saw the emergence of online shopping businesses, which is quite a phenomenon today. It has become so convenient and easy, that anyone can shop for anything right from a living room, with just a few clicks. This has evolved more with the emergence of smartphones, where now, you can shop from anywhere and anytime, with a wireless device connected to the Internet. Now you can search for almost any product or service online, without having to go anywhere physically.

Importance of e-Commerce

With the use of mobile devices and laptops increasing every day, there are a lot of advantages of e-commerce like:

- Global market reach
- A global choice for consumers
- Short product/service distribution chain
- Lesser costs and pricing.

Disadvantages of e-Commerce

And there are some risks too with e-commerce:

- Fraud and online insecurity
- Data privacy issues
- No testing or checking of services or goods
- Dependence on electronic technologies.

Impact

- **Impact on Markets and Retailers:** e-commerce markets are growing at noticeable rates. The online market is expected to grow by 56% in 2015-2020. Traditional markets are only expected 2% growth during the same time. Brick and mortar retailers are struggling because of online retailer's ability to offer lower prices and higher efficiency. Many larger retailers are able to maintain a presence both offline and online by linking physical and online offerings.

- **Impact on Geographical Barriers:** e-commerce allows customers to overcome geographical barriers and allows them to purchase products anytime and from anywhere. Online and traditional markets have different strategies for conducting business. Traditional retailers offer fewer assortment of products because of shelf space where, online retailers often hold no inventory but send customer orders directly to the manufacture. The pricing strategies are also different for traditional and online retailers. Traditional retailers base their prices on store traffic and the cost to keep inventory. Online retailers base prices on the speed of delivery.

- **Impact on Supply Chain Management:** For a long time, companies had been troubled by the gap between the benefits which supply chain technology has and the solutions to deliver those benefits. However, the emergence of e-commerce has provided a more practical and effective way of delivering the benefits of the new supply chain technologies.

- **Impact on Employment:** e-commerce helps to create new job opportunities due to information related services, software app and digital products. It also causes job losses. The areas with the greatest predicted job-loss are retail, postal, and travel agencies. The development of e-commerce will create jobs that require highly skilled workers to manage large amounts of information, customer demands, and production processes. In contrast, people with poor technical skills cannot enjoy the wages welfare. On the other hand, because e-commerce requires sufficient stocks that could be delivered to customers in time, the warehouse becomes an important element. Warehouse needs more staff to manage, supervise and organize, thus the condition of warehouse environment will be concerned by employees.

- **Impact on Customers:** e-commerce brings convenience for customers as they do not have to leave home and only need to browse website online, especially for buying the products which are not sold in nearby shops. It could help customers buy wider range of products and save customers' time. Consumers also gain power through online shopping. They are able to research products and compare prices among retailers. Also, online shopping often provides sales promotion or discounts code, thus it is more price effective for customers. Moreover, e-commerce provides products' detailed information; even the in-store staff cannot offer such detailed explanation. Customers can also review and track the order history online.

Narendra Modi : The Mighty PM

A Preview

- ❖ Full Name
- ❖ Parents & Livelihood
- ❖ Joining RSS
- ❖ Higher Education
- ❖ Rise in Politics
- ❖ Becoming Indian PM
- ❖ Birth and Childhood
- ❖ Marriage & Education
- ❖ Emergency Time Activities
- ❖ Joining Politics
- ❖ Becoming Gujarat CM
- ❖ Award and Honours

Narendra Damodardas Modi was born on September 17, 1950 in Vadnagar, a small village in Mehsana district of Gujarat. He was third of the six children of Damodardas and Hiraba Modi. His father was a tea stall owner and quite often Narendra would accompany his father to work. However, at 17, he made the exceptional decision of leaving home and travelling the country. His family was shocked by the decision, but let him go. He travelled to the Himalayas, to West Bengal and even the north-east.

Modi was married young but the marriage remained unconsummated. He kept the wedding a secret as he imbibed the spirit of selflessness, social responsibility, dedication and nationalism. In 1972, Modi became an RSS pracharak, dedicating his entire life to the organisation and service. He worked hard, waking up at 5 a.m. and accomplishing difficult tasks late into the night. In 1973, he also got the opportunity to meet senior Jan Sangh members.

Modi was at the core of the anti-emergency movement. He became the general secretary of the Gujarat Lok Sangharsh Samiti and his primary role was to coordinate between activists in the state. It is said that to avoid arrests and the Indira government's ire, Modi began disguising himself—dressed as a Sikh one day, an elderly man another day.

After Emergency, the Indira Gandhi government was routed in the polls and the new Janata Party government ascended to power. At the same time, Modi was promoted to sambhaag pracharak, the equivalent of a regional organiser, and soon, he began travelling far and wide, spreading the RSS word.

Even as he embraced politics, Modi graduated in political science from Delhi University and went on to do his Masters from Gujarat University. Modi won the admiration of seniors for his hard work and efficiency. In 1987-88, he was deputed to the BJP's Gujarat unit as organizing secretary, marking his formal launch in mainstream politics.

Recognised as a master strategist, Modi was trusted with the municipal elections in Ahmedabad. Taking on the challenge head-on, Modi began touring the entire state, campaigning and spreading the BJP's word and worked tirelessly to ensure a victory. His labour bore fruit when the party won the elections.

It was in the late 1990s Modi started to emerge as a key player when he became the general secretary of the party in Delhi. It was then that he was handed over the responsibility of carrying out national yatras. He was tasked with ensuring that L K Advani's Somnath to Ayodhya yatra went off without any hitch. The task was not easy, but Modi carried it off to perfection.

In 2001, Modi received his huge break as chief minister of Gujarat. Successful with his development model, he became the Chief Minister of Gujarat for four successive terms. Finally, he received a huge majority in Lok Sabha elections and sworn in as the 15th Prime Minister of India on May 26, 2014.

After becoming the Prime Minister, Modi has embarked on his journey for the all-round development of India. He has rebuilt friendly relations with almost all the countries of the world. He has started many ambitious programmes for the development of India, such as, Prime Minister Jan Dhan Yojana, Shramev Jayate, Make in India, Digital India and Swachch Bharat Mission. Demonetisation of ₹ 500 and ₹ 1000 notes is his master stroke to curb the black money and corruption in India.

Narendra Modi on February 22, 2019 received the prestigious Seoul Peace Prize 2018 for his contribution to international cooperation and fostering global economic growth. In October 2018, he received UN's highest environmental award, the Champions of the Earth. He also received the Order of St. Andrew, the highest civilian honour of Russia on April 12, 2019.

Modi effectively tamed Pakistan by giving a befitting reply for the Pulwama attack by conducting surgical strikes on terror launchpads in POK. He contested the 2019 general election on the theme of 'Nationalism' and received a massive mandate for his second innings as the Prime Minister of India.

President Ram Nath Kovind

A Preview

- ❖ Introduction
- ❖ Early Life and Education
- ❖ Becoming Rajya Sabha MP
- ❖ Becoming the President of India

- ❖ Birth & Family
- ❖ Higher Education & Career
- ❖ Becoming Bihar Governor

Ram Nath Kovind is the 14th President of India. Previously he had served as the Governor of Bihar from 2015 to 2017 and was a Member of Parliament, Rajya Sabha from 1994 to 2006.

Kovind was born on 1 October 1945 in Paraunkh village in the Kanpur Dehat district, Uttar Pradesh in a Koli family. His father Maikulal ran a small shop. He was the youngest of five brothers and two sisters. He was born in a mud hut. He was only five when his mother died of burns when their thatched dwelling caught fire.

After his elementary school education, he had to walk each day to Kanpur village, 8 km away, to attend junior school. After graduating in law from DAV College, Kanpur, Kovind went to Delhi to prepare for the civil services examination. He passed this exam, but he did not join and started practising law.

Kovind enrolled as an advocate in 1971 with the bar council of Delhi. He was Central Government Advocate in the Delhi High Court from year 1977 to year 1979. Between 1977 & 1978, he also served as the personal assistant of Prime Minister of India, Morarji Desai.

He was elected and became a Rajya Sabha MP from the state of Uttar Pradesh in April 1994. He served a total of twelve years, two consecutive terms, until March 2006. He has also represented

India at the UN and addressed the United Nations General Assembly in October 2002.

On 8 August 2015, the then President of India appointed Kovind as Governor of Bihar. Ram Nath Kovind took the oath as the 14th President of India on 25 July 2017.

The Cricket Champ : Virat Kohli

A Preview

- ❖ Introduction
- ❖ Coming into Spotlight
- ❖ ODI Debut
- ❖ Birth & Family
- ❖ Becoming Under-19 Skipper
- ❖ Achievements & Awards

Virat Kohli is an Indian International cricketer. He is the captain of the Indian cricket team in all three formats.

Virat Kohli was born on 5 November, 1988 in Delhi to Prem and Saroj Kohli. Virat attended Vishal Bharti and Savier Convent School. His father worked as a lawyer and untimely died in December 2006. He has an elder brother and a sister.

Virat first came into the spotlight when he played for Delhi in a Ranji trophy match against Karnataka on the day of his father's death. His team mates needed him at a crucial moment when he was much more needed at home. He preferred to do his duty and scored 90 runs. That was an act of great commitment to the team and his innings turned out to be crucial.

Virat Kohli shot into prominence as the Under-19 skipper, who led India to victory at the 2008 World Cup held in Malaysia. That accolade gained him instant recognition and made him an overnight teen sensation. Soon he made his ODI debut for India in Sri Lanka in August 2008. He played two important knocks - 37 in the second ODI and 54 in the fourth - both of which resulted in India winning, thereby enabling them to win the series as well.

Virat has a mature head on his rather young shoulders. Known to be quite an aggressive batsman, he has a sound technique, which makes him judge the length of the ball earlier than most others. He is equally adept against pace and spin, and never looks ungainly at the crease. With a penchant for using his feet against the spinners, he is known to be quite destructive when in the mood. Virat has had high expectations placed on him from the moment he picked up a bat and has shown signs that he is well on the way to fulfilling those predictions.

Virat is one of the finest fielders in an Indian side which needs more men like him to make up for the other abysmal ones. Quick on his feet and also safe with his catching, he can practically field anywhere in the field.

Virat has been the recipient of many awards such as the Sir Garfield Sobers Trophy (ICC Cricketer of the Year) in 2017 and 2018; ICC Test Player of the Year 2018; ICC ODI Player of the Year in 2012, 2017 and 2018 and Wisden Leading Cricketer in the World in 2016, 2017. He was given the Arjuna Award in 2013, the Padma Shri under the sports category in 2017 and the Rajiv Gandhi Khel Ratna, the highest sporting honour in India, in 2018. He is ranked as one of the world's most famous athletes by ESPN and one of the most valuable athlete brands by Forbes. In 2018, Time magazine named Kohli one of the 100 most influential people in the world.

Wing Commander Abhinandan Varthaman

A Preview

- ❖ Introduction
- ❖ Dogfight & Capture
- ❖ Return to India
- ❖ Education & Training
- ❖ Interrogation & Release
- ❖ Veer Chakra

Abhinandan Varthaman is a wing-commander in the Indian Air Force. In the 2019 India-Pakistan standoff, he was held for 60 hours under captivity in Pakistan after his aircraft was shot down in an aerial dogfight.

Abhinandan was born on 21 June 1983. Abhinandan's family hails from Thirupanamoor, a village about 19 km from Kanchipuram. His father, Simhakutty Varthaman, retired as an Air Marshal in the Indian Air Force while his mother Shobha is a doctor by profession.

Abhinandan did his early schooling from Sainik Welfare School, Amatavatinagar in Chennai. He was an enthusiastic reader and an outstanding speaker. He later graduated from the National Defence Academy, and was commissioned into the combat (fighter) stream of the Indian Air Force as a flying officer on 19 June 2004. He was trained at the IAF centres in Bathinda and Halwara. He was promoted to flight lieutenant on 19 June 2006, and to squadron leader on 8 July 2010. He was a Su-30 MKI fighter pilot before being assigned to the MiG-21 Bison squadron.

Abhinandan is married to a retired IAF Squadron leader Tanvi Marwah and lives in Chennai. He has 2 children.

On 27 February 2019, Abhinandan was flying a MiG-21 as a part of a sortie that was scrambled to intercept an intrusion by Pakistan aircraft into Jammu and Kashmir. In the dogfight that ensued, he crossed into Pakistan territory where he was struck by a missile. Abhinandan ejected and descended safely in the village of Horran in Pakistan administered Kashmir, approximately 7 km from the Line of Control.

Abhinandan could be identified as an Indian pilot by the Indian flag on his parachute. Upon landing, he asked the villagers if he was in India, to which a young boy replied in the affirmative. Abhinandan followed up with pro-India slogans and asked for drinking water while informing the locals of a back injury. The locals responded with pro-Pakistan slogans, after which he began to run while firing warning shots. He ran for approximately 500 metres, to a small pond, where he attempted to sink and swallow some of his documents. Subsequently, he was captured and manhandled by the villagers before being rescued by the Pakistan Army.

Later that day, the Indian Ministry of External Affairs confirmed that an Indian pilot was missing in action after a MiG-21 Bison fighter plane was lost while engaging with Pakistani jets. A statement released by the IAF also said that prior to his MiG's crashing, he had managed to shoot down a PAF Lockheed Martin F-16.

Videos and images released by Pakistani authorities showed Abhinandan being rescued from a violent mob by Pakistani soldiers, being interrogated while tied and blindfolded with a bloody face. Other videos showed him receiving first aid and being further interrogated over tea. However, he did not divulge any details to Pakistani authorities other than his name, his rank and that he was a Hindu.

After PM Narendra Modi's stern warning to Pakistan to immediately return Abhinandan to India, on February 28, 2019, Prime Minister of Pakistan Imran Khan announced at a joint sitting of the Parliament of Pakistan that the government had decided to release Abhinandan the next day as a "gesture of peace".

Abhinandan crossed the India-Pakistan border at Wagha on March 1, 2019 amid cheers by thousands of Indians. Indian Prime Minister Narendra Modi welcomed the release of Abhinandan at a political rally, asserting that the nation was proud of him.

The Indian Government has awarded Veer Chakra to Wing-commander Abhinandan for his gallantry service.

Pradhan Mantri Jan Arogya Yojana (PMJAY)

A Preview

- ❖ Health Sector in India
- ❖ Ayushman Bharat
- ❖ Wide Coverage
- ❖ Challenges Before Health Care Sector
- ❖ Benefits of PMJAY
- ❖ Health System

India has achieved significant public health gains and improvements in health care access and quality over the last three decades. The health sector is amongst the largest and fasting growing sectors, expected to reach US$ 280 billion by 2020.

At the same time, India's health sector faces immense challenges. It continues to be characterized by high out-of-pocket expenditure, low financial protection, low health insurance coverage amongst both rural and urban population.

It is a matter of grave concern that we incur a high out-of-pocket expenditure on account of health and medical costs. 62.58% of our population has to pay for their own health and hospitalization expenses and are not covered through any form of health protection. Besides using their income and savings, people borrow money or sell their assets to meet their healthcare needs, thereby pushing 4.6% of the population below the poverty line. The Government of India is committed to ensuring that its population has universal access to good quality health care services without anyone having to face financial hardship as a consequence.

Under the ambit of Ayushman Bharat, a Pradhan Mantri Jan Arogya Yojana (PM-JAY) to reduce the financial burden on poor and vulnerable groups arising out of catastrophic hospital episodes and ensure their access to quality health services was conceived. PM-JAY seeks to accelerate India's progress towards achievement of Universal Health Coverage (UHC) and Sustainable Development Goal-3 (SDG3).

Pradhan Mantri Jan Arogya Yojana (PM-JAY) will provide financial protection (Swasthya Suraksha) to 10.74 crore poor, deprived rural families and identified occupational categories of urban workers' families as per the latest Socio-Economic Caste Census (SECC) data (approx. 50 crore beneficiaries). It will offer a benefit cover of ₹ 5,00,000 per family per year (on a family floater basis).

PM-JAY will cover medical and hospitalization expenses for almost all secondary care and most of tertiary care procedures. PM-JAY has defined 1,350 medical packages covering surgery, medical and day care treatments including medicines, diagnostics and transport.

To ensure that nobody is left out (especially girl child, women, children and elderly), there will be no cap on family size and age in the Mission. The scheme will be cashless & paperless at public hospitals and empanelled private hospitals. The beneficiaries will not be required to pay any charges for the hospitalization expenses.

The benefit also includes pre and post-hospitalization expenses. The scheme is an entitlement based, the beneficiary is decided on the basis of family being figured in SECC database. When fully implemented, the PM-JAY will become the world's largest government funded health protection mission.

Health System

- ✦ Help India progressively achieve Universal Health Coverage (UHC) and Sustainable Development Goals (SDG).
- ✦ Ensure improved access and affordability, of quality secondary and tertiary care services through a combination of public hospitals and well measured strategic purchasing of services in health care deficit areas, from private care providers, especially the not-for-profit providers.
- ✦ Significantly reduce out of pocket expenditure for hospitalization. Mitigate financial risk arising out of catastrophic health episodes and consequent impoverishment for poor and vulnerable families.

♦ Acting as a steward, align the growth of private sector with public health goals.

♦ Enhanced use of evidence based health care and cost control for improved health outcomes.

5G Technology

A Preview

- ❖ Introduction
- ❖ Technology
- ❖ Salient Features
- ❖ Advance Features

5G is the Fifth Generation technology. It has many advanced features potential enough to solve many of the problems of our mundane life. It is beneficial for the government, as it can make the governance easier; for the students, as it can make available the advanced courses, classes, and materials online; it is easier for the common people as well, as it can facilitate them the internet everywhere.

Radio technologies have evidenced a rapid and multidirectional evolution with the launch of the analogue cellular systems in 1980s. Thereafter, digital wireless communication systems are consistently on a mission to fulfil the growing need of human beings (1G, ...4G, or now 5G).

5th Generation Mobile Network or simply 5G is the forthcoming revolution of mobile technology. The features and its usability are much beyond the expectation of a normal human being. With its ultra-high speed, it is potential enough to change the meaning of a cell phone usability.

With a huge array of innovative features, now your smart phone would be more parallel to the laptop. You can use broadband internet connection; other significant features that fascinate people are more gaming options, wider multimedia options, connectivity everywhere, zero latency, faster response time, and high quality sound and HD video can be transferred on other cell phone without compromising with the quality of audio and video.

If we look back, we will find that every next decade, one generation is advancing in the field of mobile technology. Starting from the First Generation (1G) in 1980s, Second Generation (2G) in 1990s, Third Generation (3G) in 2000s, Fourth Generation (4G) in 2010s, and now Fifth Generation (5G), we are advancing towards more and more sophisticated and smarter technology.

The 5G technology is expected to provide a new (much wider than the previous one) frequency bands along with the wider spectral bandwidth per frequency channel. As of now, the predecessors (generations) mobile technologies have evidenced substantial increase in peak bit rate. Then—how is 5G different from the previous one (especially 4G)? The answer is—it is not only the increase in bit rate made 5G distinct from the 4G, but rather 5G is also advanced in terms of:

- High increased peak bit rate
- Larger data volume per unit area (*i.e.* high system spectral efficiency)
- High capacity to allow more devices connectivity concurrently and instantaneously
- Lower battery consumption
- Better connectivity irrespective of the geographic region, in which you are
- Larger number of supporting devices
- Lower cost of infrastructural development
- Higher reliability of the communications.

As researchers say, with the wide range of bandwidth radio channels, it is able to support the speed up to 10 Gbps, the 5G WiFi technology will offer contiguous and consistent coverage—"wider area mobility in true sense."

The Concept of Metro Rail in India

A Preview

- Population growth in Delhi
- Increased pollution
- Various metro projects
- Reduced travel time
- Employment opportunities
- Growing Vehicles
- Formation of MRTS
- Better connectivity
- Ease of living
- Fillip to local business

Delhi had been experiencing phenomenal growth in population in the last few decades. So, the number of vehicles had been increased to 40 lakhs, these were more than that of Mumbai, Kolkata and Chennai put together. The traffic on the roads of Delhi was a mix-up of cycles, scooters, buses, cars and rickshaws, resulting in fuel wastage, environmental pollution and increasing number of road accidents.

To rectify the situation the government of India and the Government of National Capital Territory of Delhi, in equal partnership had set up a company in 1995 named Delhi Metro Rail Corporation Ltd. (DMRC).

This necessitated a policy shift to discourage private modes. So, introduction of a rail based (MRTS) Mass Rapid Transport System was called for. MRTS resulted in time saving for commuters, reliable and safer journey, reduction in atmospheric pollution, reduction in accident rates, reduced fuel consumption, reduced vehicle operating costs and increase in the average speed of road vehicles.

With rapid urbanization, the pressure is mounting on the public transport system from the people living in cities and towns across the country. Mass Rapid Transport System, MRTS has emerged as one of the most effective means of mobility for the citizens in tier-1 and tier-2 cities and Metro Rail has been a major player.

Metro Today—Currently 585 km of Metro lines are operational. Approximately another 60 km of metro lines are likely to be opened soon in the cities of Ahmedabad, Lucknow, Nagpur and Ghaziabad. With a modest beginning with 8 km in 2002, modern metro rail have shown phenomenal growth in the country.

In the financial year (2018-19), 140 km of metro lines have been opened for the public (till 10 February 2019). Out of the 585 km of operational metro lines as on 10 February 2019, 326 km have been made operational after May 2014. Since May 2014, 258 km of metro line have been sanctioned by the Govt. of India. Currently there is about 600 km of sanctioned metro lines under construction which will be operational in next five years.

There are about 1000 km of metro line proposals under planning. Govt. of India has taken various steps for standardization and growth of metro rail in India. The Metro Rail Policy 2017 of Govt. of India enables rapid and sustainable growth of metro rail in the country.

Metro Progress in India
(As on 10.02.2019) Operational: 585 km

- Delhi & NCR (327km)
- Noida-Greater Noida (29.7 km)
- Bangalore (42.3 km)
- Hyderabad (46 km)
- Kolkata Metro (27.3 km)
- Chennai (45 km),
- Jaipur (9.6 km)
- Kochi (18.2 km)
- Lucknow (8.5 km)
- Mumbai Metro Line 1 (11.4 km)
- Rapid Metro Gurgaon (12 km)
- Mumbai Mono Rail Phase-1 (9.00 km)

Under Construction Metro/MRTS Projects: 622 km

- Delhi and NCR including extensions (23 km) ✦ Kolkata (108 km) ✦ Bangalore (72 km) ✦ Chennai (10 km) ✦ Kochi (7.5 km) ✦ Jaipur (2.5 km) ✦ Mumbai (171 km) ✦ Hyderabad (26 km) ✦ Nagpur (38 km) ✦ Ahmedabad (36 km) ✦ Lucknow (14 km) ✦ Pune (54 km) ✦ Bhopal (28 km) ✦ Indore (32 km)

Expansion of Metro services sanctioned by Ministry of Railways Metro Projects have not only added to connectivity, it has reduced the travel time and hence enhanced the ease of living substantially in the urban areas. It has also led to creation of direct and indirect employment opportunities.

It is expected that with the expansion of Metros in the cities, local and intercity travel will be easier, mobility and connectivity will be enhanced giving a fillip to local business as well.

Infrastructure Development in India

A Preview

❖ Infrastructure sector a key driver

❖ Foreign direct investment

❖ Requirement of Investments

❖ Government initiatives

❖ Achievements

❖ Road ahead

Infrastructure sector is a key driver for the Indian economy. The sector is highly responsible for propelling India's overall development and enjoys intense focus from Government for initiating policies that would ensure time-bound creation of world class infrastructure in the country. Infrastructure sector includes power, bridges, dams, roads and urban infrastructure development. In 2018, India ranked 44th out of 167 countries in World Bank's Logistics Performance Index (LPI) 2018.

Foreign Direct Investment (FDI) received in Construction Development sector (townships, housing, built up infrastructure and construction development projects) from April 2000 to December 2018 stood at US$ 24.91 billion, according to the Department of Industrial Policy and Promotion (DIPP). The logistics sector in India is growing at a CAGR of 10.5 per cent annually and is expected to reach US$ 215 billion in 2020.

India has a requirement of investment worth ₹ 50 trillion (US$ 777.73 billion) in infrastructure by 2022 to have sustainable development in the country. India is witnessing significant interest from international investors in the infrastructure space. Some key investments in the sector are listed below:

✦ In 2018, infrastructure sector in India witnessed private equity and venture capital investments worth US$ 1.97 billion.

✦ In June 2018, the Asian Infrastructure Investment Bank (AIIB) has announced US$ 200 million investment into the National Investment & Infrastructure Fund (NIIF).

✦ Indian infrastructure sector witnessed 91 M&A deals worth US$ 5.4 billion in 2017.

The Government of India is expected to invest highly in the infrastructure sector, mainly highways, renewable energy and urban transport.

The Government of India is taking every possible initiative to boost the infrastructure sector. Announcements in Union Budget 2019-20:

✦ The Government of India has given a massive push to the infrastructure sector by allocating ₹ 4.56 lakh crore (US$ 63.20 billion) for the sector.

✦ Communication sector allocated ₹ 38,637.46 crore (US$ 5.36 billion) to development of post and telecommunications departments.

- ✦ The Indian Railways received allocation under Union Budget 2019-20 at ₹ 66.77 billion (US\$ 9.25 billion). Out of this allocation, ₹ 64.587 billion (US\$ 8.95 billion) is capital expenditure.

- ✦ ₹ 83,015.97 crore (US\$11.51 billion) allocated towards road transport and highway.

- ✦ ₹ 3,899.9 crore (US\$ 540.53 billion) to increase capacity of Green Energy Corridor Project along with wind and solar power projects.

- ✦ Allocation of ₹ 8,350.00 crore (US\$ 1.16 billion) to boost telecom infrastructure.

- ✦ Water supply to be provided to all households in 500 cities.

- ✦ Allocation of ₹ 888.00 crore (US\$ 110.88 million) for the upgradation of state government medical colleges (PG seats) at the district hospitals and ₹ 1,361.00 crore (US\$ 188.63 million) for government medical colleges (UG seats) and government health institutions.

Following are the achievements of the government in the past four years:

- ✦ The total national highways length increased to 122,434 kms in FY18 from 92,851 kms in FY14.

- ✦ India's rank jumped to 24 in 2018 from 137 in 2014 on World Bank's Ease of doing business—"Getting Electricity" ranking.

- ✦ Energy deficit reduced to 0.7 per cent in FY18 from 4.2 per cent in FY14.

- ✦ Number of airports has increased to 102 in 2018.

India's national highway network is expected to cover 50,000 kilometres by the end of 2019. National highway construction in India has increased by 20 per cent year-on-year in 2017-18.

India and Japan have joined hands for infrastructure development in India's north-eastern states and are also setting up an India-Japan Coordination Forum for Development of North East to undertake strategic infrastructure projects in the northeast.

High Speed Rails in India

A Preview

- India's position in the world
- Beginning of Indian Railways
- One of the largest rail network
- Some other famous trains
- Mumbai-Ahmedabad high-speed rail corridor
- Diamond Qudrilateral
- Chennai-Delhi corridor

In the current scenario, India reaches the world class apparatus and ready to compete with the top leaders of the universe. India succeeds in launching the missiles and satellites, got well trained and unbeatable defence force to protect the nation and holding high class transportation facilities within it.

India grown into the prime role of transportation and rail industry is the key point of the Indian transport system. In the field of rail transportation, India got so many experiences while implementing the recent technologies.

Indian Railway is the most ancient railway network in India. The first train was operated in the year 1853 from Mumbai to Thane. Bharatiya Rail is the native name of Indian Railways and it was established on April 16, 1853. Indian Railways, becoming one of the largest railway networks in the world.

Indian Railways operates lengthy tracks as well as residential rail tracks on the multi gauge networks. It is functioning in the local lands and also having limited services to Bangladesh, Myanmar, Nepal and Pakistan.

Indian Railways having fragmented into seventeen zones and they were further sub-divided into sixty eight divisions. Each zone and division having their own zonal headquarter and divisional headquarter respectively.

In recent years, Indian Railways has been placing so many efforts to initiate some effective promotional schemes in its traditional structure and develop the quality of service. High Speed Rail is the most emerging goal of Indian Railways and it should have a unique network in the field of railway industry.

The semi high speed train Vande Bharat Express is the fastest train in our nation in the present situation. Shatabdi, Rajdhani and Duronto trains are some fast trains in our landmark.

Some other trains like Vivek Express is the longest railway line in India which runs between Kanyakumari and Dibrugarh; Samjhauta Express is a train that runs between India and Pakistan; Thar Express connecting Khokhrapar (Pakistan) and Munabao (India); Palace on Wheels is an exclusively constructed luxury tourist train service to promote tourism in Rajasthan.

MUMBAI-AHMEDABAD HIGH-SPEED RAIL CORRIDOR

Mumbai–Ahmedabad high speed rail corridor is a government approved high speed rail corridor project of connecting the cities of Mumbai and Ahmedabad. It will be India's first high-speed railway track, when it trails it first attempt. It was announced a joint high speed railway project of India and Japan in September 2013.

This high speed rail project links the locale of Maharashtra and Gujarat in a high-tech way. This track will have 12 stations on its route, it includes 7 stations of Maharashtra and 5 stations of Gujarat. This will be a fully air-conditioned high speed rail and expecting to travel between the stations at speeds of 320 km/hr which will take nearly two hours to cover the two dimensions. At present, the fastest train operating on this line is the Ahmedabad Duronto Express, running between Mumbai Central to Ahmedabad which takes approximately 7 hours and it is a non-stop vehicle that runs between these two cities at a maximum speed of 120 km/h.

DIAMOND QUADRILATERAL

The Diamond Quadrilateral is a high speed railway project that connects the four metro cities in India namely Delhi, Mumbai, Chennai and Kolkata. To improve country's rail infrastructure there is a need to implement high speed trains. So to fulfill this demand the Diamond Quadrilateral project was planned. The leading countries like Japan, China, France, US are ready to fund the Diamond Quadrilateral high speed rail project.

CHENNAI-DELHI CORRIDOR

China is carrying out feasibility studies for high speed railway lines on the 2,200 km Chennai–New Delhi route and the 1,200 km long New Delhi–Mumbai corridor. The projected Chennai–New Delhi high speed railway corridor will be the second largest high speed railway track in the world, after the 2,298 km long Beijing–Guangzhou line, which was launched three years ago in China.

The corridor is likely to cost ₹ 2 lakh crore and is proposed to be developed jointly with China, home to the world's longest high speed railway line. The Delhi–Chennai corridor is part of Prime Minister Narendra Modi's "Diamond Quadrilateral" project.

Criminalisation of Politics

A Preview

- ❖ What does it Mean?
- ❖ Who are Criminalising Politics?
- ❖ Who are Responsible for their Growth?
- ❖ What are the Reasons?
- ❖ Lacuna in the Law
- ❖ Muscle Power & Money Power
- ❖ Criminals Escaping Punishments
- ❖ What is the Remedy

When we say criminalisation of politics, we mean to say that the political system has been eroded of the good political people or people with selfish gains have entered the political arena. These days people with criminal background find it easy to become members of Parliament or legislative assembly. This gives rise to a kind of situation where there are great deal of erosion of values, dearth of security of life, lack of transparency and accountability, rampant corruption etc.

Today in order to win an election a candidate requires only manpower, muscle power and money power. People with these three cannot think of losing an election—though a person with good leadership qualities and devotion of service to society may lose his security money. Bad practice seems to have driven out clean traditions of political behaviour. The voters, political parties and the law and order machinery are all equally responsible for the criminalisation of politics. These days political parties look for people with criminal background who will be having muscle power and who can extract money from general public to meet up their election expenses and win the election by hook or by crook. People within a party must have the courage to speak against and turn out such candidates from the elections.

Masses in India are not educated enough and can be easily influenced by money or muscle power. Middle class is either manipulative or apathetic to the whole electoral process, which provides scope for criminal elements in politics.

Under the current law, only people who have been convicted at least twice can be debarred from becoming candidates. This leaves the field open for chargesheeted criminals. Does it not seem that the political parties themselves are not interested in changing the system? In certain constituencies it has been observed that people vote for a particular candidate not in support of his agenda or his previous work done but because of the dire consequences that they may have to face after elections. The failure of the state machinery in ensuring free and fair elections is apparent here. Political parties continue to seek support of the criminals for electoral malpractices like booth capturing and rigging.

Today the biggest problem in our country is the weak law enforcement and the Indian Penal Code. People take law for granted. Even on committing a serious crime like murder, the criminal may escape punishment in lack of ample evidence or may get the benefit of doubt due to slackness of an investigating officer. These situations make the criminals more bold and they get encouraged.

In the interest of practical and immediate solution, it is easy to state that one must depend on the power of force and coercion to put an end to criminalisation of politics rather than vague notions of morality.

Assuming that the election process is sufficiently corruption free, voters only have themselves to blame if they elect a criminal. A candidate's friends and family may vote for him but it is upto the individual voter to reject that candidate if he or she suspects that the candidate may be corrupt. Highly educated and capable people generally do not opt politics as a career, they will rather prefer business or some good job or may even go abroad for further studies or job opportunities. It requires courage and bravery to contest an election.

More the educated and capable people leave politics as career, more the criminals will enter into it. Violence and criminalisation can be effectively tackled by inspiring leadership. Political parties must break ties with armed gangs and shun violence in political activities. Election Commission should act to prevent convicted criminals from entering politics. Every citizen who fails to take part in the process of discouraging criminalisation of politics even in any small way should be held responsible for the degeneration of politics to such an extent that it is today dominated by convicts and historysheeters.

The Value of Books

A Preview

- A treasure house of knowledge
- Sound advice
- Byron
- Tennyson
- Milton
- Sources of mirror light
- Africa
- Libraries
- Children's school bags
- Nature
- Lives of our ancestors
- Milton
- All books not good and great
- Lord Bacon
- The Vedas
- Civilization
- Joad
- All subjects
- Pope
- Internet

Books are, no doubt, a treasure house of knowledge. They contain all the wisdom of the past ages, as they are often written by vastly learned and experienced men and women. To respect the books is to respect our past, our cultural heritage.

Why are books so precious to us? Books enhance our knowledge. From them we learn about the lives of our ancestors. We learn how they were successful in certain spheres or why and how they failed in certain others. Great men of the past convey their sound advice to us through the medium of books.

It is not for nothing that Milton said, "A good book is the precious life blood of a master spirit." It is attributed to Byron that he said, "A book is a book even if there is nothing in it."

All the books cannot be considered good and great. There are millions of books in the world. There can be thousands or at least hundreds of books on almost every topic. No one can read all the books. Even what Tennyson calls "life piled on life" is not enough to enable a man to gain full knowledge that is contained in books. That is why one has to be very judicious in the choice of books.

Lord Bacon analysed the value of books elaborately about four hundred years ago. In his "Of Studies", he says, "Studies serve for delight, for ornament, and for ability." The following of his words have become proverbial:

"Some books are to be tasted, others to be swallowed, and some few to be chewed and digested."

It is good to form a habit of reading books. On the matter of reading, Bacon says,

"Read not to contradict and confuse nor to believe and take for granted, nor to find talk and discourse, but to wait and consider."

It is a pity that in the modern age when there is plethora of books of all kinds everywhere, people should cease showing due regard to books as if they were some dead matter. Long ago said Milton,

"Books are not absolutely dead things, but do contain a potency of life in them to be as active as that soul was whose progeny they are."

In his own inimical style, Milton advises us not to destroy a good book. "As good almost kill a man as kill a good book; who kills a man kills a reasonable creature, God's image; but he who destroys a good book, kills reason itself, kills the image of God, as it were in the eye."

We have the ancient Upanishadic prayer to God: "Lead us from darkness to light." The Rigveda was perhaps the earliest book that man got. The Vedas were composed by the sages and seers and committed to memory by the common people. They were given the written shape much later.

What led mankind from darkness to light was the agency (or vehicle) of books. Over the ages, books have transformed man from primitivism to modern civilized state. They are the chief carrier of knowledge and civilization. As C.E.M. Joad says, they spread knowledge in space and make it endure in time. To illustrate his point, he gives the example of Africa. According to him, Africa has lagged behind in civilization because of lack of books. He attributes lack of books in Africa because of presence of white ants that eat up all books whenever they are produced.

When we have realized the great importance of books, we can now quite understand the value of libraries which not only preserve books but also increase the reading habit of people provided they are well stocked with all kinds of books.

As these days professions are rapidly on the increase, so are subjects and topics and so are books. Now we have books on, besides traditional subjects like languages, arts, literature and sciences, on sports, music, health, education, technology, space, mountainering, chess, astrology astronomy, defence, horticulture, acupunture, Reiki, Feng shui, cartooning, starring, cooking, drawing, painting, embossing, computers (IT), taxation system, commerce, business, marketing, management, meditation, yoga, engineering and, may be, cloning, etc. and hordes of highly specialized subjects.

We know that a school child's bag has gone too heavy in the present times. Although one would wish the bag to grow lighter, there is no denying the fact that knowledge is a must for every human being and that knowledge can best be acquired through books. "Knowledge is power," said Bacon. It is knowledge which distinguishes man from other animals.

Alexander Pope, the renowned English poet of the Augustan period says, "A little learning is a dangerous thing." Let us try to gain more and more knowledge. Let the wind of knowledge blow to us from all four sides as the Atharva Veda says, "Let noble thoughts come to me from all sides." Jawahar Lal Nehru has pointed out that isolation can only make a nation stagnate. That is true of an individual also. This is the age of interaction and that interaction is best possible through books.

No doubt, the books now face a stiff competition from Internet or www. But the fear of many that books might at one stage become extinct is only misplaced. Books are and will remain best friends, guides and nurses of man. They advise him, provide him guidance and console him at the moment of adversity.

The Value of Trees

A Preview

- The shape of a tree—a canopy
- Religious concept of trees
- Rain, etc.
- Grow more trees
- In ancient times
- Photosynthesis
- Uses of trees

The very shape of a tree is akin to that of a canopy. A canopy provides shelter from rain, sun and any thing extraneous and is considered a sort of religious symbol. Thus, it is deemed a part of a holy and sacred plan. This lends sanctity to a tree and brings it closer to a part of some holy plan, designed and devised by some divine force.

In ancient times, an overwhelming area of the earth was covered with lush green trees. Thanks to the modern times, the area has diminished in major parts of the world, particularly in countries that are either highly urbanised or have mammoth populations. India is one of the countries where forests have been cut down ruthlessly. It is said that when the Europeans migrated to the American continent the first thing they did was the axing down of the trees in an unprecedentedly ruthless manner. The end result was that the central part of America, particularly South America changed to a desert—a condition which since has only partly been retrieved and that with strenuous efforts of some enlightened people.

It is of not little significance that the Vedas sing highly of trees and in ancient India, some trees were particularly looked upon with a great amount of reverence and even worshipped. We know that certain trees are like *pipal* and *'jind'* are still worshipped in temples and elswhere in India. Many trees are associated with great myths, stories and legends of the past heroes and are not allowed to be felled down.

Today even small children know that trees absorb carbon dioxide from the atmosphere and release oxygen in the presence of sunlight. The process is known as photosynthesis. Thus they clean the atmosphere and keep a balance of oxygen with other gases.

Trees make the air cool around them. This coolness makes the water vapour in the air heavier and causes clouds to rain down. The areas where there are no or few trees such as Sudan and Ethiopia, often go dry. Thus deserts are caused which get perpetuated for want of dense forests. Rajasthan is such an area in India and such is Sahara in Africa. Now great efforts are going on to plant trees, in such areas. The Sri Ganganagar area of Rajasthan in now overgrowing with vegetation because of the supply of water through a canal. Also efforts are going on to store rain water in Rajasthan to facilitate the plantation of more trees and crops.

Most of the trees except a few such as Eucalyptus provide us shade. In olden times (and probably still in some villages) the people used to sit under shady trees. The children played games under huge oak and *pipal* trees and the village elders held their meetings and *panchayats* delivered their judgements under the trees.

In modern times, Rabindranath Tagore, a man of great vision, expected the Shantiniketan University started by him, to be able to teach the students in the shade of trees. We know that no less a person than Indira Gandhi got a part of her education in the austere atmosphere of the Shantiniketan.

Trees give us various kinds of fruits. The leaves of some trees are used as fodder for animals. Bark of some trees proves useful in tannery. Trees provide us gums, rubber and certain medicines like quinine. Trees are useful in several other ways. Their wood is used for making doors, windows and ventilators for homes. It is also used for making furniture. Almost all the paper industry depends upon trees.

Some people, particularly the villagers, use the wood of the trees as fuel and use it for cooking and other such purposes. Actually, wood should not be used as fuel, as just for this reason so many trees have to be cut down, such that there is a constant depletion of the forest area and this is a dangerous sign for environmental good health.

It is, therefore, of paramount importance that we grow more trees instead of cutting down the existing trees. Of course, sometimes trees which go dry due to several reasons have to be axed. But fresh trees must be grown in their place.

It is in the fitness of things that "Afforestation" or "Vanmahotsav" is celebrated every year in India on first July. On this day saplings of trees of various kinds are grown in large numbers all over the country. The celebration was started after partition by the famous leader, K. M. Munshi, then a Union Minister. Let us all participate in this great event and grow more and more trees not only on this day but also during the whole of the rainy reason in July-August when the saplings catch roots in the soil readily and grow quickly into tall trees. This way we can increase greenery and get more fresh oxygenated air and rain besides several other gains.

As regards the usefulness of the wood of certain trees which we may normally think to be not of much use, here is an extract from the detail given by an expert in a newspaper about the utility of the wood of the spruce tree, which is a tall, handsome, evergreen pine tree growing in temperate and arctic regions: Its knotfree logs are highly priced for the timber required for building aircraft. The rest of the wood, whether knotted or free of the lacuna, is highly prized for packing cases, making cheap furniture, bedsteads, drawing boards, plane tables, roof ceiling, wall planking, shingles, paper pulp, matches, etc.

The Value of Water

A Preview

- ❖ Water — a common commodity
- ❖ A fish
- ❖ A thirsty man
- ❖ Condition in India — 70 years after Independence
- ❖ Example regarding scarcity of drinking water
- ❖ Elixir of life
- ❖ Earth comprises 2/3rd water
- ❖ Water essential to all kinds of life
- ❖ Sources of water
- ❖ All the beauty on the earth due to water
- ❖ Coleridge's poem
- ❖ Management of water
- ❖ Water therapy — new research
- ❖ Water for heart, kidneys, etc.
- ❖ Mineral water
- ❖ Overall importance of water
- ❖ The Ganga

We often pay scant regard to the real value of water. It is because water is such a common commodity.

If we want to know the real value of water, we should just give a thought to a fish out of water or a man dying of thirst or a man in "sorest need" of water, as the famous American poet, Emily Dickinson, would put it.

It is, indeed, shameful that even more than seventy years after attainment of Independence, we have not been able to provide clean and enough potable water to all.

Water is called "the elixir of life". This is, indeed, the name which the Indian Nobel Laureate, C.V. Raman, has given it in his celebrated essay of the same name.

The earth comprises two-thirds of water and one-third of land. Water is essential for all living beings. There can be no life without water. Human beings, animals and all kinds of plants all need water. Much of the beauty of the earth is because of the presence of plenty of water on it.

The main sources of water are rain, rivers, lakes and underground water, besides seas and oceans which are the main storehouses of water. Rains are caused by clouds. This rain helps the forests to grow which in turn also cause rain. Rain also feeds the rivers. The rivers mainly get replenished with the melting of snow on the mountains.

We amaze at the beauty of the clouds, the colourful rainbow, the snow-capped peaks of mountains, the undulating sea waves, the sounding cataracts, the transparent lakes, the lush green forests, plants, crops, vegetables and multicolour flowers. We should be thankful to God for his bounties and, above all, for his creation of water which is the source of all beauty and life on our planet which is in no way less than heaven, only if we have an eye to behold, a mind to see and a heart to love, enjoy and be thankful.

Man's misery in the absence of the availability of drinking water is thus highlighted by the renowned supernatural English poet, S.T. Coleridge in his celebrated poem, the Rime of the Ancient Mariner:

> *"Water, water everywhere*
> *When all the boards did shrink;*
> *Water, water everywhere,*
> *But not a drop to drink."*

Man should manage water properly. Much of rain-water goes waste. We should build large tanks and reservoirs for irrigation and drinking purposes, particularly in areas where canals cannot be constructed because of the stony and difficult terrain.

Now research has shown that water can serve a useful purpose in maintaining good health and in increasing longevity. According to a report,

"Researchers at Loma Linda University in California found that people who drank at least five glasses of water each day were less likely to die from a heart attack than those who drank two or fewer glasses per day.

In contrast, people who drank a lot of other fluids were more likely to die from heart attack than those who drank less, with high levels of non-water drinking in women associated with a more than twofold increased risk of death."

This gives an inkling in the use of water therapy for improving the soundness of our heart. It is known to almost every educated person that sufficient consumption of water during the day helps us keep our kidneys in proper order. It is said that all adults should daily drink at least eight glasses of water. The general formula: "The more, the merrier," also seems useful in the matter of water, "The more consumption of water for drinking purposes, the better." However, too much water should not be drunk immediately after meals as it dilutes the necessary hydrochloric acid in the stomach which is essential for the purpose of digesting food.

At present, there is great awareness among the masses about the necessity of pure drinking water. So, mineral water of many brands is sold in bottles at exorbitant rates in the market. Much of this water is spurious. So, we should be very careful while purchasing such a bottle. A bottle of mineral water should be purchased only from an authorised dealer who is a reliable one.

Thus the overwhelming importance of water for various purposes such as drinking, washing, bathing, irrigation, etc. cannot be overestimated.

We know the beauty of the rivers is because of their water. A river is not a river if it is devoid of the flow of water. Let us have a glance at the visual description of the Ganga, India's river in particular, as given by Nehru in his famous "The Last Will and Testament:"

"Smiling and dancing in the morning sunlight, and dark and gloomy and full of mystery as the evening shadows fall, a narrow, slow and graceful stream in winter, and a vast roaring thing during the monsoon, broad based almost as the sea, and with something of the sea's power to destroy, the Ganga has been to me a symbol and a memory of the past of India, running into the present, and flowing on to the great ocean of the future."

—Jawaharlal Nehru

The Value of Rain

A Preview

- India— an agricultural country
- Agriculture mainly depends upon rain
- Other uses of water
- Overall dependence on rain
- Effects of rain
- Superiority of rain over other means of irrigation
- Power generation
- Artificial rain
- Drought-conditions
- Effect on creatures and plants
- Children
- Dickinson
- Wordsworth
- Demerits
- Merits—overwhelming

India is an agricultural country. The mainstay of the Indian economy is the produce from the agricultural sector. This produce depends mainly upon the availability and proper management of water. The main sources of water in India are:

1. Rain water.
2. Rivers and rivulets that flow from the mountain areas and glaciers.
3. Tanks, pools and dams storing rain water and (generally surplus) water from rivers.

If we have a close look at all these sources of water, we shall realize that the main source of water in India is by and large only one and that is rain-water. All other sources of water are dependent upon this main source. If it does not rain enough on the mountains and in hilly areas, there will not be enough water in the rivers, in dams, tanks and pools storing this rainwater.

As far as underground water is concerned, if it does not rain sufficiently in an area, the table land water level in that area goes down. This also happens if too much water is utilized on the surface land for irrigation, drinking, washing and other purposes.

It does not need much emphasis to say that all kinds of fruits, vegetables and crops depend upon the availability of water. It is also admitted on all hands that rain water is the best for all such purposes and no other water supplied on the ground can compare with the conducive effect of the rain water. Rain water not only percolates down through the roots of plants, but it also makes the surrounding soil moist such that the roots which find it difficult to acquire nourishment for the plant through the hard soil, can do so easily through the soft and moist soil.

Moreover, rain also causes coolness in the air and spreads moisture in the atmoshpere which makes it easy for the leaves and branches to absorb food from air and proliferate. No doubt, there is now drip system of irrigation which is an imitation of rain. But it cannot equal real rain in effect.

In the modern age, rain is also essential for generation of power. If the water level in the dams is miserably low, power generation becomes almost impossible. This is what happened in 2002 when for lack of rain, water in the Ranjit Sagar and Pong Dam went abysmally low. The result was that there were long cuts in electricity in Punjab, Haryana and Delhi. The people who could afford the use of generators, made use of such devices. Others had to sit in the dark and live without fans and desert coolers in the scorching heat of June and July.

As a result of these power cuts and for lack of rain, the standing crops of paddy were destroyed, thus resulting in huge losses to the farmers and a loss of many crores of rupees to the national exchequer. The farmers who could afford, had to run their tubewells on diesel, but that was too costly and this way even the cost of inputs of farmers could not be recovered.

Another unhealthy aspect of these long power cuts was that in certain villages in North India, the people got so restless and infuriated that they gheraoed the state electricity board offices and even caused huge damage to power stations at some places. The board employees got scared and felt danger even for their lives and at certain stations, even police protection had to be sought.

When the drought conditions got unpredictably prolonged, the people began to pray to God Indra, the rain god and performed *yajnas* and resorted to other means to incite rain.

These simple facts give us a glimpse of the importance of rain. Rain is caused by the monsoon in summer in India. Among other factors, the forests play an important role in causing rain. Hence, forests must be preserved and expanded at all costs.

It is well-known that now science has the means and methods to cause artificial rain. But that is possible only if some clouds loaded with water are floating in the sky. Science can even cause artificial clouds, but that also depends upon availability of water on the ground and other factors. All these factors are very costly and have only limited effect.

There are certain countries like Ethiopia and Sudan where it does not rain at all for years together. Some years back, it was reported that it rained in Ethiopia after twenty years, that is, two decades. Even in Laddakh in Kashmir it rains only once in a blue moon. The significance of rain can be learnt from these countries and states.

Drought often hits Gujarat and Orissa. In 2002, it hit Haryana, U.P., Karnataka, Andhra Pradesh, etc.

We can recall Emily Dickinson's lines, "Success is counted sweetest by those who never succeed." Similarly, rain is the most charming thing to those who have never (or only rarely) seen and experienced it.

However, there are certain pet categories of those who are very fond of rain.

Besides men, animals, birds and plants in general, children in particular are very fond of rain. They like to bathe in rain, sometimes much to the chagrin of their parants. They are sometimes seen floating paper-boats in rain.

Birds are also very fond of bathing in rain. If it rains heavily, it is a nuisance to them. But when it is drizzling, they like to sit in it and enjoy it for sometime. Particularly, after the rain, they move to pools of water, have a quick dive there, one after the other. As they come out of each snap dive, they preen their feathers, and look so charming to the on-lookers.

The buffaloes also like to keep standing in rain, particularly if it rains after a long spell of drought. The fishes and water animals of all kinds swim and jump in water. The fishes which are in fishery pools, can survive only if water is available in abundance. If it does not rain and rivers and canals get dry, it takes a heavy toll of these of fish and other water life.

After the rain, frogs can be heard croaking loudly at all places where there is water. Thus rain has its paramount effect on all and sundry living beings, more or less, in one way or the other.

A poet has thus sung about the beauty of rain:

"After the dust and heat, In the broad and fiery street,
In the narrow lane, How beautiful is the rain!"

The rainbow appears after the rain. Is there a child who would not like to look at the colourful rainbow? This is what Wordsworth says about it:

"My heart leaps up when I behold a rainbow in the sky."

Rain may cause some discomfort as roads and streets go slippery. Many have to use umbrellas to go in rain. Some old houses may start leaking. The low-lying localities may be flooded with rain water. Rivers may cross their danger marks, if it rains in excess. There may spread some diseases and even epidemics during or after rains. But all these things are manageable. The merits of rain far overwhelm its demerits.

The Value of Sports

A Preview

❖ Who is a sportsman?
❖ Qualities
❖ The real purpose of sports
❖ The present situation
❖ Qualities one learns in the playground
❖ Role in development of personality
❖ Match-fixing

A person who plays a game seldom is not said to be a sportsman. A sportsman does regular practice and that punctually.

A sportsman is always possessed with the spirit of doing something wonderful and unbelieveable in his field. He does not like to be corrupted or to corrupt anybody. It is because of his performance that he is acclaimed which he has to prove in the ground where many hundreds of people watch him. So, transparency is one such quality which always lives with him.

Thus complete transparency is one of the qualities which is connected with the world of sports. As a matter of fact, this quality should be observed in all walks of life to have a clean and healthy society where all individual members can enjoy a life of peace, tranquillity, happiness, mutual cooperation and contentment.

The qualities imbibed in the field of sports in youth stand a person in good stead all his life. The first and foremost quality is the sportsman spirit. This quality persuades a man to remain cheerful even when he loses a match. It means that one should play a game for the sake of game and not just for victory.

Life is also a field where one acts. It is one's choice to accept it as a happy field full of sports or joys or a valley of misery. One who knows the art of happiness takes life as a game of sports where one is expected to play honestly and with complete sincerity to the best of his knowledge, skill and capability. A true sportsman never tries to hoodwink others. Similarly, a really happy and contented man plays only a fair game in life. On the contrary, a cunning and selfish man ultimately brings misery to himself and all others connected with him.

At present, we see so many tricksters, scamsters and scandal-mongers in society who cause misery to so many innocent and honest men and themselves finally rot in jails and hospitals. Had they been sensible and learnt some art of living in the sports at school or college or taken a cue from true and geniune sportsmen, they would have spared themselves and others of this sorry state of affairs.

It is in the playground that we learn certain qualities such as leadership, discipline, team spirit, healthy competition and the like. Mr. Gladstone, the Prime Minister of England, is said to have stated once, "If you want to be a good leader, first learn how to be a good follower." It is rightly said, "If the two ride a horse, one must ride behind." It is also said, "Rome was not built in a day." So, it takes its own time to build up one's personality, just as it takes time to raise a majestic building.

Sports help us in developing our personality. It is a pity that much attention is not paid to sports in our country. Most of the funds are wasted on trivial items not connected with sports such as dinners, tea parties, honouring some personages from outside the realm of the sports, etc.

Our players do not even get sufficient diet. Infrastructure for sports in our country is lacking. Then there is so much bungling in the matter of selection of teams. It is no surprise that we get very few medals in the Olympics when we shamefully realize that we are a country of 1.25 billion, or we comprise one seventh of the total population of the world. Certainly, something must be done to overcome this malaise at the highest level. Just the creation of a ministry of sports at the union level is not enough.

In April 2000, there was a sort of upheaval in the world of cricket when the revealations regarding match-fixing became a part of the public debate. Every lover of cricket was appalled.

As a result of all this turmoil, many voices were heard demanding banning or abandoning of the game of cricket altogether. Let us hope this is not going to be done. Instead, we should hope that the detractors, if any, are going to be suitably punished to ensure a fair game so that it can continue providing entertainment and inspiration to millions of spectators and TV viewers the world over.

Life In A Big City
or
Is A Big City A Hell or Heaven ?

A Preview

- ❖ Very tiring — a cliche
- ❖ A country in miniature
- ❖ A big desert
- ❖ Ennui, depression
- ❖ Life goes on for all 24 hours
- ❖ Traffic jam
- ❖ Neighbours
- ❖ Training centres
- ❖ Pollution
- ❖ Employment, educational avenues
- ❖ Means of measurement, health, study
- ❖ Offices, universities, schools, colleges, places of worship, hospitals, libraries, theatres, parks, swimming pools, stadiums, etc.
- ❖ Life of the rich
- ❖ Life of the common men
- ❖ Life—lovely
- ❖ TV
- ❖ Watchman
- ❖ Telephones
- ❖ Markets, offices, etc.
- ❖ Transport system
- ❖ Avenues for women

It has become a cliche to say that life in a big city is very tiring. Ask those who live in big airconditioned bungalows, as for instance, in posh colonies of South Delhi, and move in big air conditioned luxury cars which carry them not only to offices and places of works with comfort but also to five star luxury hotels, dancing halls, singing auditoriums, musical concerts, theatre halls, art galleries, swimming pools and the like and then decide if the life in the cosmopolitan city of over two crore souls is tiring to them.

The saying, however, is right if we concern ourselves with the common people only. Of course, most of the people lead a miserable life in a big city. But in that sense too, the big city is only our country in miniature. It is common knowledge that in our country, a small percentage of people enjoys all the luxuries while most of the people, particularly the poorest to lead life of abject poverty.

It will however, be more pertinent if we confine ourselves to life in a big city only. A philosopher has said, "A big city is a big desert." It is because we often feel isolated and lonely in a big city and suffer from ennui which can lead to self pity, a sense of guilt and depression. Of course, now we have in almost every home a TV set where we can watch films, serials, sports or listen to educational or religious lectures or songs and hymns. We can also have an audio system to hear songs and hymns of our choice. Over the TV we can also play video-games. But such a thing is possible in any city or town and even in a village and it cannot be called the peculiarity of a big city only.

In a big city, life goes on for all the twenty four hours. There is traffic on the roads day and night. The vehicles continue to ply on the roads till midnight. Thereafter, when one goes to bed, one can hear the warning voice of the watchman, calling, "Keep awake!" Alongwith his words comes the sound of his whistle and a tap of his big heavy club on the road. He may also be having a cell-torch in his hand as electric breakdowns are now common even in big cities. During the rainy season, he may be holding an umberella in his hand as he is supposed to do his duty at all costs and in all kinds of weather. But a watchman may be available in any other city or town, though in a big city he is much more pressed to perform his duty, come what may.

There are frequent traffic jams in different squares and parts of a big city. Already, it takes a lot of time in reaching from one place to another in a big city, as the city has a sprawling area. If once a person, particularly one in a four wheeler like a car or bus, is caught in a stubborn traffic due to any reason, one's almost the whole day or a big chunk of it is wasted. Since frequent visits and meetings among friends and relatives are not possible in a big city, specifically when the two are living at long distances or at the remote corners in the same city, the telephone, emails, chats and couriers and sometimes even postal communiations serve the means of exchanging news, views, greetings and the like.

A big city is a strange place where the neighbours do not know each other and hardly come to help each other even in a case of emergency, though exceptions are always there.

There are so many offices, shops and markets in a big city. One who has money, in his pocket, can get anything done. All the bureaucrats can be contacted in their offices. Anything can be purchased. Any kind of business or trade can be started if one can make a handsome investment. Moreover, there are so many training centres for all kinds of skills, studies and trades and one can earn while learning the study or skill of one's choice in accordance with the latest modern trends. This definitely is a great positive point in favour of the life in a big city.

The availability of so many avenues for studies and employment makes thousands of people from the adjoining areas and even remote quarters to visit a big city like Delhi. To bring in the morning and take back home in the evening all these outsiders hundreds of trains, buses and taxis ply from the big city to other places and *vice-versa*. There is also an elaborate public transport system in a big city to carry the people from one part of the city to the other.

All these vehicles cause a lot of pollution which has to some extent been reduced by shifting toxic factories, as, for instance, from Delhi, Agra, etc. and by the use of CNG gas in buses taxis and autorickshaws.

There is an elaborate police system in a big city. But still, many dacoities, burglaries, murders and other crimes take place. Noise pollution is also a big bane of a big city.

We should not, however, lose sight of so many plus points of a big city. So many universities, schools and colleges for education, theatres, musical halls, etc. for entertainment, parks and gardens for relaxation, market complexes for trade, big and small manufacturing corners for workers of all kinds, facilities, etc., hospitals for medical aid, hotels, restaurants and other eateries of different standards for all, historical monuments, swimming pools, places of worship, tourist spots, etc. for tourists and others, libraries for studying books, etc are available only in a big city. So, life in a big city is a mixed fare of plus and minus points.

Now, let us see what a famous writer says about life in a big city:

"This planet" the man said, "is not good enough for me." "You presumptuous, ungrateful rat!" said God. "So this planet is not good enough for you. I will, therefore, send you to Hell where you shall not see the sailing clouds and the flowering trees nor hear the gurgling brooks and live there for ever till the end of your days." And God sent him to live in a city apartment. His name was Christian.

—Lin Yutang in Paradise Lost

Human Rights

A Preview

- ❖ The Americans and the Human Rights
- ❖ Violations of human rights in developing countries
- ❖ The Punjab and Haryana High Court Judgement
- ❖ Situations demanding curtailment of human rights
- ❖ Various human rights organisations and commissions in India and abroad
- ❖ Role of such commissions

The USA, in particular, claims to be the guardian of human rights the world over. But in USA itself President Advisory Board reported:

"Evidence presented to the board makes it clear that many whites, in general, are unaware of how colour is a disadvantage to most members of other groups."

"To understand fully the legacy of race and colour with which we are grappling, we as a nation need to understand that whites tend to benefit, either unknowingly or consciously, from this country's history of white privilege", the report stated.

Of course, there have been many violations of human rights in India as in countries like Pakistan, Bangladesh, Sri Lanka and other developing countries. Sometimes, the security forces do over-react and there is a clear violation of human rights which should not be allowed.

Certain western organisations like the Amnesty International have often taken serious view of such violations. There is the well-known Human Rights Commission in the UN also. But the point is that the terrorists also should not be allowed to violate human rights.

The Punjab and Haryana High Court while disposing of the position against Prevention of Terrorism Act (POTA), observed:

"The terrorist causes a terrible trauma to the innocent. His acts pose a threat to the human society. A person who threatens the sovereignty and integrity of the country is certainly different from a person who merely threatens an individual......."

The learned court expressed in sufficient detail its views on the question of an individual's liberty which is often declared to be inviolable by the human rights protagonists:

"Every right rests upon some degree of restriction. Social obligations limit the individual's liberty. The society has its own science. Liberty can never mean license. It does not mean doing what one likes. Nor can it lie in destroying the rights of others. In a civilised society, liberty should only ensure that a person is able to do what he ought to be doing. Every man has to respect the rights of others before he can justifiably assert his own. Liberty has to be earned before it can be enjoyed. Men of intemperate habits cannot be free. Their passion forge their fetters. While advocating the cause of human rights, this basic truth has to be remembered".

Thus, the human rights are very important to man. They include right to life, liberty, freedom of speech, etc. But, it has to be borne in mind that when by a particular action of an individual or organisation there is a threat to the peace and smooth working of society or when the existence or sovereignty of the state itself is jeopardised, the said human rights may be curtailed according to the law. Thus liberty is a relative term and not an absolute one and so are human rights. But whenever there is a gross violation of human rights in utter disregard of social and moral norms, the culprits must be brought to book effectively whoever they may be, whether terrorists or men in uniform, and their ill-gotten property should also be confiscated to deter them from committing such serious crimes or violations of law in future.

In India, human rights commissions have been formed at the union and state levels. All violations of such rights should be reported to these commissions. There are also National Minorities Commission and National Women's Commission. They are doing good service to the nation. But they must still be considered nascent bodies which are not effective to the desired extent, even if they are to be considered not entirely toothless. At least, they can highlight violations of human rights and reasonably bring such violations to the notice of the general public.

Let us hope the members of various human rights commissions the world over express their views more fairly and fearlessly after studying all the pros and cons of a situation.

Place of Women in Society
or
Empowerment of Women

A Preview

- For a healthy society
- Shivaji, Gandhiji, etc.
- Women in ancient India
- Women in almost all professions
- In England
- Panchayats
- Domination of husbands
- Woman not inferior to man in any field
- Behind every great man
- Antony and Macbeth
- Some great women
- A woman's view
- Indian Constitution
- Reservaion for women
- Shakespeare and Tulsidas
- A Supreme Court judgement

It is very important that we make our women more powerful if we want a healthy society. It will be a platitude to say that woman is not only the one who gives birth to man, but she is also the maker of man.

Behind most of the great men, there is a woman. She may be a mother or wife, more often a mother. Men like Shivaji and Gandhiji had great mothers. A woman can sometimes also spell doom for man, particularly if a husband is an uxorious or a henpecked one, as for instance, Antony in history and Macbeth in literature.

In books of ancient history we read that in ancient India, women enjoyed an exalted place of respect. No *Yajna* could be considered perfect without the participation of women. Even many of the hymns in the sacred Vedas were written by women.

In history, we have had several great women like Queen Elizabeth I, Queen Victoria, Florence Nightingale, Madame Curie, etc. Valentina Tereskova was the first woman who went into space. In India we have had Sita, Savitri, Draupadi, Razia Sultana,

Chand Bibi, Mira, Rani Lakshmi Bai of Jhansi and others. In recent history, we have had Vijayalakshmi Pandit, Sarojini Naidu, Sucheta Kripalani and others. Even some of the Prime Ministers the world over have been women, *e.g.* Margaret Thatcher of England, Golda Meir of Israel, Mrs. Bandaranaike of Sri Lanka, Mrs. Indira Gandhi of India, Mrs. Benazir Bhutto of Pakistan, Shaikh Hasina and Begum Khalida Zia of Bangladesh and so on. Mrs. Chandrika Kumaratunga has been the President of Sri Lanka.

Now, we have women ambassadors, journalists, fashion designers, teachers, authors, doctors, nurses, pilots, engine drivers, officers, lawyers, etc. Fatima Bibi was the first woman to become a judge of the Supreme Court.

It is all right that women now get better facilities of education and rise to high posts in all fields and departments. But, unfortunately, discrimination against women, including even highly qualified and competent working women continues even now.

According, to Pallavi Jha, former Chairperson of the CII (Maharashtra): "A few years ago, a researcher came to interview me about why women were not doing as well as their male colleagues after graduation from business schools. The young women that she had interviewed told her that despite their getting higher marks than the young men and performing better, they received less approval and recognition from male bosses and were slower to be promoted. They felt dejected and despondent."

We must remember that in England, women could get even their right to vote after a long and strenuous struggle. They are fortunate in India to have got it without their asking, as it is enshrined unequivocally in the Constitution. This does not mean that women should grow lukewarm or become complacent. To organise any women's organisations like violent or aggressive women's libs is not the answer. Instead, they should assert themselves in a more effective and convincing way.

In our country, it is imperative for the Panchayats to have at least one woman member. Similarly, a number of legislative and parliamentary constituencies are reserved for women candidates. That is well and good, at least on paper. The fact is that the election campaign is mostly carried out by their husbands. And in case a woman candidate wins the election, it is virtually her husband who runs the show.

Sometime back, there was an outcry to reserve at least 33% seats for women. After so many lengthy sessions, nothing emerged finally. However, the impact of the deliberations and discussions does not seem to have gone down the drain, as women are now getting more and more awakened.

"It is common knowledge that women generally do not resort to deceit and cunning and are usually simple and straight in their statements. But the problem arises when they are guided by cunning men."

Thus, women can become effective only if they shun off their total dependence on their husbands. Guidance or assistance in even their official work, they may take from their husbands. But, it must be transparently clear and convincing to all that they themselves are running the main show. Only then they can deliver the goods and earn a state of credibility among the people. For this, they must give clear proof of their genius, integrity, candour and courage. This is how they can take a bold step forward.

Women must forget such lies as—

> *"Frailty, thy name is woman"*

or what Tulsi Das said—

> *"The fool, the drum, the shudra and women,*
> *Are all whom we must condemn."*

The real purpose of Tulsi Das was probably to warn us against lust. This is what he says in Aranya Kanda of Ramcharitamanasa:

Lust, wrath, greed, pride and all other violent passions form the sturdy army of infatuation, but among them all the most formidable and calamitous is woman, illusion incarnate.

—Shri Ramacharitamanasa, Aranya Kanda

All that was ages ago. Now, woman is living in the new era, era of space, science and computers, the twenty first century. And she is not inferior to man in any respect, not even biologically. Once this realization comes to woman, she can even outdo many as in education to a great extent she is already doing.

Although most of the rural women and those belonging to poor families are still living in a miserable condition, yet the winds of change are also there. There is a loud clamour for women's rights and reservation in offices and legislatures. A few years ago the Supreme Court ruled that a widowed daughter, if she has no income of her own or no estate of her husband to fall back on, can claim maintenance from her father or mother.

It is the duty of all of us to have a high regard for the rights of the girl child and the women. The empowerment of women means the empowerment of the nation.

The Secret of Success

A Preview

- ❖ Nothing ... like success
- ❖ Perseverence
- ❖ Discipline
- ❖ Gandhiji
- ❖ Duties
- ❖ Necessary qualifications
- ❖ Courses
- ❖ Strong will and mind
- ❖ Key to success
- ❖ Planning
- ❖ Disraeli
- ❖ Napoleon
- ❖ Luck
- ❖ Entrance Tests
- ❖ Persistent labour required

It is a common saying that "Nothing succeeds like success." Hitler is sometimes quoted to have said, "Success is the sole earthly judge of right and wrong."

Whatever may be said about success but the fact remains that nothing can be achieved without hard work. Hard work is the key to success. Sometimes, desired results may not be available even through hard work. This may happen for quite some time. But a persevering person is sure to achieve success in the long run.

Success demands a long story of meticulous planning behind every effort. An unplanned effort in any direction may not enable a person to reach the goal. A ship without a rudder is liable to go astray or be swept away by violent sea storms. The same thing can happen in human life also.

Success demands discipline at every step in life. One must be regular and punctual. A student who does not take regular morning walk or exercise and a balanced diet, cannot maintain good health. If he does not go to school at the right time and attend every period and remain attentive in the class and do his homework regularly, he cannot show good results.

It is said about Benjamin Disraeli, one of the most renowned Prime Ministers of England that when he started to speak the first time in the British Parliament when he became an MP, he was so much confused and had such a horrible stage fear that he could not utter a single word. He left ashamed and sat down.

Later, the same Disraesli, who later became the Earl of Beaconsfield, learnt the art of speaking and shed his initial hesitation by standing before the mirror and speaking loudly for an hour or so. Thus, he simulated to be speaking in the Parliament. In course of time, he began to be hailed as one of the greatest orators of the world.

It is said about Mahatma Gandhi that he was a very shy man by nature. He could not speak a single word when he appeared before a judge in a court for the first time as a lawyer. He must have felt awfully small at that time. Later, as we know, Gandhiji became one of the greatest men in history and appeared umpteen times before judges of different courts in connection with not only his legal practice but also the Independence movement.

Mahatma Gandhi's case is an eye-opener in another way also. He has demonstrated beyond an iota of doubt that even the greatest empires in the world can be shaken to the roots just through peaceful, passive and non-violent means on the basis of truth and well meaning, hard, self sacrificial struggle.

Once Napoleon was told that the Alps awfully came in his way in connection with one of his campaigns. Napoleon politely brushed aside the idea, saying, "There will be no Alps."

We can achieve success only if we are as conscious of our duties as our rights. What Horatio Nelson, the famous British general said at the Battle of Trafalgar is a common knowledge, "England expects every man to do his duty", and "Thank God, I have done my duty."

Thus, it is not difficult for us to understand that luck is not as important as it is made out. Dame luck is important in life, no doubt, but hard work and other virtues are no less important.

If a person wants to be a doctor or an engineer or some artist, teacher, or technocrat or even a mechanic, he must first of all acquire the necessary qualifications. This can be done only by studying in a recognized institute and not only by passing the examinatin or getting the diploma or degree with low or just qualifying marks but by getting fairly high marks.

Most of the courses now require the mandatory passing with fairly high marks in entrance test as getting through a board or university examination is not considered enough. Even after completing a course, one may be required to sit in a competitive course and come off with flying colours.

All this requires very hard persistent labour from the beginning. One who wants to reach a particular destination, must start quite early. We can ponder over these points and think of many others which can lead us to success. That is only if we have a strong will and mind.

Here is an extract from the self-story of a successful man (now Managing Director of a famous company concerned with plastic industry) as it appeared in an important daily:

"From the very first day, I decided that I will be honest in my dealings. Never have I till date made an attempt to make a fast buck by dubious means. It is perhaps this reason that my product is made from one of the purest forms of plastic. Besides we adhere strictly to the norms prescribed by the Supreme Court with regard to manufacturing of polybags."

The two most important points revealed in this self-story are that—

1. One must be honest to the core.
2. One must abide by all laws concerned.

It is stupid to try to make fast buck by violating laws. Laws are made for the good of all of us and if we abide by them, the good will flow to us automatically in course of time.

The Secret of Happiness

A Preview

- ❖ Common belief—state of mind
- ❖ The Buddha
- ❖ Wordsworth
- ❖ Leisure and hobbies
- ❖ We should give up negative thoughts and qualities
- ❖ A writer's views
- ❖ Bacon
- ❖ Ancient & medieval poets, etc.
- ❖ Pope
- ❖ Work
- ❖ Virtues
- ❖ Avoid tension
- ❖ Sweetness of temper, etc.
- ❖ Swami Ram Tirth

It is a common belief, and it is right in itself, that happiness is a state of mind, and that it has nothing to do with one's possessions, physical charms and even intellectual attainments.

Many poets and philosophers in ancient and medieval times considered life and this world a vale of sorrow. Even the Buddha is said to have stated that the world is a home of sorrows and miseries.

Many romantic poets of England regarded this world as a valley where sorrow and nothing else rules. John Keats, perhaps the greatest among the romantic poets said about this world:

"Where but to think is to be full of sorrow."

Even PB Shelley, sometimes considered an optimistic and revolutionary poet, said in his celebrated poem Ode to the Skylark:

"We look before and after,
And pine for what is not,
Our sincerest laughter,
With some pain is fraught,
Our sweetest songs are those,
That tell of saddest thought."

Thus, unfortunately, man cannot find free happiness even in laughing and singing. Surprisingly, man cannot enjoy even the sweetest music until sadness is mixed in it. Antonio, the real merchant of Venice in Shakespeare's drama "The Merchant of Venice," has the most characteristic quality of sadness which further lands him in a state of utter misery which in the modern context may be called a "catch-22" situation.

We must remember that when the Buddha calls the world "A home of misery," he also tells us the solution to get out of this state of misery. According to him, the fundamental reason for man's misery is his endless desire. One can get rid of misery by giving up this desire for possessing more and more materialistic things. The Buddha advises us to follow what is called "The

Middle Path." In other words, the extreme desire for anything is the basic cause of misery. The Buddha further advises us to follow what is known as "the eight fold path" which comprises eight truths, such as true living, true thinking, true knowledge, true word, etc. We should bear in mind that the Buddha is the most rational among the philosophers and he considers ignorance a sin and hence the cause of misery. Hence, it is our duty to attain knowledge and increase the stock of learning that we have.

Admittedly, contentment is a great source of happiness. Alexander Pope, the famous Augustan poet, says in his "Ode on Solitude":

> *"Happy the man whose wish and care*
> *A few paternal acres bound."*

In the modern world of sick hurry, we often forget to relax. Relaxation, both physical and mental, is essential to give rest to our tired nerves. Instead of taking sleeping pills at night or pushing ourselves to heart attacks and paralysis and strokes, we should just learn how to meditate and relax for a few minutes daily.

According to a survey, happiness cannot be the monopoly of the well-to-do or the high and the mighty. Even a poor man can find happiness in certain things. It is often seen that the labourers toiling in the sun and the housemaids doing menial jobs go on singing while they are busy in their boring chores. Hence, Wordsworth, the renowned English poet says about a Highland lass in his famous poem : "The Solitary Reaper"

> *"Behold her ! single in the fold,*
> *Yon solitary Highland lass,*
> *Alone she sings and cuts the grain*
> *And sings a melaneholy strain."*

Incidentally, the poet also tells about the power of music in the same poem:

"I listened motionless and still,
And as I mounted up the hill,
The music in my heart I bore,
Long after it was heard no more."

There is no denying the fact that to improve the quality of life and even to exist, we need money and some minimum material possessions. An unsound man or a recluse has no value in the modern world.

In order to earn some money and get other basic necessities, one has to work. Work in itself is a source of happiness. The thing that makes us sorrowful is our attempt at over-reaching ourselves. We should have the right means to achieve the right ends. We should not be afraid to maintain the dignity of labour. We should remember:

"Work is worship."

In order to be happy in the real sense, we should train our mind to turn away from the unpleasant thoughts and move towards sweetness. We should learn the value of leisure and pursue some good hobbies to keep our mind busy in healthy and entertaining pursuits instead of just being overwhelwed by gloomy thoughts and baseless forbodings.

We should follow the path of truth, righteousness and sincerity to maintain peace of mind and give up such negative qualities as anger, desire, vanity, avarice, attachment, sloth, etc.

Above all, tension should be avoided. Let sweetness in thought, temper and talk become our habit. Then happiness will pursue us rather than the other way about.

A writer thus expresses his views on the attainment of happiness while laying stress on the "Middle state":

"Middle state is the most suited to happiness, not exposed to miseries and hardships, the labour and sufferings of the lower part of mankind; nor embarrassed with the pride, luxury, ambition and envy of the upper part of mankind... The calamities of life are shared among the rich and poor, but the middle station has the fewest disasters, and is not exposed to so many vicissitudes...."

Swami Ram Tirth, the renowned spiritualist of India, considered self-sacrifice and self effacement (for the good of others), the greatest sort of happiness. He gave the example of a lamp in one of his famous lectures at the Tokyo University, Japan. He said that the lamp is able to spread the light only by getting its wick burnt. Similarly, a man can get enlightenment and happiness by being useful to others through selfless work and sacrifice.

Bacon says that one can find joy in doing free service to others.

Child Labour
or
Rights of the Child
or
Children's Charter of Demands

A Preview

- Children's rights
- SC judgements
- Child labour
- UN
- International Conference of Mountain Children 2002
- 17 point charter of demands
- Explanation
- Prof Sen's scrutiny
- Public schools
- Teachers

The child is invested with certain rights which must be recognized by the society. Children must not be deprived of such rights.

Some of these rights are:

1. Right to protection from all forms of exploitation.

2. Right to survival, including right to life.

3. Right to development

4. Right to education

5. Right to social uplift

6. Right to social security

7. Right to leisure and recreation

8. Right to freedom and expression, etc.

In the M. D. Mehta *vs* the State of Tamil Nadu (AIR 1991-SC 4777), the Supreme Court prohibited children below the age of 14 from being employed in any "construction work (which) is clearly hazardous occupation."

The Supreme Court also said that "employment connected with manufacturing process in the match factory is not to be given to children, they can, however, be employed in packing process."

In Sheela Barse *vs* Secretary, Children Aid Society, the Supreme Court observed:

"Children in Observaion Homes should not be made to stay for long and as long as they are there, they should be kept occupied and the occupation should be congenial and intended to bring about adaptability in life aimed at bringing about a self confidence and picking of humane virtues." (AIR 1987–SC 659).

In spite of all this, children's rights are being violated most blatantly. Child labour is a common right in kiln, construction work, in restaurants, in shops, in houses, in factories and almost everywhere.

The poor children whom their parents cannot feed but want extra hands to augment the income of the family are exploited by the vested interests. It is their time to attend the school and they should not be deprived of their genuine right to education.

The UN too admits certain rights of children like right to education, right to be well-treated and nursed properly etc.

At an important meeting, the following rights of children were recognized:

  (*i*) improvement in buildings of schools;

  (*ii*) provision of modern facilities for practical subjects in schools;

 (*iii*) participation of students in assessments carried out by teachers;

 (*iv*) high standard in appointment of teachers;

  (*v*) provision of regular attendance of teachers;

 (*vi*) disciplinary action on teachers who force students to undergo tuitions;

 (*vii*) provision of facilities for games;

(*viii*) promotion of cultural activities and establishment of libraries;

 (*ix*) strict implementation of child marriage and child labour laws;

  (*x*) mass awareness for equal opportunity in education for the girlchild;

 (*xi*) free education for children of economically weaker families;

 (*xii*) elimination of evils of society like drinking liquor and gambling;

 (*xiii*) special attention to the education of physically challenged children;

 (*xiv*) saving of rivers and the environment;

 (*xv*) facilitation of guidance to children;

 (*xvi*) participation of children in formulation of all policies related to development of children, and

(*xvii*) equal opportunity of education for children

If we have a close scrutiny of children's demands, we will realize that they are the minimal and are genuine. Nobody can deny that for the healthy growth of society, it is imperative that we should have healthy and well-informed, enlightened children. It is of utmost importance that the children should be allowed to have an all-round development of their personality which is possible only if they get a congenial atmosphere at home and school and all facilities for proper growth without any let or hindrance.

If the children have to study in a class-room even devoid of proper ventilation and the minimum facilities such as fans, fluorescent tubes and even a black-board as in many Government primary schools, how can children be expected to grow into good students fit for higher studies matching international standards? The study conducted by Prof. Amartya Sen, the Nobel Laureate under a special programme PROBE revealed that a very large number of schools in our country lacked such minimum facilities and had either dilapidated buildings or no buildings at all.

We know that many so-called public schools charge high fees and donation money from students' parents and give almost nothing in return. They appoint substandard teachers who are not even qualified for their jobs. What justice can these teachers do? Then so many teachers compel children to engage them privately for tuitions at their residence. For this, the students' parents have to shell out more money. Poor parents, indeed! What can they do? They are helpless.

Gone are the days when the teachers were a dedicated lot. But the teachers' grievances also seem genuine. They are not paid salaries equal to their qualifications. And even those meagre salaries are not paid regularly. So, they have to find out other means for subsistence. Let us all work honestly to let our children grow into great men and women.

Discipline

A Preview

- ❖ Nature and discipline
- ❖ A student
- ❖ Sportsmen
- ❖ A farmer
- ❖ Rights and duties
- ❖ An average man
- ❖ An employee
- ❖ Army
- ❖ Liberty and discipline
- ❖ Kinds of discipline

Discipline is the law of nature. Man is an inseparable part of nature. Hence, he has of necessity, to follow and observe discipline in all walks of life.

Nature follows all its laws very scrupulously. The sun rises in the morning and sets in the evening regularly. The seasons come and go in proper order annually. Day and night alternate each other. The heavenly bodies all observe discipline. Then why should not man?

A man who does not observe discipline has to suffer in life. He has to lead a miserable life. He becomes lethargic and may grow errant or intemperate which are but the impending signs of disaster and misery.

A student who does not go to school or college regularly and punctually, nor does he do his homework with full sincerity, cannot be expected to be a brilliant student. Sometimes, such a student may not even get through his examinations. Thus, ultimately, he has to meet with failure in life when even his nearest friends and relations foresake him. Then he repents, but that is of no use. It is rightly said, "It is no use crying over spilt milk."

An employee who does not work properly in his office may be sacked any time. In such a case, not only he but also his entire family has to suffer for his indisciplined life.

Sportsmen have to be very particular about discipline. A team, the members of which are not well disciplined, cannot hope to get success in any match. A team has to observe team spirit without ignoring the mandates of the captain.

In the army, discipline is of utmost importance. Discipline is the essence of any good army. An army cannot be just called an army if its soldiers are not well-disciplined. No army can win a battle unless it is highly disciplined.

Rightly did Tennyson say in his celebrated poem, "The Charge of the Light Brigade."

"There's not to make reply
There's not to reason why?
There's but to do and die."

Even Mahatma Gandhi has said that it is not the duty of a soldier to criticize the orders of his officer. His duty is only to obey.

We can easily understand that a disciplined army like "The Charge of the Light Brigade" must get victory in the end notwithstanding the heaviest odds. Hence, when Tennyson says the following lines, while celebrating the victory of the Light Brigade in spite of getting wrong orders and despite being outnumbered, he is not at all exaggerating their success:

"When can their glory fade?
O the wild charge they made.
All the world wondered.
Honour the Light Brigade,
Honour the charge they made,
The noble six hundred!"

A farmer who does not sow seeds in the field at the right time and then does not water the plants regularly, cannot hope to get a bumper crop.

Discipline is of utmost importance on the road. One must run one's vehicle in the proper lanes and always keep to the left normally. A careless pedestrian can get crushed under the wheels of a vehicle.

Many people confuse liberty with complete freedom to do anything they like. They think that discipline and liberty are antagonistic to each other. As a matter of fact, liberty and discipline are complementary to each other. One helps the other.

No man can hope for any concession regarding liberty from others if he is not ready to give any such concession to others.

Accordingly every right has a corresponding duty. Thus, if we think, we have the right to do something, we are then also under obligation to let others also do the same thing. In this way, though seemingly, discipline and liberty seem to cut each other, in reality they only ensure and guarantee the possibility of the other. Take, for instance, the case of the Prevention of Terrorism Act (POTA).

Though the POTA might seem to be imposing restrictions on individual activities, it was, in fact, passed by Parliament to ensure liberty to vast sections of society and sovereignty to the state itself. Thus, it was a part of displine which safeguarded liberty. Even the UN had asked member countries to pass laws in their states against terrorism for the sake of peace and security.

Discipline is said to be broadly of two types:

(*i*) Physical discipline   (*ii*) Moral (or higher) discipline

Physical discipline may be observed by anybody by just being bold in the face of danger. But moral discipline demands the controlling of emotion and giving up many things like greed, attachment, ego, desire, anger, etc. That is a more difficult task particularly for a worldly man. Only a stoic or a recluse can observe it in letter and spirit.

Certain virtues like truthfulness, honesty, sincerity, unflinching faith in God, patriotism, etc. must also be considered examples of moral discipline. Those who do not get corrupted even in the face of all temptation and allurement must be deemed great and brave souls.

Let us try to develop in us both kinds of discipline. That is easy in childhood and impressionable years of adolescence and youth. A disciplined person is an asset to himself, to his family, to the society, to the nation and to the whole of mankind.

Leisure

There is a Sanskrit maxim: *"Siddhir bhavati karmaja"*, that is, "success comes through work." Of course, work is very important to have the smooth flow of life for one and all. Jawaharlal Nehru's saying, *"Aaram haraam hai"* is a byword among the people of India.

We should, however also try to understand the significance of the saying, "All work and no play makes Jack a dull boy," and "A sound mind lives in a sound body."

How can one have a sound body? Certainly not by working day and night. Of course, work is worship. But a bout of hard work demands at least a fraction of the time for recoupment and replenishment. Human body is after all, like a machine. When a machine has worked for some time, it requires some rest, so that the effect of friction and its adverse effects is lost or at least mitigated.

When we are doing any physical or intellectual work, our body and brain are constantly demanding a constant flow of oxygen and glucose. No doubt, nature has fixed in our body certain mechanism that constantly works to fulfill the demands of our brain and body cells. Still like excess of any things else excess of work is bad.

When we consider the art of living, our minds go to the aim of life. When we think of the aim of life, our hearts *ipso facto* go towards the creation of God which is sprawling before us.

According to Gandhiji,

"The aim of life is that we should serve the power that had created us, and on whose mercy or consent depends our very breath, by heartily serving its creation. This means love, not hate, which one sees everywhere. We have forgotten that aim and are either actually fighting each other or preparing for that fight."

If we make service to mankind our aim in life, we can never feel any tension or stress and strain in life. Otherwise, as Gandhiji says, we are always "fighting each other or preparing for that fight."

When we work with a such a mean and selfish mentality as to rob somebody or let him down or see him insulted and humiliated and get savage pleasure not of our doing, we are actually not doing any work but our life of this type is only a bundle of obnoxious pieces of mischief, callousness and cruelty. It is better not to do any work than to do such heinous type of work. Unfortunately, most of us are working only for selfish purposes to the disadvantage of others. Our interests clash and we quarrel or indulge in plotting, scheming, strategies, scandals, scams and embezzlement, and this we call work. Is this work ? Can we honestly answer this question?

It is for this reason that a famous thinker says:

"All the evil in this world is brought about by persons who are always up and doing, but do not know when they ought to be up nor what they ought to be doing. The devil, I take it, is still the busiest creature in the universe, and I can quite imagine him denouncing laziness and becoming angry at the smallest waste of time. In his kingdom, I will wager, nobody is allowed to do nothing."

W.H. Davies, in his beautiful poem, "Leisure" says—

> *"What is this life if full of care?*
> *We have no time to stand and stare.*
> *No time to look at beauty's glance,*
> *No time to see how her feet can dance."*

We can enjoy leisure by pursuing one or the other hobby. We can read some fascinating book. We can have the hobby of stamp collecting or gardening or photography or we can see some interesting and absorbing movie or TV serial. Or we can have a stroll in a garden or park or in the courtyard of our house.

We should feel contented with our lot. Doing overwork for any reason only borders on or is actually a symptom of avarice and the evil of a possessive spirit in one's mind. Alexander Pope, in his celebrated poem "Solitude" teaches the lesson of contentment.

Khushwant Singh in one of his essays published in the column "This Above All" says emphatically that (excessively done) hard work is futile.

Thus the celebrated author-thinker points out in his own simple, but highly impressive inimitable style that we cannot escape the fact that America is an amazingly prosperous country. But neither can we escape the fact that society there is in such a condition that all its best contemporary writers are satirists. Curiously enough most of the great American writers have not hesitated to praise idleness.

So, the best way of leading a happy life is, which, indeed, should be our aim, to alternate work and leisure in such a way that neither leisure hinders work nor work encroaches upon the domain of leisure.

Life Is Action, Not Contemplation

A Preview

❖ Life—a process of action
❖ History
❖ To think, plan, etc.
❖ Ambani
❖ Browning
❖ Kings, saviours and conquerors
❖ Devices for human welfare
❖ Joy technique
❖ Reciprocity
❖ Positive thoughts, etc.
❖ Self-respect
❖ We should do good deeds only
❖ No discrimination
❖ Students

It has been rightly said that— "Life is a process of action. The entire content of man's consciousness—thought, knowledge, ideas, values—has only one ultimate form of expression: in his action, and only one ultimate purpose: to guide his actions."

—Ayn Rand

from (the novel—Four Major Attributes)

If we look at the history of mankind, we shall realize that the greatest good to mankind has been done by those who have been the men of action. Mere contemplation is of no use. It is true that every man who wants to do something for mankind, and even for himself and his family, has first to chalk out a plan or strategy. He must also have a strong will and determination to act, that is, to translate his dreams, his imagination, his ideas and thoughts into action.

The late Dhirubai Ambani who is rightly considered one of the greatest men in business history, had the motto: "Have an ambition and also have the determination to achieve your ambition." Nobody can deny his monumental or phenomenal success.

Robert Browning, the great Victorian poet, was imbued with the spirit of undying optimism. He had been a fighter all his life, at least, in his poetry. Hardly ever, if at all, did he lose ground to despair or pessimism. In his celebrated poem "Prospice", he challenges death and says that he had always been a fighter and so let there be another fight:

"The last and the best."

In Indian history, kings like Chandragupta Maurya, Samudragupta, Akbar, Maharaja Ranjit Singh and many others were all men of action. We cannot forget that the greatest saviours of mankind like Lord Krishna, Prophet Mohammad and Guru Gobind Singh ji were all men of action. The greatest known warriors and conquerors like Alexander, Caesar and Napoleon were also men of action.

Action is not only important in the battle-field, but also in every field of life. The people who invented the boat, the ship, the bullock cart, the way of joining bones and such others who discovered or invented devices for the welfare of mankind, were all men of action in their own way. Madame Curie discovered radium for the benefit of mankind and even sacrificed her life in this noble cause. Can her sacrifice or, for that matter, that of any man or woman who has done yeoman's service to mankind, be forgotten?

As an extra bonus, action done for the good of others brings joy to the person concerned himself or herself. As a practitioner of the real technique of joy says:

"Everybody really knows what to do to have his life filled with joy. What is it? Quit hating people, start loving them. Quit being mad at people; start liking them. Quit doing wrong; quit being filled with fear. Quit thinking about yourself and go out and do something for other people. Everybody knows what you have to do to be happy."

Of course, selfless service is the best one. But even if one wants to get joy in equal measure as one distributes joy, the same "joy technique" practitioner advises us—

"Still another good technique is this: increase proportion as you give joy, you will receive joy. It is a law of exact reciprocity. Joy increases as you give it, and diminishes as you try to keep it for yourself. Actually, unless you give it, you will ultimately lose it. In giving it you will accumulate a deposit of joy greater than you ever believed possible."

It is quite clear that a man of action should act only for the good of others. He should neither have negative notions and ideas, nor he should do anything which can be detrimental to the cause of others. He should not hurt others' feelings or sentiments. Just as he needs to be a man of self-respect, he should realize that self-respect for others is equally important.

This brings us to a wider aspect of life. It is that we should not hate others or treat with discrimination anybody on the basis of religion, race, caste, creed, region, nationality or sex. We should look at all with an equal eye and work tirelessly for the welfare of mankind.

Even if we try to surmise the value of positive action even for a student, there is no difficulty in realizing very soon that only an active student can show good results. A shirker or a lethargic student can make no headway in life. The goddess of success appears in its full glory before those only who work and act whole-heartedly and not those who just think, imagine and contemplate.

A real man of action would like to do an adventure even for the sake of adventure which is a fascinating and delectable experience to such people. Let us read what Dennis Tito, the famous, astronaut says about himself:

"I was taking a risk to realise my life's dream and I think I was in denial about the level of danger. I had wanted to go to space since 1957 when the then Soviet Union launched its satellite, Sputnik. It fascinated me that there was another world up there. I went to univesity to study aerospace engineering. So my interest wasn't a recent thing. Now I have a much better understanding of why people put their lives on the line to go and fight in Afghanistan, for example. Your desire to accomplish a certain mission is stronger than life."

Patriotism

A Preview

- Place of one's birth
- A cock
- Scott
- Rani Jhansi
- Rich cultural heritage
- Iqbal
- No discrimination
- Swami Vivekananda
- Isolation and cause of downfall
- Our determination for national reconstruction
- To live and die for the country
- A sparrow
- Self confidence and a source of inspiration
- Tennyson
- Spirit of toleration
- Unity in diversity
- Freedom fighters & martyrs
- Tagore

Every living being loves the place where it is born. The place of one's birth is one's home and everybody, especially a rational being, tries to defend it and keep it in proper order with all his might, capacity and capability.

Even a sparrow tries to defend its nest and its fledglings with all the power within itself if they are attacked by some prowler like a crow, etc.

The saying : "Every cock fights best at its own dung-hill" is not without a deep meaning. It implies that a person (or for that matter, any creature) has the maximum amount of self-confidence and inspirational energy at his (or its) own native place or ground.

Rightly did Sir Walter Scott say,

"I bow to thee my country,
All earthly things above."

The determination of a typical John Bull is:

"My country, right or wrong."

We have in literature several stories and poems which inspire the spirit of patriotism in us. In Hindi we have a famous poem on "Jhansi ki Rani Lakshmi Bai" in which the lines run like this:

"Khoob ladi mardani, Woh to Jhansi wali rani thi."

(*i.e.* she fought very bravely like brave men; she was the Queen of Jhansi)

In English, Tennyson has written the famous poem:

"Charge of the Light Brigade" which includes such inspiring lines as—

1. *There's not to make reply,*
   Thre's not to reason why,
   There's but to do and die.

2. *Cannon to right of them,*
   Cannon to left of them,
   Cannon in front of them,
   Volleyed and thundered.

3. *Stormed at with shot and shell,*
   Boldly they rode and well,
   Into the jaws of death,
   Into the mouth of hall,
   Rode the six hundred.

4. *Flashed all their sabres bare,*
   Flashed as they turned in air,
   Sabring the gunners there,
   Charging and army,
   While all the world wondered.

In India, the spirit of patriotism has not been lacking, except perhaps in the modern times, though still not among the common people.

We have a rich cultural heritage of which we must be proud. We have a composite culture which is another matter of pride. Then in spite of such a vast variety in our society and in our various regions and states, we have the immortal spirit of "unity in diversity."

It is our good luck that we have taken birth in a country where we have the people who are the most tolerant of all kinds of variety and even adverse criticism and practices. We are a secular society where there is no discrimination on the basis of caste, creed, race, religion or region.

Can a true patriot forget Iqbal's famous line—

"Sare Jahan se achha, Hindustan Hamara;
Hum bulbulen hain iski, Yes gulistan hamara."

As per the mandate of the Constitution, we should not discriminate between men and women. Woman is no longer the weaker sex. Science has already proved it abundantly.

We have had a long history of freedom struggle. Thousands of our young men kissed the noose willingly to attain freedom for us. Many others suffered in jails and bore untold miseries and tortures hurled upon them by the cruel Britishers. Let us not forget the sacrifices of these freedom fighters and martyrs. Can we afford to forget Mahatma Gandhi, Nehru, Lala Lajpat Rai, Subhash Chandra Bose, Sardar Bhagat Singh and his companions, Sukhdev and Raj Guru, Chander Shekher Azad and many others?

Pitiably we have forgotten even the names of hundreds of freedom fighters who died or suffered in other ways for us.

This is how Swami Vivekananda, the famous Indian philosopher, orator, patriot and religious, spiritual and cultural ambassador of India, says about this country—"If there is any land on this earth that can lay claims to be the blessed *'punya bhumi'* (holy land), to be the land to which all souls on this earth must come to account for *'karma'*, the land to which every soul that is wending its way Godward must come to attain its last home, the land where humanity has attained its highest towards gentleness, towards, generosity, towards purity, towards calmness, above all the land of introspection and of spirituality—it is India."

Such positive thoughts about India may not be found anywhere else. That is why Tagore says—

"If you want to know India, study Vivekananda. In him everything is positive and nothing negative."

Swami Vivekananda says,

"I am thoroughly convinced that no individual or nation can live by holding itself apart from the community of others...."

Swami Vivekananda's views are very close to those of Jawahar Lal Nehru who also opines that the main reason for India's downfall was her aloofness from other countries. In ancient times, India had trade relations with neighbouring countries and even with countries as far as Italy, Greece, Arabia, Mongolia, Japan and not to speak of Sri Lanka, Malaysia, Indonesia, Singapore, Thailand, Afghanistan, Iran, China, etc. In (early) medieval times, India isolated herself and lost her glory, importance and power. Caste system, purdah, the custom of 'sati' and other such evils are life-hindering practices which not only brought a bad name to her, but also weakened her internally and nibbled at her inner soul and substance.

Let us now all gird up our loins to serve our country and try to uplift the lot of the poor, women, dalits, orphans, the handicapped, the children, the senior citizens and the youth of our country. Let us give attention to such problems as population explosion, unemployment, poverty, crime committing, drug taking, illiteracy, disease, AIDS, etc. and do whatever we can for national reconstruction and saving our people from natural and other disasters. Let us join hands and brain to make our country strong and free from the menace of communalism, social justices, cruelty to animals, deforestation, pollution, etc.

If we, particularly the students and the youth, play honestly a constructive role, we can change our country into a veritable heaven. That will be the manifestation of the true spirit of patriotism in us.

Last but not the least, we should always be ready to die for the defence of our country. We should be ready to make any sacrifice for our country.

We should, however, understand that patriotism does not mean hating other countries. Our catholic spirit of universalism and internationalism should not dampen our spirit of true patriotism and nationalism. Similarly, patriotism and nationalism in us should not lead us to the dark den of chauvinism and jingoism. Let us love all mankind and be altruistic philanthropists while simultaneously being true patriots.

Nationalism and Internationalism

A Preview

- Nationalism and patriotism
- M.S.N. Menon
- Globalisaion and nationalism
- In medieval India
- Ashoka, Chanakya
- English
- Pilgrimages, functions
- Nehru, Tagore, Gandhi
- An observer's view
- Internationalism
- British rule in India
- In ancient India
- Shankaracharya
- Akbar, Aurangzeb
- Modern nation state
- Various "issues"
- Vivekananda

Nationalism and patriotism are sometimes used inter-changeably, being treated as synonymous. They, of course, have a similar connotation and they overlap in meaning. But whereas patriotism shows intense love for the country and a desire to participate in all its activities in weal and woe and to defend it at any cost, nationalism gives more stress on its sovereignty, integration and unity.

Internationalism rests on the idea of a cosmic or world citizenship. It expresses concerns and interests of the whole of mankind and prompts an active role in world affairs and to matters generally pertaining to all or most of the countries of the world.

Now, it is the age of globalisation when all social and economic (if not political) forces in the world are getting mixed up. But this conglomeration presents a strange enigma. In the opinion of the celebrated writer, M.S.N. Menon, as expressed by him in his article, captioned: "Politics only follows expediency."

"Nationalism is emerging in many countries. Even in America and Japan. Isn't it strange that in the age of globalisation, ethnicity has become the most emotive factor in the world? This is because the nation state can no more deliver what it promises. And in an inter-dependent global economy, the promises of the nation states are hollow. The party manifestos are frauds. And promises of politicians are worse."

As is amply clear from all sources, globalisation is the order of the day, but it has not suppressed the fading of nationalism among the nations. Even through globalisation, nations try to promote their own causes in general, irrespective of the effect their activities may have on other states. Thus, as for instance, in our own country, multinational companies are most careful about their own interests or intersts of their respective countries instead of the interests of the countries in which they operate.

In ancient India, we had the holy people who travelled from one shrine to the other in the remotest corners of the country.

Thinkers like Chanakaya thought of not only a national but a world empire for Chandragupta Maurya. Ashoka's empire spread on almost the whole of the Indian subcontinent and even in Afghanistan and, may be, other countries, no longer a part of India.

Then we had Adi Shankaracharya who spread his Upanishadic message all over India and established his *'maths'* (monasteries) in all the four corners of India. Even in middle ages, Mughals, particularly Akbar and Aurangzeb had their sway more or less, on the major part of the Indian subcontinent.

When the British came to India, by and by they conquered the whole of India, leaving aside the principalities and native states over whom they held partial suzerainty. They set up a network of railway lines and adopted several other means to knit India into one unit. They introduced English in schools to make convenient easy communication through this foreign link language which practically became the *lingua franca* of the country. Of course, they did all this for their own convenience. But, the fact remains that this system brought all parts of India together as never before and now it was only a matter of some effort to give it a concrete shape. This made the matter easier for our leaders. However, we have to admit without any hitch that the idea of nationalism had already taken roots in the western world before it came into India.

It is, however, true that prior to the British rule in India, though India had a semblance of unity in the religious and cultural matters (for instance, besides pilgrimages, in the matter of celebrating festivals), yet India could not be called a nation, strictly according to the political science theory.

In fact, all such things as nationalism, globalisation, internationalism, unionisation, etc. can co-exist as has been demonstrated by our great thinkers like Tagore, Gandhi, Nehru and others. But like anything else, excess of nationalism or any of the "isms" is bad.

However, when Swami Vivekananda talks of India's merits, he cannot be said to be overpraising India at the cost of other countries. It is because he does not talk of imperialism, chauvinism, conquest or possessiveness but of gentleness, generosity, purity, introspection and such virtues:

"If there is any land on this earth that can lay claims to be the blessed *punya bhumi* (holy land) to be the land to which all souls on this earth must come to account for karma, the land to which every soul that is wending its way Godward must come to attain its last home, the land where humanity has attained its highest towards gentleness, towards generosity, towards purity, towards calmness, above all the land of introspection and of spirituality—it is India."

—Vivekananda

Prayer and Meditation

A Preview

- Tennyson
- Shelley
- Newton
- The rich and the poor
- Babur and Humayun
- Pope
- Meditation
- Yoga
- A saying
- Shakespeare
- Science
- Einstein
- A reader's view
- A science teacher
- Lack of a social security system
- Difference
- Tagore
- Prayer also for others

*"More things are wrought by prayer
Than this wild world dreams of,"*

Says Tennyson, the representative poet of the English Victorian period.

Even Shakespeare says,

"More things are there in heaven and earth,
Than are found in your philosophy Horatio."

Those words are spoken to Horatio (hero's friend) by Hamlet, the hero of the play of the same name and who is probaly the mouth-piece of the playwright to a great extent if not entirely.

In science, we know all laws, sometimes considered absolute or inviolable are shattered one by one by the new discoveries and experiments. Thus, Newton's laws of motion were proved false by Einstein's Theory of Relativity, which itself is now under a strong threat and is virtually on the verge of being proved falacious or wrong under the formidable new researches and experiments that are going on at various places in the world.

Hence, when man becomes helpless, whom should one approach with the fervent hope of providing a sanctuary or a place of protection from physical, mental, spiritual and psychological turmoils?

It is rightly said:

"Prayers can do miracles". At times, when doctors also turn away the patients who are mortally sick, the patients can doing nothing but pray to God for recovery. It is reported that now even in this present age, many people in India and abroad, have been healed at 'prayer meetings'.

So prayers cannot be dismissed easily nor can be the medicines and the doctors.

One can only admire Babur for having tremendous faith in God when he took three rounds of Humayun's bed. His son was miraculously cured whereas Babur himself died a slow death.

Without going into the merits and demerits of the case or even while refraining from passing any personal view or subjective judgement, we can note with some surprise that even Newton was a firm believer in God and Einstein had a strong faith in the existence and omnipotence of God.

Then, it will not be a surprise if we note, without endorsing or rejecting what a science teacher said the other day, "I definitely have faith in God's curative powers. A patient will recover faster if people are praying for him with sincere hearts.

The role of the doctor is very important, and if the doctor also has faith in God, most of the times his diagnosis will be absolutely correct. His patients will recover quickly because he will prescribe the right medicines."

We have to note that when a man has attained a desired standard of living and a sure system of social security, he considers himself safe in all respects and does not find any need for God. But when a person is poor such that the rich people or even the government are not ready to help him, as there is no social security system worth mentioning as in India, Pakistan and Bangladesh and such other poor, developing countries, it is only God who is left for man to sustain his hope and optimism in life.

It is perhaps rightly said that God lives in the countries where there is no social security system.

It is not to defend this system lacking social security. It simply means that a helpless person can get relief only in faith and prayer. It is also noticeable that man cannot live without hope. As Alexander Pope, the famous poet of the Augustan period in England says,

> *"Hope springs eternal in the human breast,*
> *Man is never but ever to be blessed."*

Meditation is closely related to prayer. The difference lies in the fact that in prayer man may demand something of God, but in meditation this is not the case. Meditation is for attaining peace of mind, relaxation and physical and mental health. However, all meditation, based on the system of yoga aims at attaining a union with the Almighty as its ultimate aim. Such things have been elaborately explained by such stalwarts as Swami Vivekananda and Shivananda.

Even prayer, studied in the right perspective, does not mean any request to God. It is just another form of meditation. Rabindranath Tagore says in one of his poems that he need not request God to grant anything, as God knows better than man what is good and useful and necessary for the latter. Hence Tagore says,

> *"I do not choose the best,*
> *The best chooses me."*

It is often said, "Whatever happens, happens for the best." Prayer is, however, done for others also, for the patients, the invalid, for those in adversity, etc.

Tourism

A Preview

- ❖ India has a vast potential for developing tourism
- ❖ Details
- ❖ Tourism not very popular in India
- ❖ Reasons
- ❖ Explanation of dangers of war
- ❖ Remedy lies in removing obstacles through conscious and persistent efforts.
- ❖ An example how local officials and people can help in promoting tourism which can prove beneficial to the common people

India has a vast potential for developing tourism. For example—
1. We have innumerable areas of scenic beauty;
2. We have green lofty hills and mountains, lakes, cataracts, glaciers, skating and skiing rights, bird and animal sanctuaries, wild and adventure game centres;

3. A chain of hotels and motels and tourist spots and halting places along the main national highways

4. A ministry of tourism at the centre;

5. Great ancient and medieval times temples, mosques and historical buildings and monuments;

6. Arrangements for boating, etc. as in Dal Lake, Kashmir;

7. Wonderful strange sights such as the Darjeeling sunrise, the Amar Nath Ice Shivlinga, etc.

In all these and other factors, tourism in India is not that flourishing as in several other even smaller countries as Singapore, Thailand, Hong Kong (now under China) etc. There may be several reasons for this, some of which may be mentioned below:

1. Lack of good hotels

2. Heavy rates of hotels and consequent high rates of food available there

3. Lack of good quality food and food liked by tourists from different parts of the world.

4. Bureaucracy armed with the spirit of red-tapism.

5. Poor investment avenues in India.

6. Lack of interest among the common people

7. Lack of initiative in the government officials in coaxing tourists to visit India.

8. Lack of leadership to enthuse the people like taxi drivers, auto drivers and shopkeepers to be highly respectful to the sentiments and feelings of the tourist and not try to fleece them.

9. The prevailing conditions of uncertainty in the country.

10. Law and order problem

11. Terrorism, as in Kashmir

12. Communal riots

13. Lack of proper facilities or any priority measures being allowed to the tourists in the matter of travelling as by rail, air or road conveyance, stay in rest houses, etc.

14. Excessive checking or harassment at airports, railway stations, etc.

15. Lack of proper or cheap (or at affordable price) the medical aid particularly in case of emergency

16. Lack of proper or adequate arrangements regarding entertainment, sports, free or easy access to all kinds of reasonable information, not detrimental to national interests.

17. Lack of availability of information regarding India's past history and present politics, economy, scientific progress, etc. at information centres or offices of organisations such as the Archaeological Survey of India, etc.

18. Lack of such important centres as zoos or zoological parks, botanical parks, music concert halls, auditorium for discussion on literary, economic, scientific, art, technological or any current political matters, etc.

19. Constant dangers of nuclear war between India and Pakistan.

We all know that when in May-June 2002, the danger of nuclear war between India and Pakistan was looming large, the countries like America, Britain, France, Australia, Japan etc. took back a large number of their citizens from these two countries and other citizens of those countries were advised by their respective governments to avoid India and Pakistan except when the visit was unavoidable or indispensable.

Japan stopped her flights over India. Even the British Council Library in New Delhi was closed. So, how could one expect any promotion of tourism in India in such circumstances ? Thank God, the danger is over or has subsided, at least for the time being.

Now, of course, remedy lies in removing the obstacles through conscious and persistent efforts.

It must, however, be understood that it is not very difficult to develop tourism in India, if conscious, concerted and correlative efforts are made by both the government and the people, and if new areas and avenues for tourism are developed.

My Best Friend

A Preview

- Friendship of themes
- So many friends
- My best friend
- How friendship developed
- As a salesman
- Beyond description
- Birds of a feather
- True friends rare
- Description—virtues, etc.
- Adversity is the best test
- Great sacrifice

One can have any number of friends if one has money and the will to lead a glamorous life. It is commonly said that thieves always make good friends among themselves. But it is difficult to have many friends and then those good ones if one doesn't have enough money and the will to compromise with one's integrity, dignity and self-respect.

I am a fortunate one and must be considered a rare person who has so many friends and most of them quite good ones. It is always dangerous to indulge in self adulation. But it is at least a matter of pride for me to realize the veracity of the dictum: "Birds of a feather flock together."

It will be presumptuous if I claim that there must be something good in me that has enabled me to attract good friends towards me.

Though I have many friends, yet my best friend is Saleem. Needless to say, a good friend must be a good person and this is what Saleem is, though he does not belong to an affluent family, nor do I belong to one. I do not acquiese to the view that only riches can make good friends. It is my personal view that even more than riches, one's credibility, uprightness, spirit of sacrifice, mutual trust and sincere support at the time of crises make good friends.

What should one expect of a good friend, particularly from a friend whom one calls one's best friend? I think, he must have all the great virtues of a common man. He must be truthful, honest, cooperative, self-effacing, considerate, sympathetic, and above all, a person of high moral character and the one who keeps his promise at any cost. He must be a reliable, highly dependable person. As for broken reeds, they are so commonly roaming about in streets that you cannot count them like the stars in the sky. All the positive qualities are there in Saleem and all the negative qualities are singularly absent.

Saleem is an early rising bird. He doggedly pursues the saying:

> *"Early to bed and early to rise,*
> *Makes a man healthy, wealthy and wise."*

He goes out for a walk in the morning and regularly takes exercise. Consequently he is healthy and glowing with a pinky face, loving warmth, pleasant demeanour and a cool head.

It is said that a period of adversity is an acid test for friends, and this is how Saleem stands tested positively and that without any such deliberation on my part.

Unfortunately a few years ago, my father lost everything in business. Then he met with a serious accident. We had no means for keeping the pot boiling. Even the treatment of my father became a problem for us. All the members of our family decided to get electricity and telephone sets disconnected and even began to sell our household goods. Our TV and refrigerator were sold off. We had even decided to forego one meal daily.

I had not informed Saleem about all this. Per chance he visited our house. He was shocked to see all this. The next day he came with a small bag containing ₹ 50000 and compelled me to accept it. He got back our TV set and refrigerator and also got for us the electricity and telephone connections restored. The reader must have rightly imagined that Saleem moved heaven and earth to get my father cured, and he, indeed, was hale and hearty in a few days.

In fact, Saleem was then a stranger to us. He had visited our house as a salesman of a washing machine company. We had promised him that we would purchase one. He himself was not in good financial health. He sold for us his plot of land. This is how we became friends. He is my alter ego and I am ready to sacrifice my life for him. I have no more words to describe his goodness.

My Country

A Preview

- ❖ Scott's lines
- ❖ Nationalism & Internationalism
- ❖ A big country
- ❖ Population
- ❖ Unity in diversity
- ❖ Federation with a democratic set up
- ❖ Panchayati Raj
- ❖ Problems
- ❖ Native land
- ❖ NRIs
- ❖ Neighbours
- ❖ Progress
- ❖ Terrain
- ❖ A republic
- ❖ A peace-loving country

India is my country and I am proud of it. I believe in letter and spirit what Sir Walter Scott, a famous poet and novelist has said about one's native land:

"Breathes there the man with soul so dead,

Who never to himself has said,

'This is my own, my native land?"

Scott believes that such a man just cannot exist.

Even a small sparrow living in a small nest, loving dearly its young ones, loves the nest more than its own life. Then why should man be less than even a sparrow? It will be the height of ingratitude on the part of a man not to love his country, his native land.

Many people in the world believe in the dictum: "My country, right or wrong." But extreme nationalism leads to chauvinism which is harmful to the interests of mankind. We should try to be nationalists as well as internationalists like Gandhi and Tagore. In the modern world, of course, the geographical boundaries are fast disappearing as more and more men and women are emerging as citizens of the world.

Even from India, many people have emigrated to countries such as America, England, Australia, New Zealand, Italy, Canada, etc. Many of them hold green cards and others have obtained citizenship there.

Even the Non-resident Indians (NRIs) love India, at least, most of them. There is a couplet in Urdu in this connection which can be thus translated into English:

"Far from the orchard the nightingale recalls its nest;
Away from my native land, I recall my home with zest."

India is a vast country. Even in the matter of total land area it is a big country by any stretch of imagination. Therefore, it is called a sub-continent. Once the areas comprising Pakistan and Bangladesh were also part of India. At the time of partition, they got separated from India as West and East Pakistan. Later in 1971, East Pakistan, after a bloody, revolutionary struggle attained freedom from the cruel, partisan rulers of West Pakistan who virtually controlled East Pakistan as their fiedom. Still earlier in history, even Sri Lanka, Myanmar (Burma), Malaysia, Indonesia, Thailand and even major parts of Afghanistan were part of India, as probably in the reign of King Ashoka, the great.

In the matter of population, India is second only to China, India is a densely populated country. This mammoth population is a great problem for India. Although she has rich resources and was once known as "the Golden Sparrow," yet now she is a poor developing country even more than seventy years after attaining Independence, mainly because of this rapid increase in population.

India has made tremendous progress in various fields like agriculture and irrigation, industry, engineering and pharmaceutical goods, in particular, in Information Technology, in Space Research and nuclear science. At the time of Independence, India was a country which depended for most of its necessities on foreign countries. Now, India is making and manufacturing almost evertything for its needs—from the smallast pin or needle to the biggest ship, aircraft, atom bomb and even spacecraft.

India has the lofty Himalayas to the north, a large part of which lies within India. In the south, she has the Indian Ocean and the countries like Sri Lanka, Malaysia and Indonesia. India's boundaries touch Bangladesh and Nepal in the north-east, Myanmar and China in the east, Pakistan and Afghanistan in the north-west. She has the Arabian Sea in the west and far at some distance lies the large continent of Africa. The imaginary Equator is situated not very far off from the southernmost tip of India, while the Tropic of Cancer passes through the middle of India in the dry tracts of Rajasthan.

India has a unity in diversity in all respects. She has cold lofty hills of Siachen and Kargil and hot dry regions of Rajasthan. The south, being near the Equator is a hot region almost the whole year.

There is extreme of climate in Punjab, Haryana and most of north India. The Himalayan peaks and some peaks in Himachal Pradesh and Jammu and Kashmir remain covered with snow almost the whole year.

If most of Rajasthan remains a dry desert almost the whole year because of the Tropic of Cancer and the structure of the Aravali hills which are shaped parallel to the direction of the monsoon winds from the Arabian Sea, Assam is wet almost the whole year. Mawsynram which is situated in Meghalaya state is the wettest place on the earth, recording about 1,141 cm of rain per year. The Indian people belong to different religions, castes and races. They speak different languages. They wear different dresses. They have different food habits. Yet, they are Indians, first and last.

India is a federation of 28 states and 9 union territories as in August 2019. It has a democratic set-up based on the Parliamentary system of government. It is a republic with the President as the head of the state. The real power lies in the union cabinet headed by the Prime Minister.

There are two houses of Parliament—the Lok Sabha, the lower house and the Rajya Sabha, the upper house. The main legislative power lies with the lower house which is elected by the people for a term of five years. There is a similar system in the states. The President is the head of the government, while the Prime Minister and his council of ministers are the elected representatives of the people.

India has a Panchayati system at the grass roots level. There is an independent judiciary to interpret the Constitution which is the longest in the world. There are High Courts at the state level and district and other lower courts at lower level. There are also municipal corporations in big cities and municipal committees in small towns.

Unfortunately, India has a hostile neighbour who, like India, is a nuclear power but is always at loggerheads with India. India is the land of great peace-lovers like the Buddha, Guru Nanak and Gandhi. She has friendship with all countries. Only Pakistan has spurned all her peace offers and the Kashmir problem has become a great headache for India.

About 30 per cent of population of India still lives below the poverty line. There are also other problems like unemployment, wide-spread corruption, etc. Indian government is trying to overcome and solve all the problems with the cooperation of the people. Let us hope for the best.

Resurgent India

A Preview

- ❖ Swami Vivekananda's call
- ❖ Freedom struggle
- ❖ International forums
- ❖ Food production
- ❖ Lal Bahadur Shastri
- ❖ Chinese war
- ❖ Nuclear power
- ❖ Terrorism
- ❖ Globalisation
- ❖ UNDP Report
- ❖ Jawaharlal Nehru
- ❖ Impact on Asian & African countries
- ❖ Independence
- ❖ Industrialisation
- ❖ Atal Behari Vajpayee
- ❖ Pak wars
- ❖ Missile programme
- ❖ Problems
- ❖ A study
- ❖ Drought, 2002
- ❖ Awakening political, economic and social

Before thinking of Resurgent India, let us give a positive response to Swami Vivekananda's call to his countrymen in his own inimitable, irresistible way—

"Let new India arise. Let her arise out of the peasant's cottage, grasping the plough, out of the hut of the fisherman, the cobbler, and the sweeper. Let her spring from the grocer's shop, from beside the oven of the fritter-setter. Let her emanate from the factory, from marts and markets. Let her emerge from the grows and forests, from hills and mountains."

Nobody can deny that India is at last on the march. Rightly did Pandit Jawahar Lal Nehru predict when he said that India was like a sleeping elephant which when woke up, nothing could stop her from marching foward. And, now, at last India has woken up to the reality of the world at large.

Even when India got her freedom after a long, long struggle which was full of sacrifices of her brave sons and daughters in various ways, she became a symbol and a model of freedom and democracy to all mankind. Taking a cue from India's achievement, many Asian and African countries struggled hard for freedom and at last won it by making untold sacrifices and facing unrelenting miseries. Countries like Indonesia, Algeria, Congo and many others got their freedom, not only through their own efforts, but also through India's most positive and well directed efforts at various international forums.

When India got freedom, her food production was only about 3.5 crore tonnes per year. Now, it has crossed 28 crore tonnes. As the population began to grow rapidly, India had to go out to foreign countries with a bowl in her hand. Today, she is a food-surplus state.

India has made a tremendous progress not only in the field of agriculture but also in industrial, scientific and defence fields. Lal Bahadur Shastri, the then Prime Minister of India, had given the slogan:

"JAI JAWAN JAI KISAN".

Later Atal Behari Vajpayee expanded the slogan to—

"Jai Jawan Jai Kisan Jai Vigyan"

When China attacked India in 1962, India had to suffer a humiliating defeat. Then she made up her mind to improve drastically the defence sector. In course of time, she has become a mighty military power as also an economic giant. She gave a crushing defeat to Pakistan in all the wars fought in 1965, 1971 and 1999 just as she had earlier done in 1948.

Today India is a nuclear power and has a powerful indigenous missile system which is second to none in the world. No country can look towards India with an evil eye.

Certain terrorist activities in various parts of India, including December 13, 2001 attack on Parliament, November 26, 2008 attack on Mumbai, etc forced India to have a stand off with Pakistan on the borders and on the line of control in Kashmir.

Now, India has a well orchestrated voice in the world affairs. Foreign countries, including the USA have started recognizing India's voice. It is indeed, impossible for any country of the world to ignore India at international level. However, much more still has to be done to further improve and raise this level of understanding India at world level.

India has a number of problems like the rapid increase in population, poverty, unemployment, illiteracy, disease, etc. But, all-out efforts to solve these problems are already being made.

Globalisation came to India as a mixed fare. It had its positive and negative aspects. To the affluent sections of the society, it gave immense scope and opportunities to grow. But to the poor or less affluent people and particularly those below the poverty line, the poorest of the poor it did not show any sudden change and amelioration.

Still, according to a study in a renowned daily by a veteran, India has shown tremendous growth after globalisation:

"Today few years after the reforms, India is a changed country. It has become one of the fastest growing economies in the world—having grown at a smart more than 7.0 per cent a year during the decade. Second, its population growth has begun to slow down for the first time in decades. Third, literacy growth doubled—from its historic climb of 0.7 per cent a year to 1.4 per cent—hence, literacy rose from 63.83 to 73.0 per cent during the decade, with the biggest gainers being women and the backward states. Fourth a 125 million Indians rose out of poverty as the poverty ratio declined from 36 to 29 per cent—this is almost the same pace as China's in the 1980s."

According to the report (2018) of the United Nations Development Program (UNDP) India occupies 130th position among 189 countries of the world in the matter of human resources development. The UN study is based on various factors like per capita income (the poor being counted a person who has an income of less than a dollar in a day), literacy, longevity, health measures, etc.

In spite of all the points which may be deemed negative, India's march forward (which, may be termed as a leap forward, using the Chinese terminology) cannot be denied or witheld. Despite the devastating drought faced in most of the states in India mainly due to failure of the monsoon in 2002, the fact of India's being one of the fastest growing economies in the world cannot be denied.

Two of the greatest awakenings felt by India are in the field of social and political fields. In the political field India is well-entrenched and well ensconsed as a democracy in spite of the lack of any towering leader and general moral fall of politicians. In the social field which is connected with the economic field, people are well-awakened and they demand their rights and well-being from the leaders and bureaucrats. Their voice is bearing some fruit as corrupt politicians and bureaucrats are being nabbed. Let us hope India will rise to the pinnacle of glory in times to come.

My Aim (or Ambition) in Life
or
What I Want to Be

A Preview

- ❖ It is not easy to know the purpose of life
- ❖ All men are not equal in all respects
- ❖ My friends, want to go in for money earning professions
- ❖ I want to be a college teacher
- ❖ Teacher—a nation builder—moulds impressionable minds
- ❖ Must be a dedicated one
- ❖ Leaders' interference in matters of education
- ❖ My aptitude—I'm fond of research and higher study—not possible in schools
- ❖ Not easy to become a college teacher
- ❖ I'm a brilliant student and working hard
- ❖ College teachers—now well paid
- ❖ Hope to become a college teacher
- ❖ Atmosphere at home is also academic

Of course, it is very difficult for a common man to know the purpose of life. We, human beings, as Shelley puts it, don't know "what we are, whence we are and why we are." But, as human beings we have, have to live in the world for a few decades and as such, we have to chalk out the best manner in which we can live, so that it is most beneficial to us and to others.

Nature has not made us equal in all respects. We all have different aptitude. Hence, while everybody is at liberty to aim or aspire as he likes, it is better to do so in consonance with our aptitude, milieu and resources.

Of course, there our many of my close friends who have the ambition to become doctors, engineers, lawyers, manufacturers or successful businessmen or traders. Some want to go in for the IAS or other services. However, my aim is humble, as I want to become a college teacher.

It may be argued that my aim is driven by necessity, since I do not belong to very rich family and, as such, cannot afford expensive education needed for medical, engineering or other technical courses. That may be as it is, but the crux of the matter is that I am also fervently goaded by a strong national and social spirit within me.

There is no denying the fact that most of us must, keeping in view the social respectability, like to go in for some lucrative jobs and professions, and even the college teachers may sometimes be lured to earn more money by taking tuitions at home instead of delivering the goods in the classroom, yet I am not the person to be swayed by such superficial and material considerations.

The basic thing which is demanded of a teacher is that he should prove to be a true nation builder. For that a teacher may be a primary, a secondary or a college teacher. A teacher is essentially a teacher, and a teacher must realize this fact abundantly well. That he should be a dedicated and devoted one, does not need to be over stressed.

A teacher deals with the most impressionable minds and his impact on his students is everlasting. A nation will have the kind of youth it has, and the youth's mind is moulded by the teachers. Hence the teacher occupies the centre-stage in the matter of nation building.

It is true that nowadays the power hungry and money loving leaders and others belittle the role of teachers. Sometimes, they interfere in the affairs of universities, colleges and schools and other educational institutions. But that must not be allowed at any cost. The teachers should be allowed to teach in the manner most suited to them.

When this much power is pleaded for the teachers, this *ipso facto* also implies great responsibilities on the shoulders of the teachers. They must have some introspection and give up lethargy. They must come well prepared to the classes. They must continue research and study and transfer their treasure of knowledge to their students.

Of course, I am aware that it is not easy now to be a college teacher. Of course, I could become a school teacher. But, as per my aptitude, I am more fond of research and higher study and that is not possible in a school. To be a college teacher, one must have obtained very high marks in lower classes besides in the master's degree examination and also must clear the UGC's test in the subject concerned.

Fortunately, I am a brilliant student and very good in English. My father and brother are also college teachers. They are a beaconlight to me. I can learn a lot from their vast learning and experience. Thus, we do already have an overwhelming teaching atmosphere at home. I think, I shall be able to get high marks in higher classes also. It will not be hard for me to clear the UGC test.

Even if money is not to be totally ignored, we have to bear in mind that the college teachers are no longer ill-paid. After the implementation of new grades, they draw handsome salaries, and I don't think they need to take tuitions. At least, I'll never go in for such a practice. I shall work hard in the class and give free guidance to any student who comes to me for the purpose outside the class room.

Thus, in all probability, I am set to become a college teacher. I pray to God to fulfil my ambition as I am working hard for it.

Students' Role in National Reconstruction

A Preview

- Primary duty of a student
- Freedom struggle
- National policies and progresses
- Slum
- Politics
- Modern world
- The Gita
- Responsibilities
- Sports, exercise, etc.
- Healthy adults
- Proper atmosphere for studies
- After Independence
- National calamities
- Rural areas
- Kinds of courses
- Milton
- Extra-mural activities
- Health
- Students must vow
- Patriotism

The primary duty of students is to pursue knowledge. As such a student is expected to pursue his aim of gaining knowledge with a single-minded devotion and a spirit of dedication.

However, even studies can be pursued if proper atmosphere for this exists. As such, all sections of society have a duty to maintain calm and congeniality in their homes and elsewhere to let these future leaders of the country do their job diligently.

The Indian students, by and large, did a yeoman's job during the freedom struggle. On the call given by our political leaders, they came out of their institutions and took a major part in the freedom struggle.

After Independence, now the students' role in India is limited to the pursuit of knowledge and taking active part in such national policies as census, pulse polio, T.B., malaria, AIDS, Hepatitis-B and C eradication programmes, as also such programmes and campaigns as Adult Education, literacy, etc.

It is heartening to note that the Indian students have often shown great alertness and enthusiasm in promoting national programmes and policies. They have risen to occasion on such crucial times as the Gujarat earthquake, Orissa supercyclone, floods in different parts of the country, famines in certain areas, controlling of communal riots and other problems.

It must, however, be remembered that students can do a lot more. They can go to slums and teach the slum-dwellers the value of cleanliness, family welfare programmes, etc. Similarly, they can go to rural areas and tell the people to learn the value of literacy, rejecting drugs, alcohol, tobacco, etc. They can also tell them about the benefits of a small family.

It is deplorable that the innocuous students are sometimes misled by the crafty politicians and other vested interests, such that politics enters the portals of knowledge and learning and the real aim of education and studies is lost in the unnecessary turmoil.

It is also important that while at school and colleges, the students should also be given some training in cerain arts, crafts and simple technologies, such that they develop a scientific bent of mind and shun superstitions and faith in fate. They should be taught the dignity of labour such that they do not go after white collar jobs and have confidence in self-help and self-dependence.

There is no doubt that in the modern world of rising prices yawning unemployment and yawning disparities in incomes and all-pervading atmosphere of tension, stress and strain, angst, multiple dangers even to the existence of mankind on this planet and uncertainty, it is, indeed, very difficult, if not impossible, even for a sincere person, may be a student or anybody else, to deliver the goods in right earnest.

Still, as Milton says—

"What though the field be lost?"

The Gita teaches us that we should do our duty in all circumstances, irrespective of the visible consquences, as the fruit or result is in the hands of God.

It is the duty of a student to pursue his studies and do other national jobs with heart and soul and he should not desist from doing so in any kind of situation.

At any institution, a student must try to develop all round personality by taking part in extra-mural and cocurricular activities such as speech-making, painting competition, debates, declamation content histrionics, musical concerts, fancy dress show, dance or acting competition, poetical recitation, paper reading, quiz competition, seminars, workshops lectures, social and national campaigns etc. He should not fight shy of doing his duty when he is asked to shoulder some responsibility such as organising a camp, a seminar, a match, a function, etc. Such experiences can prove very useful to him later in life and as such, he can also prove an asset' to the nation.

A student must also take care of his health and character. About character it is rightly said—

When wealth is lost, nothing is lost;
When health is lost, something is lost;
When character is lost, everything is lost.

If the student is healthy, he can study better and come off with flying colours at all examinations. As such, he must take part in sports. He should go out for a daily morning walk and take light exercise every morning when the so called spirit of "feng shui" is at its best.

The students must vow—
1. never to use violence.
2. not to break or destroy public property.
3. never to take or give dowry.
4. never to copy in the examinations.
5. never to vote (as they become major) on caste, religious or regional grounds.

They should work for the nation and try to grow into physically, mentally and emotionally healthy adults such that they can take the reins of the country in the most suitable way as the time comes. They should even be ready to die for the country, if need be.

The Choice of a Profession

A Preview

- Division of Labour
- Modern world
- Teacher
- Lawyer
- Doctor
- An arduous job
- Government's new policy regarding loan for studies
- Parents
- Heart surgeon

- Contrary opinion
- Professions
- Engineer
- Commerce executive, etc.
- To be a doctor
- Reasons
- Selfless service to humanity

- A psychologist's view
- Wordsworth, etc.

According to the Law of Division of Labour, if a profession is pursued for generations, the pursuers become specialists and can deliver the goods in a better way. Contrarily, a technique, if it is followed from father to son and so on, gets fossilised and further progress in the development and use of new technologies remains almost halted.

The modern world aims at constant growth and evolution. As such, it is essential that our youths learn new technologies, techniques and methods and skills which are now available in almost all fields.

As far as I am concerned, I have considered several professions. For instance, I can become a school or college teacher. But I know that the teachers, though quite well-paid now, have very few avenues for progress or promotion.

Moreover, the teachers do not enjoy the same status and respect in society now as they enjoyed some decades ago. Moreover, a teacher's knowledge remains limited to classroom teaching only and with due apology to teachers, it is often seen that they lack worldly wisdom and money mindedness, and it will only be a miracle if a teacher is ever seen to be a millionaire.

Since I am quite good at science also, I can also become an engineer. The modern age is the age of science and technology. Many kinds of new technology is there in the market. Computer engineering and allied courses have a great market value. Several degrees and diplomas are available in several fields. Then there is also much scope for commercial professions, as commercial executives, marketing representatives, etc. are in great demand.

Another profession which can attract one's eyes is law. It is not difficult to do LLB or even LLM. But I have no aptitude for law, engineering or any commercial or managerial profession. All such professions are dry and aim only at Mammon worship. It is said that a lawyer has to tell lies whether he likes it or not. Ironically, even if a lawyer's aim may be noble, it seems strange to me to try to get justice by practising lies and trapping methods.

Similarly, I reject all other professions for one reason or the other. I want to become a doctor. No doubt now it is an uphill task to become a doctor. The fee is very high at the medical colleges and universities. The period of study is also very long and hard. The student must have a sharp brain and stamina to keep standing or sitting at one place for hours together.

Fortunately, I am a brilliant student. My father and elder brother are also doctors, and I can get good guidance from them and can discuss critical cases with them. I also enjoy good health. It is because I get balanced diet at home and have the habit of taking regular morning walks and exercise in the open. I also take a keen interest in sports. Football is my favourite game.

Moreover, I belong to a well-to-do family and can afford the high fees and all kinds of other expenses in connection with studies. If for one reason or the other, the expenses are still likely to go out of hand, I can get government help in the form of easy loan on cheap terms. The government have a scheme for early loans for studies in India and abroad. I want to fully avail myself of this opportunity without becoming a burden on my parents. I understand that the loan amount is to be repaid only after the completion of my studies and as a I get some job and start earning.

However, the most important factor which impels me to become a doctor is my naturally philanthropic bent of mind which I have inherited from my parents. My father does selfless service to humanity. He charges no fees or only nominal fees from poor patients. Similar is the case with my mother who is a midwife and runs her independent clinic. I want to follow in their footsteps in the best family traditions. Here the point of continuing the old parental profession is also vindicated.

I, however, want to be a heart surgeon. As such, I want to learn the latest techniques and the use of ultra-modern equipment and machinery for the purpose. I want to be an expert in ballooning, bypass surgery, angiography and such things.

I know that for this, I'll have to work very hard and that perseveringly and untiringly, but I am ready to pay the price. My father has also consulted a renowned psychologist to learn about my aptitude and he has also advised that I shall prove most successful as a heart surgeon.

I'm confident my cherished dream of serving humanity will be fulfilled. Indeed, I cannot bear the sight of a suffering human being. I have the spirit of Weltschmerz in an overwhelming measure in me. I want to disprove Wordsworth's lament:

"What man has made of Man?"

I want to make all and best of 'Man' by serving men who are the image of God on earth. O God, let it be! Amen!

Hostel Life
or
Life in a Hostel

A Preview

- Home, home...
- Parents and elders, etc.
- Freedom in hostel
- Often one study room for all siblings
- Separate room
- Room-mate
- Opportunity to make friends
- Healthy competition
- Regular programmes
- Canteen, etc.
- Competition
- Opportunity to learn, get guidance, etc.
- Some fall prey to bad company and habits
- Discipline essential
- Supervision by warden and parents' visits essential

It is often said, *"Home, home, sweet home."*
It is also said, *"East or west, Home is the best."*

We need not dispute such statements. But life in a hostel is different from life at home. It has its advantages and disadvantages.

At home, one lives under the supervision and guidance of parents and elders. In many homes where there is joint family system, one's grand parents also live in the same house. One's brothers and sisters also live under the same roof. Sometimes, even uncles, aunts and one's cousins may also be living in the same building.

At home, the elders give instructions to the children to do this or that and not to do something. A docile and obedient young boy or girl may accept it meekly and depend unquestionably on the wisdom of his/her parents and other elders. But, a more modernised youth, even though while obeying his/her parents, may feel some sort of interference in his way of thinking or acting.

On the other hand, in the hostel, one is free to act and behave as one likes except that he/she has to obey certain hostel rules under the supervision of the warden, who is at least not present there every moment over his head.

At home, one rarely has a separate room for study except in very well-to-do families. Normally, one has to study along with his brothers and sisters in the same room. Thus, one cannot study according to one's own desire. Sometimes, a particular time for study may not suit one of the siblings or one may like to go to bed at a particular time and the other one at a different time. There may be difference of opinion even in such minor matters as keeping the window shut or open, switching on or off the A.C., the cooler or the fan and so on.

In the hostel, often every student has a separate room, at least, in higher institutions. And even if there is a mate, it is not very difficult to adapt and adjust. Often both the room-mates are equally matured and there are very little chances of a dispute arising between them, at least, not over trivial matters. At home, the brothers, and sisters are not of the same age and have different standards of maturity. Thus, differences can arise more easily. Moreover, they have been living together for years and, we know that the children of the same family often quarrel among themselves over petty matters. This is a psychological fact as we know quite well that familiarity breeds contempt.

In the hostel, one rises and goes to bed according to one's own free wish and will. This is one of the many reasons that some students do not like to go home even during the long summer vacation.

In the hostel, one finds a great opportunity to make friends. If one has studied a book like "How to make friends and influence other people" by Carnegie or read Lord Bacon's essay "Of Friends", one can be in a greatly advantageous position in this venture. It is because one cannot develop deep friendship with every kind of hosteler. One has to study the other person's tastes, aims and aptitude and attitude to life.

The hostel life gives a student a great opportunity to discuss varied topics such as some burning problem, some book or film or some idea.

Hostel life creates a healthy competition among the hostelers in the matter of studies, games and extracurricular activities. If one has a good reliable confidant, one can discuss even personal problems and hesitations with him/her.

There is no denying the fact that hostel life provides one a great opportunity to develop one's personality. It inculcates in the mind of the students such virtues as love, sympathy, mutual cooperation, etc.

A student weak in studies may get the necessary help and guidance from his room-mate or some other hosteler in the same wing. As a matter of fact, as is often seen, students in a hostel live like one family. They have regular programmes of amusement, competitions such as general knowledge, science and other quizzes, 'antakshri', etc.

Sometimes, they may have eating competitions, and thus those students who suffer from chronic hunger, give up their shyness in the matter of eating and improve their health by increasing their diet. Moreover, in good hostels, particularly in hostels attached to medical and engineering and such other colleges, diet is often rich and balanced. It is also not very costly and is hygienic, as often such hostels run their canteen and cafeteria on cooperative basis, under the supervision of students themselves with overall supervision of the warden and other officials.

As in the case of eating, so in the case of public speaking, singing, debating, acting, etc. The students shed their shyness gradually and at last attain a fully developed personality. In the case of studies, careless students try to emulate their brighter colleagues and they also work hard to reach their level.

Of course, there are certain students who instead of gaining anything from the hostel life, in reality lose a lot. Such students waste their precious time in undesirable pursuits. For instance, they may get addicted to drugs, drinking, smoking, gambling or seeing too many movies. They live and move in bad company and play drakes and ducks with their parents' hard earned money. Naturally, all this is done at the cost of their studies and thus their parents' golden dreams are shattered.

We should not find fault with the hostel life, as such. The wardens and other college authorities should keep a proper check on the students living in hostels. It does not mean that they should restrict all their freedom and even apply unwanted inhibitions on them. But discipline is a must. Like any other field, hostel life cannot be quite fruitful without the proper enforcement of discipline in its right degree and form.

At the same time, parents should also keep in touch with their wards and frequently enquire of the college authorities concerned with the hostel about their wards' activities. But unnecessary and too much interference should be avoided. In reality, just a simple visit by parents off and on to the hostel will be enough to keep their ward in the right gear.

How I Spent My Last Summer Vacation
or
A Summer Camp

A Preview

- ❖ Previous practice
- ❖ The winds of change
- ❖ A summer camp in our school
- ❖ Arrangements—groups etc.
- ❖ Activities and hobbies
- ❖ The best memorable item
- ❖ Well worth it

Previously, I used to go to some hill station like Shimla, Mussoorie, Kasauli, Dharamsala or Nainital during my summer vacation. But I spent my last summer vacation in a different way. Although, at first, I was haunted by the memories of the scenic beauty of the hill stations I had visited during some of the previous years, yet my father was the main moving force who persuaded me to change my mind, and I really realize now that he was right.

My father had read the following report in a newspaper regarding a mega city which goaded him to make me realize the tone and tenor of the winds of change sweeping the social fabric all around.

"With thousands of kids heading for summer camps being organised in schools and other private centres here, there has been a tremendous response to such activities this summer.

Parents do not want their children to idle away their time at home. Instead, they want them to explore their hidden talents, brush up their skills and become more creative. While most of the parents prefer their kids to join coaching for dance, music and painting classes, others want them to take up sports activities like skating, karate and swimming."

My most loving father ran from pillar to post to get me a seat for the summer camp in some hi-fi school in the mega city. He always made it a point to take me with him. As he presented me to the principals of different schools, one after the other, I felt small as if I were an animal for sale or some saleable commodity. But I knew my kind papa was only after my long term benefit.

We got the reply big "No" everywhere since every school was allowing only the students of its own school for the summer camp for which there was so much rush everywhere.

We wondered if our own school, though quite a good one but situated in a small town, could adapt itself to the changing milieu. At last my father met the Principal of our school and the idea clicked. In fact to our surprise Ms. Saroj Rai, the enlightened Principal of our school had already made the arrangements for the summer camp and only the announcement regarding the same was to be made on the day my father met her. The announcement was made with enhanced excitement. She thanked my father for the idea, all the same.

Now, let me recall the summer camp itself, held in our school campus. I need not explain that though the participation was on voluntary basis, the response was tremendous.

The students were advised to attend the camp wearing school uniform only, and they did as they had been advised to do.

In all, about 800 students participated in the summer camp.

They were divided into five groups as under :

1.	Nursery to Class I	Group A
2.	Classes II to IV	Group B
3.	Classes V to VI	Group C
4.	Classes VII to VIII	Group D
5.	Classes IX to XII	Group E

Students of Group A were taught to learn painting, music and dance for two hours daily.

Games based on mathematics, English and painting were taught to students of Group B.

Group C students learnt scanning of photographs and playing games using joy sticks.

Students of Group D were taught surfing the Internet, slide presentation on Powerpoint and the concept of making software.

Group E students learnt Windows and HTML. I was in this group.

Although different groups were taught certain basic concepts and made to participate in certain specific activities, yet there were certain common activities in which anybody and everybody could participate at the particular times and days meant for such activities. Only one had to inform a day or so earlier, so that proper arrangements could be made for him or her alongwith others who had given their consent earlier.

Such activities included hobbies like art, vocal and instrumental music, giddha, bhangra, classical and kathakali dance, science, model making, making soft toys, casting, public speaking, etc.

There were certain activities which were done on daily basis. These included group discussion, mono-acting, histrionics, election, poetry recitation in English, Hindi and regional language, debates, declamation contests, paper reading, extempore public speaking, G.K. Quiz, etc.

There were several other activities such as yoga, P.T., sports, races, gymnastics, swimming and boxing contests, judo, karate, kho-kho, etc.

Then there were some activities including lectures by experts on personality grooming, uses of meditation, dignity of labour, etc. Practical meditation classes were also held on voluntary basis.

For pre-primary wing students there were about two hour activities such as block printing, papier mache, collage making, puppet making, mask making, free hand painting and drawing, etc. These little kids were also taken to the crystal clear cool water shallow swimming pool with colourful sides as reflected in the ambrosial water.

The thing which left an undying mark upon my mind was the artificial snowing on the vast floor of our now made air-tight school hall were I with my friends even skated for a while. How our worthy school Principal had arranged it for us made me wonder. Everybody was marvelled at her resourcefulness. Neither my father nor I nor anybody in the house grudged the amount we had to pay for the fifteen day camp. Our school, always first was first to arrange such a camp in our town.

A Rainy Day in Summer

A Preview

- ❖ Monsoon in India
- ❖ Very hot
- ❖ Drizzling
- ❖ Heavy downpour
- ❖ Low-lying areas
- ❖ A particular day
- ❖ A cool breeze
- ❖ Lightning, thunder of clouds
- ❖ Streets inundated
- ❖ The Yamuna
- ❖ Huts, trees, the condition of the poor
- ❖ Pleasant weather after the rain
- ❖ Disruption of routine life as also sports world

A rainy day in summer is often a boon, though not to all. But a rainy day in winter is often a curse to most of us.

Fortunately, I am to describe here a rainy day in summer.

India is a country where the monsoon clouds rain with full fury during the rainy season on major parts of the country. Some areas get more rains, others less. Only a few regions like certain parts of Rajasthan, Gujarat and Laddakh remain almost dry sometimes.

I am, however, talking about Delhi, the capital of India. It gets mediocre rain every year. But last summer was said to be the wettest one in the history of Delhi.

Let me take up a particular day during the rainy season. It was the tenth July, I still remember. The Sun had been scorchingly hot during the entire month of June. There was no sign of cloud. The people were tired of this heat and were praying to God for a merciful eye. Whereas it had been raining heavily for one week in the neighbouring Haryana and Uttar Pradesh, Delhi had just been skipped off by the cruel, crafty dark clouds that passed over Delhi daily as if to tease and pester the Delhites. Many superstitious people had started believing that it was so because the maximum number of sinners lived in the capital of India.

Let me come still closer to the main point. Ninth July was certainly a very hot day. Even on tenth July when I got up early in the morning, it was not cool by any standard. But soon I felt a cool breeze springing up. My eyes fell towards the sky. I witnessed huge fluffy lamb shaped clouds rushing past overhead.

Suddenly, there was a dazzling flash of lightning in the sky. The clouds began to thunder and roar with an ear-piercing sound. It appeared as if they had been engaged in some fierce battle and were booming guns.

All at once it began to drizzle which lasted only for a few minutes. It was followed by a heavy downpour which increased in quantity as the velocity of the wind that had followed the flow of soft breeze began to drop.

Now, there was all dark everywhere in the atmosphere. It appeared as if rain drops as big as a one-rupee coin were falling on the ground and creating a loud pattering noise, particularly when they struck the window-panes.

It need not be stressed that it was an uphill task for anybody to go out in such a heavy rain. Everybody had to keep indoors. It will also be needless to say that everybody had heaved a sigh of relief and thanked God for his merciful gesture.

The streets, lanes and markets were soon inundated. They presented the scene of fast-flowing rivulets. The sun had so disappeared as if it had been vanquished by the revengeful rain-god. Water entered some lowlying houses and it created a great problem for them. The situation grew particularly alarming in the sub-level localities. Some houses began to leak. The huts of several poor people collapsed and some of them, the wooden ones in particular, were carried away by the fast-flowing swirling water current.

The rain god remained furious till the afternoon. Then its fury slowed down. People came out of their houses with umbrellas in their hands. Water had subsided in main markets. Still at certain places where the roads were kutcha or were in the process of being built, they got slippery and many people slipped their feet on them.

Late in the afternoon, the rain completely stopped. I came out of my house. A cool breeze had started blowing again. The weather was very pleasant. I looked towards the sky.I was overjoyed to find a multicolour rainbow in the sky. I was at once reminded of William Wordsworth's famous line:

"My heart leaps up when I behold a rainbow in the sky."

Many of the shops had reopened. People were very happy. I was somewhat sad to learn that the daily wage-earners had lost the day and their income for the day was nil. Some of them, at least, might have had to forego their meals.

In the evening news bulletin it was reported that Yamuna had crossed the danger mark. Many huts and head of cattle had been washed away. One washerman had lost his life as heavy rain suddenly came when he was washing clothes. I went to see the Yamuna. I looked at the trees on its banks. They looked greener and more charming than ever before.

Heavy rain causes disruption not only in normal life but also in the sports world. In the next day's newspaper, I learnt about the cancellation of a test match between India and West Indies due to heavy rain. I, like all the cricket fans, felt sad about this cancellation of match.

Annual Prize Distribution Function in Your School

A Preview

- Recognition of merit
- Discipline and teamwork
- Rehearsal
- Chief guest
- Special rooms and calms
- Arrival of chief guest
- Speeches
- Items presented
- Closing ceremony
- A cup of tea
- Lesson of one campus family
- Cleanliness
- Cultural programme
- Campus
- Spectators
- Headgirl
- Reception Committee
- Prize distribution—prize winners
- Professional artists
- National anthem
- Excitement over

Annual Prize Distribution function is a regular feature in almost every institution. The apparent purpose of this function is to give prizes to the meritorious students who have shown their mettle in the field of studies during the year. Such a function encourages the young scholars. It is a sort of recognition of merit which impresses even those who have not been able to win a prize.

There are several other benefits of such a function. All the class rooms are thoroughly cleaned and kept spick and span by the students themselves who do so with full devotion and enthusiasm. Thus, they learn the importance of cleanliness, and the lesson of discipline and teamwork.

Since there is invariably cultural programme after the distribution of prizes, it gives a golden opportunity to young artists who thus learn various items such as speech-making, singing, dancing, histrionics, acting, mono-acting, music, drum-playing, dressing, presenting skits, etc.

The rehearsal for the function often starts much earlier, may be a fortnight or so earlier. The headboy or headgirl is asked to write a speech which is thoroughly checked and corrected by the class-teacher and the principal. A large number of students are involved in various activities. One or the other duty is allotted to almost every student.

Several groups or committees are formed. Those are headed by teachers and students' representatives. Each student is a member of one or the other committee, society or group. School houses, clubs and societies such as Cultural society, Drama club, Dance club, Music society, Literary society, Bhangra Party, Giddha, Chila, School Welfare society, Students' Welfare society or club, etc. all play a prominent role in the matter of rehearsal.

The Annual Prize Distribution function of our school was held last Sunday in our school auditorium. It was held from 10. a.m. to 2.00 p.m. Mr. Prem Mukerjee, the Deputy Commissioner (North Zone) was the chief guest.

Preparation for the function had started about a fortnight before. The whole school presented the picture of a bride. It was full of colour and glamour. One could see colourful banners and ribbons fluttering in the air all across the campus.

There were created special-rooms and cabins as Reception-cum-Enquiry office, Volunteers for Guidance office, visitors' room, etc. The parents of the Prize winners and other prominent citizens had been invited to the function. Everybody had been requested to reach the venue by 9.30 a.m. sharp.

The stage was meant for the artists and photographers, etc. Behind the space left open for the cultural programme, sofas were placed for the chief guest, the principal the vice-principal and the members of the school managing committee. A corner seat was meant for the stage secretary. This honour was given to Ms. Malti, the headgirl and the most brilliant student of the school, who every year herself won several prizes in academic, cultural, extra-curricular and sports matters and was a good orator and debator, and had been decorated with school colours and the rare honour of being declared the School Scholar last year and that by none other than the Lieutenant Governor.

The teachers occupied the first and second rows in the school hall. Behind them sat the prize-winners and then the parents and behind them other students.

About a week before the function, a rehearsal function had been held in the school hall. There the principal and some other teachers had spoken to the students with inspiring words and several examples and illustrations from history and mythology. The purpose had been to bring home to the students the importance of discipline, decorum and good manners. Accordingly, there was a pin-drop silence all through the function which was only punctuated by well-deserved clapping and laughter wherever, appropriately required.

The chief guest was punctual to the minute. He was received and garlanded at the gate by the Reception Committee comprising The President of the school Managing Committee, the Principal, the Vice Principal, some senior teachers, the headgirl and the other student representatives. Immediately, the school band sprung into tune.

As the chief guest entered the hall, all present in the hall stood up silently. They occupied their seats only after the chief guest had occupied his seat. First of all, the Principal delivered a speech, highlighing the academic achievements of the school. Then the chief guest was asked to deliver a speech. Thereafter, the headgirl stood up. She thanked the Chief guest and also delivered her speech.

Thereafter, the prize distribution ceremony started. Each prize-winner whose name was announced with the reading of citation by the headgirl, arrived on stage and collected his/her prize from the chief guest who shook hands with him/her with a smile, as he/she went to his/her seat. Some prize-winners smiled, some looked on and others were just indifferent as the photographers, flashed their cameras.

After the prize distribution ceremony was over, the cultural programme started. It was a hilarious success. Mock rehearsals for all the items presented by the students had been performed a number of times. Items such as bhangra, giddha, skits, short dialogues, fancy dress, hymns, folk dances, music tunes based on various popular Hollywood and Bollywood films were especially liked by the spectators. Some prominent professional singers and dancers who had been invited on the occasion, also presented their brief items which made the students clap like mad.

As the function came to an end, the curtain was drawn. Everybody stood up as the National Anthem was sung in its proper time and tune.

The members of the managing committee, the teachers, the prize-winners and their parents and volunteers had been requested to stay back for a cup of tea with the chief guest who had a round of the school campus and some class-rooms and showed a great admiration for everything he saw and heard. Everybody was impressed with his dynamic presonality and qualities of head and heart.

Thus, came to an end the fortnight of great excitement for one and all in the school, right from the students of the lowest to the highest class and from the Principal to the least significant person in the school. It was well-demonstrated, consciously or unconsciously, that all within the campus, irrespective of their status or emoluments, were members of one school family and parts of one indispensable and unbreakable chain in which none was redundant or dispensable or insignificant.

A Railway Journey

A Preview

- ❖ Individual experiences
- ❖ Journey described
- ❖ Experience at the booking window
- ❖ The platform
- ❖ The compartment
- ❖ The experience
- ❖ Strange mood
- ❖ Effect
- ❖ Arrival at the destination
- ❖ Friend's remarks
- ❖ Personal feelings

It is rightly said that everything in the world is relative. Nothing is absolute. Most of us are prone to form impressions and opinion of the world in accordance with our personal experience. When someone else has some dissimilar exprience and expresses a divergent view of the world, we feel disdainful and sceptical of the veracity of his statement.

I'm sorry I've had the necessity or audacity to throw up all this harangue over a petty matter like "A Railway Journey." It is because I had a strange experience with a fellow the other day.

I admit I'm a bit of a short-tempered fellow and I am prone to losing my temper over trivial affairs.

It so happened that I foolishly began to describe a railway journey to a haughty fellow. Here is what I narrated to him:

"I had to go to Amritsar. That was some day in the hot month of June last. I boarded the Chhattisgarh Express at night from the Delhi railway station. It had taken me about an hour in obtaining the second class general ticket by standing in a queue and get a fare amount of pushes and punches when the queue was broken up.

The same thing happened to me while boarding the train. There was so much rush of the passengers trying to board the train and those who wanted to alight that I had to tolerate with strict forbearance even a punch on my nose and the music of a tearing sound from my worn out shirt.

As I entered a compartment I got sandwiched between the columns of passengers who seemed arrayed as if they had been the soldiers of some blackguard army of bygone days, perhaps ready to "do and die" for some cruel despot. I had to tolerate the smell of biri fumes despite the judicial prohibition and heavy enclosed breathing all around. Many mouths gave out the nauseating smells of tobacco, gutaka, *paan* and the like.

Sometimes, as the train moved, a whole mass of human avalanche seemed to be falling on me as if ominously telling me, "Your doom is not far off."

The hurtling sound of the train could hardly be heard in the pandemonium and cacophony of the packed, suffocating compartment which gave me a grand opportunity to pray to God most sincerely, "O God ! send me to hell eternally through some other means, instead of torturing me thus."

Not only I could hear nothing but also I could see nothing in the gloom of sulphurous hell-pit I found myself to be in. Even as small stations passed by, I could hardly see their otherwise glaring lights except as shadows in the twilight.

I learnt two lessons. One was the lesson of silence. I was reminded of Keats' line:

> *"Heard melodies are sweet,*
> *But those unheard are sweeter."*

I tried to hear in my inner mind the unheard melody of the running train like the echo of the Highland lass in the music saturated valley.

I was reminded of Gandhiji's words:

"We are frail human beings. We do not know very often what we say. If we want to listen to the still small voice that is always speaking within us, it will not be heard if we continually speak.

Experience has taught me that silence is a part of the spiritual discipline of a votary of truth..."

The second lesson was the lesson of seeing nothing, as I even shut my eyes (while standing between the seats) as like one of Gandhiji's monkeys. I tried to recall in my mind the beauty of a rose as Tagore advises us to do, in one of his poems. I felt hilarious even in the midst of those tribulations as I recalled the beauty of flowers in a garden I had recently visited, as I recalled in my mind Wordsworth's famous concluding lines in his "Daffodils":

> *"For, oft when on my couch I lie,*
> *In vacant or in pensive mood,*
> *They flash upon that inward eye,*
> *Which is the bliss of solitude.*
> *And then my heart with pleasure fills.*
> *And dances with the daffodils."*

I was in a state of deep meditation and in such a delectable mood that I suddenly cried out spontaneously, "Oh God! Thank you!" Fellow passengers heard my involuntary cry and finding me in such a strange mood, declared: "Here is a big yogi; let us arrange a seat for him." Everybody was then busy to look after my comfort.

I unpremeditatively went on singing praises of God and all in the compartment bent low to me and jostling in the crowded through came forward to seek my blessings. They forgot their mutual acrimonious gestures and ephemeral exchanges of abuses.

I reached Amritsar comfortably well in the morning. I went straight to the Golden Temple and the Durgiana Temple and prayed there to God and begged forgiveness for any errors of omission and commission during the journey."

As I had finished my narration, the fellow said to me: "You are a big dunce, indeed, the biggest one I have ever seen in my life. First, why did you go to Amritsar by the Chhattisgarh train when about half a dozen better trains are available for that holy city? Secondly, you could spend a little more and travel first class."

Then the man volunteered to say, "I always go by the Shatabdi or the Rajdhani. I like A.C. compartments. I relish mineral water, meals, coffee, chocolates, fruitee, ice-cream and such things supplied free of cost to the happy and lucky passengers."

He concluded : "You, the fool can't understand that it is below the dignity of a civilized man to travel by such trains as you did."

I thought it even more stupid to argue with the man that a vast majority of Indians were so poor that they found it very difficult even to pay for the fares of "such ordinary trains, and observed the golden principle of silence, saying to myself, "If speech is silver, silence is golden." I regret only the role of "Swamiji" I played, though never deliberataly or purportedly.

My Favourite Author/Leader (India) (Jawaharlal Nehru)

A Preview

- Birth
- Education
- Gandhi's influence
- Independence Movement
- Great Writer
- Prime Minister
- Parents
- Practice
- National Congress
- Jailed
- Children's Day
- Non-Aligned Movement

My favourite author Jawaharlal Nehru was born on 14th November, 1889, at Allahabad. He was the son of Pt. Moti Lal Nehru and Swaroop Rani. Moti Lal was a rich lawyer. As such, Jawaharlal was born with a silver spoon in his mouth.

Jawaharlal received his early education at home. He went to England in 1905 for higher studies. He studied at the Public School at Harrow. Later, he received education at Cambridge. He was called to the bar.

He returned to India in 1912 and started practice at the Allahabad High Court. He, however, came under the influence of Mahatma Gandhi. He joined the Indian National Congress and jumped into the National Independence movement.

He spent the prime of his life in the jail. It was in the jail that he did most of his writing work.

He is known not only as a great patriot and stateman but also as a great writer.

His most famous works are—

i) Discovery of India

ii) Glimpses of World History

iii) An Autobiography

He is acknowledged as a great humanist, prose-stylist and historian.

Both as a man and writer, Jawaharlal was larger than life. He served as a bridge between the east and the west.

His prose style is simple, lucid and free from dogma. He has the knack of expressing his viewpoint clearly in a simple way such that even an ordinary reader is greatly impressed. He does not believe in such complex nuances as circumlocution, inversion, use of oxymorons and the like.

He has a rational and scientific bent of mind. He is a great nationalist but he also lives all mankind. As such, he is also a universalist of the first order.

He rejects communalism and politicization of religions. He believes in broadness of mind and attitude. He is an agnostic, but he believes in the efficacy of intuition, the good or adverse effect of actions and the usefulness of true spirituality such as advocated by Sri Aurobindo, Tagore and Swami Vivekananda.

He is a great lover of India, man and nature, which is abundantly brought out in almost all his works.

Jawaharlal has geniune love for the poor. His historical studies are based as much on the effect of economic forces operating in the market in various periods of history as on the glamour of kings, rulers and generals. His broad sympathy with time toiling masses in everywhere visible.

Jawaharlal is a poet at heart who grows ecstatic as he describes some natural scenery or objects such as the Himalayas, the Ganga, the clouds, the rainbow, etc. He loves not only men and objects of nature but also animals, birds and insects.

He is rightly known as a great lover of children who still call him "Chacha Nehru". His birthday is observed all over India as Children's Day.

He became the first Prime Minister of India on 15th August, 1947, when India attained freedom. He gave stress on strengthening the democratic institutions and establishment of heavy industry. Thus, he is one of the foremost makers of modern India. As such, he will always be remembered with love and affection by every Indian.

He was a great lover of the youth and wherever he went, he conveyed his message of true patriotion, dedication, sincerity and perseverence to the youth.

He was a great lover of world peace. He was one of the founding members of the Non-Aligned Movement. He tried to establish friendly relations with all countries. Unfortunately, China stabbed India in the back when she attacked her in 1962. It was a great shock to Nehru and he died on 27th May, 1964.

He was also a great lover of books of all kinds. He loved to read English poetry or poetry written in English. Even on his death, the following lines by the great American poet, Robert Frost, were found written on his writing pad:

"Woods are lovely, dark and deep, But I have promises to keep,
And miles to go before I sleep, And miles to go before I sleep."

Thus, he was a versatile genius. It is because of the great and positive qualities in his works which are good for mankind that I love him as my favourite author as also my favourite leader.

My Favourite Foreign Author/Poet (Robert Frost)

A Preview

- ❖ Nehru's favourite poet
- ❖ Early life
- ❖ Middle life
- ❖ Later life
- ❖ Studied from different angles
- ❖ Some famous poems
- ❖ The gift outright
- ❖ The road not taken
- ❖ Mending wall
- ❖ Birches
- ❖ Popularity
- ❖ Criticism and praise

Robert Frost, the popular American poet is my favourite foreign author and poet. It is no co-incidence that many of the Indians also love him and it is a common belief that he was the favourite poet of Jawahar Lal Nehru, the first Prime Minister of India. It is said that after Mr. Nehru's death, the following lines from one of Frost's poems were found written on his writing pad:

> *"Woods are lovely dark and deep,*
> *But I have promises to keep,*
> *And miles to go before I sleep,*
> *And miles to go before I sleep."*

—Stopping By Woods on a Snowy Evening.

Robert Frost was born on March 26, 1874 in San Francisco, California. His father's name was William Prescott Frost Jr. He spent his childhood in San Francisco and then moved to Lawrence in Massachusetts with his mother and sister in 1885 after his father's death.

Frost graduated from Lawrence High School and then in 1892 attended Dartmouth College for a few months. His first poem "My Butterfly" was published in the "Independent" in November, 1894. He married Elinor Miriam White in 1895.

He wrote his first poetry from 1900 to 1910 at "Farms" and taught at a school, Pinkerton Academy, Derry Village in New Hampshire. Later, he taught psychology at New Hampshire State Normal School, Plymouth, New Hampshire from 1911 to 1912.

He went to England with his wife and four children in 1912 and lived there upto 1915. There he wrote poetry. In 1913 he wrote "A Boy's Will" while "North of Boston" was written in 1914. On returning to America in 1915, he settled on a farm, Franconia, New Hampshire. In 1916, he wrote "Mountain Interval." The same year he was elected to the National Institute of Arts and Letters.

From 1917 to 1920, Frost worked as Professor of English at Amherst College. In 1920, he became the co-founder of Bread

Loaf School of English", Middlebury College. From 1921 to 1923, he was the Poet in Residence, the University of Michigan. He again remained the Professor of English, Amherst College from 1923 to 1925.

In 1924, he won the Pulitzer Prize for "New Hampshire." Later, he won the same prize thrice for his "Collected Poems" in 1930, "A Further Range" in 1937 and "A Witness Tree" in 1943. In 1957 Oxford and Cambridge Universities and National University of Ireland conferred on him Litt. D. S. He wrote several poems and won several awards and positions in his life. He died on January 22, 1963. He, however, could not win the Nobel Prize. It might be because his later poetry was disapproved by some critics.

Frost is studied from several angles, for instance,—

1. As Frost—the Man	**2.** as a Modern Poet
3. as a Lyric Poet	**4.** as a Regional Poet
5. as a Thinker	**6.** as a Poet of Nature
7. as a Poet of Man	**8.** as a typical American Poet
9. as a Symbolist	**10.** as a Poet of Rural (or Rustic) life, etc.

Some of his most famous poems are :
1. After Apple-picking
2. The Road Not Taken
3. Stopping By woods on a Snowy Evening
4. Two Tramps in Mud Time
5. Mending Wall
6. Design
7. The Gift Outright
(**Note:** "The Gift Outright" attracted John F. Kennedy, the President of America's attention, so much so that he invited the poet himself to recite the poem at the inauguration ceremony of his being appointed President)
8. The Onset
9. Directive
10. Neither out far Nor In Deep, etc.

The simplicity and renunciation of all ornament can be seen from the lines given below from "The Gift Outright":

"She was our land more than a hundred years
Before were her people....."

The lines in which the poet recalls the history of America's colonization run like prose, as they are unsophisticated and shun of fall all the superficial ornamentalism.

Frost expresses his view that the real freedom movement in America started only when they started to their country in the true sense. He says—

"We were withholding from our land of being,
And forthwith found solace in surrender."

In one of his best known poems "The Road Not Taken", Frost says that once when he was travelling alone, he reached a point on the road where he could not decide what further part of the road he should take. After some deliberation, he chose one direction as it seemed to have been less frequented than the other. And as the poet himself says—

"And that has made all the difference." Now, he only wonders what like he would have been had he taken the other road. But the crucial point is that he could have taken only one of the two roads. Hence, his curiosity would have still been there had he taken the other road. Can we say that life is only a bundle of curiosities, wild speculations, fancies and contradictions?

Many of Frost's poems are about social situations. It is a social situation which he presents in his famous poem "Mending Wall", when he says—

"Something there is that doesn't love a wall."

He presents the opposite viewpoint in the same poem:

"Good fences make good neighbours." Thus we have to accept contradictory views in life. Frost does not probably want to thrust his viewpoint to give any message this way or that way whether all human walls should be mowed down or are they essential for human progress? He remains satisfied to convey the speaker's words:

"Something there is that doesn't love a wall that wants it down".

In "Birches", he says—

> *"Earth's the right place for love;*
> *I don't know where it's likely to go better."*

Thus Frost is a poet of man and lover of this earth. No wonder that he became very popular as much with poets as with common people. Poets like Ezra Pound, W.H. Auden, C. Day Lewis, Edwin Muir, Amyy Lowell, Macleish, etc. were all praise for him. But he has been criticized by Randall Jarrel for his less human, less social, less dramatic and heartless later poetry. In any case, Robert Graves rightly called him "a master poet by world standards."

Modern Education in India

A Preview

- ❖ Previously—stress on humanities
- ❖ Science and technology
- ❖ Computer science
- ❖ Ads
- ❖ Diplomas and courses

Previously education in India was mainly humanities based. Much stress was laid on subjects such as history, geography, political science, religious teaching, drawing, Indian languages, moral science, home science, public administration, civics, social studies, etc. Core science subjects such as chemistry, physics, botany, zoology, physiology, etc. we also taught, but they were not given much attention.

Later, as India got freedom, by and by and as a pressing necessity for the rapid progress of the country, subjects like medical science, engineering (mainly civil and mechanical engineering), architecture, textile technology, paper technology, sugar technology, microbiology, pharmacy, pharmacology, etc. began to receive attention. Still later, subjects like fashion designing, modelling, interior decoration, hotel management, commerce, business administration, engineering of various other kinds, new subjects in medical science in advanced form such as nephrology, gynaecology, cardiology, obstetrics, paediatrics, phychiatry, cardiology etc also began to be taught.

Now, with the changing times, knowledge of computer studies, commerce and business in our country are being provided.

If we have a cursory look at the advertisements of various universities in our country, we shall find that these are science subjects especially those concerning the computer in one way or the other which predominate in most of the cases.

It is not hard to realize that such courses as the following generally steal the light:

1. Bachelor/Master of computer Application. (BCA/MCA)
2. Diploma in Computing (DIC)
3. Advance Diploma in Web Programming (ADWP)
4. M.Sc. Computer Science
5. P.G. Dip. in e-com. Tech. (PGD-e-Com)
6. Dip. Med. Lab. Technician (DMLT)
7. Dip. X-Ray Technology (Dip. X-Ray Tech), etc.

This is how modern education is getting entirely transformed.

Now, there is stress on certain other types of courses concerning besides computer, library and information sciences, journalism and creative writing, health, nutrition and childcare, Rural Development, Distance Education, Tourism, Management,

Women and Youth Development, Areas Specific Awareness and Manpower Development.

Thus, the whole education system is changing, especially at the higher level. Now, courses are aplenty. Only a student has to be hardworking and intelligent.

Defects in Our Education System
or
The Importance of Education

A Preview

- ❖ Dilemma of an illiterate man
- ❖ Education and Literacy
- ❖ The real purpose of education
- ❖ Education essential for pursuit of various courses
- ❖ Defects—
    - (i) Too much stress on humanities
    - (ii) Too much stress on examinations
    - (iii) Overcrowding
    - (iv) Poor qualification of teachers
    - (v) Lack of technical education
    - (vi) Lack of moral education
    - (vii) Government and public school systems of education
- ❖ Prof Yashpal's views

The importance of education cannot be over-estimated. An illiterate man is like an animal. He cannot understand anything in the modern world. He knows nothing of the progress of the modern world in various fields.

Literacy and education have a shade of difference in meaning. A literate person is one who knows the three R's, that is reading, writing and arithmetic. Sometimes, those eager to push the figures of the literate up count just those who have been trained to put their signatures somehow among the literate ones.

An educated man is expected to be many steps up over a merely literate person. Generally a person who has got some qualification like graduation from some university or even just matriculation from some school board may be considered an educated person.

However, in the broader sense, an educated person must have certain qualities besides mere academic qualifications. He must have developed in himself a broadness of outlook, attitude and noble ideas. This is what all great educationists like Dr. S. Radhakrishnan, Krishnamurthi, Bertrand Russell and others have said.

According to Albert Einstein,

"It is not very important for a person to learn facts. For that he does not really need a college. He can learn them from books. The value of an education in a liberal arts college is not the learning of many facts but the training of the mind to think something that cannot be learned from textbooks."

In modern times, education has assumed great importance. It is because education has become essential for the pursuit of careers of most of kinds. But the present education system in India has several defects. Some such defects may be listed as under:

In spite of all the efforts to the contrary, our education system has remained mostly tradition-ridden so far. Too much stress is laid on humanities and comparatively little on subjects like science and commerce. Of course, courses, diplomas and degrees are there which are concerned with new technology, management, etc., but they are not available in all institutions of higher learning. It is generally complained, and rightly so, that students per force have to learn subjects in which they have little interest and which are not at all necessary for the furtherance of their careers.

Secondly, the classes are often so much overcrowded that teacher's voice is hardly heard, and then the problem of indiscipline in an overcrowded class is the natural outcome, particularly when the teacher's voice is inaudible. In such a scenario, most of the time of the teacher is spent in controlling the class instead of giving his real lecture in right earnest.

The third lacuna in our education system is that too frequent tests and examinations mar the spirit of true education. We have annual and half-yearly examinations. In certain institutions we have even monthly or weekly examinations. Some educationists suggest that there should be daily tests or the students performance should be adjudged on the basis of their daily performance in the school. This simply means that the students' mind should never be allowed to have a moment's leisure or any rest. He should be constantly in a state of whirl. To add to these examinations, now we have entrance tests for various courses also.

The poor qualifications of teachers reflect on their quality of teaching. Most shockingly, we sometimes hear of teachers who have got back door entries through bribe or recommendation. In a number of cases, even the selection committees were found to be substandard. The members of these committees lacked proper qualifications. How could they select the most suitable candidates?

Apart from lack of technical education, no moral education is given to the students. The result is that they grow up as irresponsible citizens in many cases. Their attitude grows materialitic and competitive, and they become ruthless in working. They have no respect or regard for their parents, teachers, country or mankind. They are devoid of qualities such as love, compassion, cooperation, sympathy and the like.

At school level, broadly speaking, we have two types of education. The education which is being given to the poor or lower middle class children in government schools and that being given to the children of the rich and middle classes. The second type of education is too costly for the poor to afford it. Whatever the contents and merits and demerits of these types of education, the basic point is the instilling of a glaring complex in the small impressionable students' mind.

The students studying in government schools learn naturally that they are inferior beings as compared to the other ones, while a sense of superiority is being created in the minds of the children studying in public schools. The result is that practically two classes of human beings—those with master will and spirit and those with slavish will and spirit are being created. And as a natural consequence the economic gap of the two classes is likely to go on widening and widening. This can ultimately spell doom for our democratic set-up.

System of examination should be well-integrated with the system of education and the latter with life. In his essay: "Gandhi came too early..." Prof. Yashpal comments on the prevalent education and examination systems as under:

"In the past few decades we have had endles discussions about what's wrong with our higher education but there are no solutions in sight. That's because we have separated education from life and that is why we can have a centralised examination system which tests a students' level of studies from books and not his or her real knowledge. There is no skill formation thus all the riches of our culture are produced by agencies and people who are outside the education system."

We should know that Prof Yashpal is a renowned scientist and educationist and a former Chairman of the University Grants Commission (UGC).

Examination System

A Preview

- ❖ Once there was much stress on degrees
- ❖ Now, we have gone the whole hog for entrance tests
- ❖ Cheap academics
- ❖ Tuitions
- ❖ Loss to class-room teaching
- ❖ How to get rid of the menace of tuitions
- ❖ The multiplicity of entrance tests also a bane
- ❖ Annual tests, monthly tests, etc.
- ❖ Gradation system
- ❖ Uniformity of courses and syllabi

In the whole education system the examination system is perhaps the most defective part of it as it prevails in India.

Once there was much stress on degrees. The marks one got in examinations like BA, MA, etc. were the yardsticks which determined a student's future. There was an outcry against this system. It was because in the technical courses such as MBBS, BE, etc. mere performance on the basis of degrees was not considered enough. It was well-known that many of the wards of influential people could manage to get high marks in practical examinations by exerting their influence on the internal as well as external examiners.

Then, as now, we have the entrance tests for almost any and every admission to any and every institution. This again is the other extreme which we have touched, and as in the case of giving too much importance to degrees, now in giving no importance at all to degrees, we have again touched the nadir point.

This scenario has led to the mushroom growth of cheap academies and the menace of tuitions against which now there is so much hullaballoo. It is quite understandable that a beleaguered student studying under the shadow of awful entrance tests will like to have ready material to vomit it out on the answer sheets.

According to one view expressed by a reader in a newspaper:

"Entrance tests have almost zeroed the value of classroom teaching. The lengthy course contents of two exams—the board/ university exam plus the entrance test—compel a student to take up tuitions and parents to part with a fat sum. The system is such that parents and students are worried about the tough competition ahead."

Thus an extremely serious consequence of these entrance tests is that the students have become totally indifferent to classroom teaching. The teachers have, as if to teach the air in the classroom. It should not be amusing if the teacher as well as the students both become neglected goods as they by virtue of necessity neglect each other.

It is true that, tuitions are a great menace, such that students like to be spoon-fed and they give up the habit of self study. Thus originality is lost and there is only surface knowledge which is reproduced in the answer sheet, as if it had been just vomitted.

Thus, "The practice of tuitions has seriously affected the study habits of students. Students want everything readymade now. They want to be spoon-fed all the time as Library reading is no more there. The students want only, helpbooks and notes prepared by teachers or by coaching centres."

This menace of tuitions cannot be got rid of by arresting and punishing teachers:

First in Haryana and then in Punjab, teachers found teaching tuitions were arrested and legal action was taken against them. But, surprisingly, no action was taken against academies and institutions doling out at exorbitant rates cheap ready-made notes prepared just in pieces and buts. But, unfortunately, the very culture of these entrance tests is fragmentary and even a student who scores a high mark is instrinsically blank in the sphere of knowledge since he/she has done no deep study.

We get another sound advice from the reader when he/she expresses his/her opinion:

"Extra coaching should be given in the school/college itself in the classes run at off times at rates much lower than what is charged by the private coaching centres. The money thus earned by the institution will add to the institution's resources, out of which to keep the teacher's interests going, the teacher can be paid extra for the extra work done. The teacher should be made liable to pay the income tax also for this additional income. Such a facility would prevent many students from going to the expensive coaching centres."

We are actually trying to cope with foreign pressure and necessity although conditions may be different to a great extent in our country where an overwhelming segment of population lives below the poverty line. Now, our young men and women have an eye on courses and tests such as LEET, TOEFL, IELTS, MBA, MCA, etc. besides innumerable computer courses. BEd is another great attraction although the scope even in this course is limited and is further shrinking. One hoary part of examination is the annual examination and allotment of percentage of marks. Now, we have other systems, besides the entrance tests, for instance, semester and monthly test systems and the gradation system.

New and new systems of testing students' knowledge and intelligence are being devised, but the fact remains that cheating in the examination in the form of copying and by several other means, even with the connivance of parents and teachers is going on and this has its adverse effect on society. Much depends on the conscience of society in which we live—whether we live in a sincere and transparent society or a hypocritical one.

Another crying need of the hour is the uniformity in the syllabi for the same classes in boards and different universities.

The student migrating from one intitution to the other in the middle of year finds it difficult to pull on with his studies if he finds the courses different. Then he has to go in for some tuitions or shell out a fat amount to pay fees in some academy selling cheap notes like fast food.

The multiplicity of the entrance tests at every test and for every class and the multiplicity of syllabi for the same course in different universities and institutions boggles a student's mind. He is at his wit's end what to do and so are his parents. The result is that even if he is a bright student, he goes in for tuition for every subject with some teacher or in some experienced academy and shells out his parents' years' hard earned money just in a few months. All this requires deep consideration from educationists and authorities.

Public School System

A Preview

- ❖ Forster's view
- ❖ Public schools—still following the British model
- ❖ High fees and other charges
- ❖ A typical example
- ❖ Prevalent attitude of public schools in general
- ❖ Rift in society
- ❖ All public schools not bad
- ❖ Poor conditions in government run institutions
- ❖ Schools getting government grants
- ❖ Public schools not getting government grants
- ❖ Under-qualified staff—poor salaries
- ❖ Bungling in books, fees, etc.
- ❖ Influential people—commercial aim
- ❖ Some schools run by dedicated people
- ❖ Courses and syllabi
- ❖ People should be cautious

The famous British novelist and lover of India, EM Forster was particularly averse to the British Public School system which was elitist and exclusive in nature. We know that Forster was a lover of the lower strata of society and it was he who agreed to write the renowned Indian novelist Mulk Raj Anand's novel "Untouchable" that saved his (Anand's) life for he had decided to commit suicide having already been rejected by 17 or 18 publishers.

Now a writer says about some famous public schools in India which still persist in following typically the British model:

"These schools would hesitate to admit it, but they are also a caste apart. Most of their students are either drawn from the twice-born castes or from communities and classes who like to see themselves in a mould of high-casteist behaviour and attitudes. While adopting and practising such attitudes, they also like to deny them in order to maintain a politically correct public posture. If at some stage someone were to suggest that these schools should be asked to reserve a minimum percentage of admissions for those who are from beyond the twice-born castes, it would certainly cause chronic turmoil in their collective blood pressure."

Even if here the writer talks of some typical public schools, still the fact remains that many other public schools though not so upbeat in their sustainned norms of superiority complex and unfounded rarity of high standards, exhibit all the resources at their command to beguile the man in the street to pick his pocket by managing to corner high donation, building fund and development fund fees by offering certain courses and hobbies such as swimming, horse riding, etc. and many others though useful yet not necessarily related to necessities of life or to essential child education.

There is a specific example of a man who when he applied for admission of his ward to a public school was asked to himself appear for interview. The man did go to the school office on the appointed day and at the appointed time.

The man with his child was summarily turned out of the interview hall and when he asked the reason for such a treatment, he was told that he was not a graduate. Then he said, "Sir, that is why I want my child to be a graduate. This rude treatment meted out to me itself proves my point. But I want my child to be a simple graduate and not a postgraduate like the members of this board as I do not want him to learn the art of rudeness to such great heights."

A learned writer who seems to have studied such schools closely, comments on the public school system as at present prevalent in India:

"Our public schools are very fearful of winds of change. They like to filter and bar unorthodox ideas from other role-models with strong screens and spikes inserted into their cultural and ideological framework. They are afraid of non-conformist, unconventional ideas and behaviour. They are afraid to subject themselves to analysis and discourse from educationists and thinkers, who might not be privy to their social mores, their utilitarian and authoritarian ways of conducting school life. The other hallmarks of these schools are competitive tension, the urge to always be in win-win situation, fear of authority, a general atmosphere of bullying and taking undue advantage of privilege."

No doubt, many of the public schools create a rift in society by separating the rich, elitist classes through lofty, often unrealistic claims and suggestive, indirect hatred of the lower strata of society which comprises the majority in our populace and which is the backbone of our democratic set-up.

This does not mean that the Public schools are not doing any service to society. For one thing, it is no secret that conditions in government run schools and other institutions are plightful and they present the other extreme side of affairs. They are often marred by poor performance, indifference, general apathy, paucity of funds, no or little teaching, lack of equipment, squalor, absenteeism and so on. The list of deficiencies and shortcomings can be expanded to any extent.

One well-known fact is that the government is unable to cater to the needs of society in the matter of education. Only private institutions can fill this gap.

There are schools which get government help in the shape of annual grant. They have to prescribe the syllabus in their schools as demanded or desired by the state government concerned. Though not always, yet often, their standard of teaching can also be said not to be very high. It is also the reason because they have often to charge fees as ordered by the government and, we know, that such fees are often not quite high. Hence these schools are also usually short of funds as the managements cannot arrange funds to the extent required.

The typical public schools do not get any grant from the government. They have entirely to fend for themselves. As they have to manage their own resources, they charge high fees from students. Often they pay less salary to their staff than that prescribed according to government prescribed grades for each category of teachers, though this cannot be said to be true of all public schools. The reputed public schools often not only pay salary according to government approved grades but even higher, sometimes much higher, to the deserving teachers.

It is natural that those schools that pay less, often very much less to the teachers, cannot get good teachers. Sometimes, the teachers in such schools are underqualified. Then how can we expect the proper delivery of goods from such teachers? Such schools are only sham public schools and demean the whole public schools system. They get recognition somehow from government through important political or bureaucratic links. Their aim is to please the poor, credulous students and make money. They even bungle in the matter of books and stationery.

They get tax concessions and sometimes concessions in the matter of electricity and water supply and may be, telephone service. They are often owned by influential persons who treat them as their private estates. Some influential persons just form trusts whose chairmen, managers and directors are they themselves and/or the members of their family or persons under their influence.

When all said and done, we must admit that some of the public schools, at least, are run by dedicated men and women with the idea of service to humanity, especially in the matter of education. They devote their whole might and even lives to the cause of education and produce great men and women with inspiring ideas.

Most of the public schools have the CBSE course in their schools under the syllabus approved or prepared by the National Council of Educational Research and Training (NCERT). But some schools claiming to be public schools follow the syllabus as approved by the state board or government. Some public schools are run on convent lines but some just call themselves as such to dupe the people.

The people should be wary of public schools, though all of them cannot be painted black. We should not just be enamoured of awesome buildings, A.C. classroom, fleets of buses or glamorous dresses and neckties or even sprawling lawns and swimming pools. We should, above all, notice what is taught in a school.

A Job in Visual Communication

A Preview

- ❖ A new field
- ❖ Kinds of jobs
- ❖ A boon to India
- ❖ The role of advertising agencies
- ❖ Plenty of potential
- ❖ Open market
- ❖ Requirements of companies
- ❖ Institutes offering courses

At present there is a huge potential for the growth of visual communication across the world. This new field offers undreamt of opportunities to the professionals skilled in this field. It is one of the rarest fields in which, as reports appear, a trainee can get even ₹ 50,000 per month which goes up to ₹ 2.5 lakh or more per month after a few years experience after absorption as a regular employee.

If you are an innovative and creative person by nature, a job in the field of visual communication may be awaiting you. You can get the job of an Art director in some advertising agency. It need not be brought to anybody's notice that at present there are innumerable advertising agencies ever busy producing new and new kinds of advertisements for various companies who want to promote the sale of their new and old products at the best possible rates, and the number of such agencies is on the increase day by day.

In the field of visual communication such professionals as artists, photographers, engineers and software designers are in great demand. There is, fortunately now a huge market in our own country for the skilled and well trained personnel who may even like to work as free lancers if they so decide for themselves. It has become possible after the market has been opened to the multinational firms and already several cartoon serials and their dubbed versions have proved a grand success is our country.

Innumerable companies, government departments, health and education organisations, including NGOs, publishers of all kinds, television companies like Zee, Star, etc., newspapers and periodicals and magazines, all require the services of visual communicators at various levels and various allied works for not only production but also marketing etc. Similarly, producers of video games, CDs, music video cassettes, etc. are always in need of highly competent designers, planners, innovators, creators, analysers, representatives, image-makers, scanners, processors, etc. Such things are required not only for entertainment items, but also for medical and health purposes, education, art, painting, graphics, comic books, video movies, commercials, etc. also. Even fashion designers, interior decorators and house furnishers require the services of such professionals.

As per information made available at present, "Toonz Animation India (TAI) in Thiruvananthpuram offers 1 and 2-year diploma course, while Xavier's Institute of Comm-unications offers a 9-month diploma for animation. Some of the other institutions that offer courses on animation or visual communication are National Institute of Design, Ahmedabad, ZICA Studios, Mumbai, Industrial Design Centre, IIT Bombay, Arena Animation Academy, Pentamedia Graphics Limited, Chennai, C-DAG's National Multimedia Resource Centre, Pune.

Some of the leading animation design studios where the professionals are employed in India are Pentamedia Graphics, Crest Communications, Uni-lazer, Toonz Animation India Ltd., Magic Shop, Universal Studios, UTV Toons, Western Outdoor, Digital Canvas, ZICA and Shri Adhikari Brothers Apart From Creative and artistic abilities, a degree or diploma in Fine Arts, Visual Art, Commercial Art, Graphic Design, Animation Design or Visual Communication Design is must. The professionals must also possess sufficient experience to handle animation and multimedia software like Maya, 3D Studio Max and Tictactoon, Flash, Giff Animator, Adobe After Effects, etc.

Generally, the undergraduate courses are said to start for one who has cleared 10+2 examination. However, those really interested, may go in to get fuller and the latest information from the relevant institutions and authorities concerned.

Science and Religion

A Preview

- ❖ Seem to be antagonistic...
- ❖ Many similarities and dissimilarities
- ❖ Religion believed to be much older
- ❖ Early man
- ❖ God
- ❖ Science makes man rational
- ❖ Science at early stages looked at with suspicion
- ❖ Donne and Keats
- ❖ Einstein and Newton
- ❖ Religion and magic, rituals, faith, etc.
- ❖ A world purely based on science dangerous
- ❖ A world purely based on religion blind,
  rigid and unprogressive—hence, both essential

Science and religion seem to be antagonistic to each other. But intrinsically, their purpose is the same—that is, to make life happy and worth living. Both claim to be based on truth, though their methods are different.

There are many similarities and dissimilarities between science and religion. The basis of science in earliest stages at least, is believed to have been observation and experience, and it is quite undersandable that man must have been observing the natural phenomena and having some experiences of varied type. Yet, religion is believed to be much older than science. It is because religion is primarily based on belief and faith which later took the shape of magic. But science in its tangible form came to be recognized much later.

It is now almost established that man has evolved from other species after the passage of numerous milleniums. As he appeared on the earth in the present human form, he was awed to watch the lightning in the sky followed by a loud thunder. As he moved on the earth, he came across or experienced floods and forest fires which made him realize the presence of some spirit behind all such things and happenings. He began to feel and realize and associate his own life and fate in the hands of some invisible power whom perhaps he gave the name of God. The fact that the name of God in different vernaculars, lauguages and dialects exists almost all over the world in all religions, among all races and countries, means that either all mankind was thinking alike at one or the other time or the people in different regions or areas of the world were having some communication system even unconsciously, may be in the form of conveying of some fact, information, secret or piece of knowledge from person to person through the mouth, as the writing process, as we know now, came much later, indeed, recently only.

Whatever might be the origin of science and religion, the main point is their area of activity and their method of working.

Science makes a man rational and free-minded. Religion wants man to believe blindly in what he is told to be true and worthy of being practised. Science asks questions and puts every thesis or proposal to test. Religion abhors such methods.

Science believes in logical experiments and wants to declare something truthful and true if it comes out finally resultant of the experiment. Religion pre-supposes the result and wants to stick to it irrespective of the outcome of investigation, inquiry or experiment.

At the early stages as science and the scientific temperament progressed, people looked at science with suspicious eyes. It was called the Devil's hand which was out to shatter all faith in old philosophy and established belief in various customs and practices.

The result of this skeptical approach towards science was that many of the scientists were tortured or even silenced with the edge of the sword. Burno was said to have been burnt alive and Galileo was believed to have saved his life with great difficulty.

Even some literary people like Donne and Keats doubted the usefulness of science which was believed to be out to destroy all human emotions and sentiments. Thus John Donne wrote during the Elizabethan period in England:

"The new philosophy calls all in doubt"

Even Keats said much later in the early nineteenth century:

"Do not all charms fly,
At the mere touch of cold philosophy?"

However, here, we should not presume that Keats is criticising science. He probably had not much faith in religion, although he uses very rich religious vocabulary in his poetry. So, he might, contrarily, be raising his doubts about all religious philosophy which seems cold to him.

Generally, science is said to lack all human touch. Scientific experiments are often performed without bearing in mind that the final goal of every human activity or research should be human welfare. As such, sometimes, research leads to an awful destination, as it happened with Einstein. It is said that the great scientist of the modern era only accidentally stumbled upon his Theory of Relativity. And this is what led to the manufacturing of atom bombs—a thought which disturbed even Einstein himself and began even to doubt the capacity of mankind to maintain its survival for a long time to come.

Religion has some fixed thoughts, ideas, rituals, ceremonies and practices which get fossilized in course of time and go on being practised and followed by the believers with no or very little changes. Science, on the other hand, believes that nothing can be said to be absolute in the world. Everything is relative. Newton's laws were shattered by Einstein and now Einstein's own theories may be proved wrong, if the new experiments that are being done, prove successful.

We can say, religion is the heart and science the brain of mankind or legs and eyes respectively. A world based purely on science will destroy itself with its highly devastating weapons of war. A world purely based on religion will go blind, dogmatic unprogressive and will be ruled by fanatical godmen, magicians, quacks, astrologers, shirkers and such others.

So, religion and science both are complementary to each other. For mankind, both are required in equal measure and simultaneously. Thus intrinsically, both are essential for man.

Cinema

A Preview

- ❖ A wonderful means of entertainment
- ❖ Cinema vs TV
- ❖ The poor, children, women like it is special
- ❖ Great educative value
- ❖ Sex and violence in films
- ❖ The Duryodhana and the Rakhshasa awards
- ❖ Their significance
- ❖ Improvement in the standard of the Bollywood films the need of the hour

Cinema is a wonderful means of entertaiment and instruction. It is a part and parcel of mass media. No doubt, with the advent of the small screen its significance has to some extent got curtailed. Still, it has a strong hold on the people's minds particularly, the people belonging to lower sections of society like the cobblers, the carpenters, the rickshaw pullers, the labourers and others who are illiterate or semi-literate. They prefer the cinema to the TV. It is because in their houses, either they don't have the TV sets or even if they have them, they feel more elated and at home in the wide and open atmosphere of the cinema hall. Moreover, the life-size pictures of men and women enthrall them more than the diminutive pictures of the heroes and the heroines on the small screen.

Children are also enamoured of the cinema shows. Of course, they often remain glued to the idiot box in their houses. But if they are given an option, they would like to see a film in the cinema hall. Even women show the same tendency.

The cinema does not show the multiplicity of programmes as we find in the TV serials, but it has its own value. It is mainly an entertainment programme through films.

In spite of the main thrust of the cinema only to provide entertainment, it has a great educative value. Some films are really very educative. But pitiably, many of the films, particularly the Bollywood films, are full of violence and sexy, bawdy scenes which are often not related to the main topic.

Although a central Censor Board is there, Chairperson of which is usually an old veteran actor or actress, yet somehow, perceptibly or imperceptibly horrible, violent and sexy scenes appear in films and in spite of the shrill outcry of the opponents of pornography and indecent social practices, they continue to be shown.

Similarly, in ceratin advertisements, some of them shown in the cinema halls also, pornography in an overt or covert way continues to creep in. Otherwise, cinema is also a wonderful means of spreading some national messages of spreading literacy, population control, etc.

To overcome the menace of sex and violence in films and advertisements, the Maharashtra State Commission for Women has instituted two strange awards. They are—

1. The Duryodhana Award for 'bad' films and sexiest advertising; and

2. The Rakshasa Award for violence against women in the media.

The Commission is a statutory body which was set up in 1993. It has the powers to investigate crimes against women and ensures that the laws regarding women's rights are implemented in letter and spirit.

Some people have objected to the institution of such awards. They think that they can be counterproductive, as the films and advertisements which get these awards may get undue publicity and many persons may like to see them just for the sake of curiosity.

However, a big functionary of the Commission, has defended these awards, saying:

"Look at the awards as a signal to improve standards. We are not being puritanical. We are looking at these awards from the standpoint of women's empowerment. We want a movement towards refinement. We are tired of seeing these one-faceted sex objects even the male is stereo-typed as a hunk with nothing in the top category. We've reduced our-selves to such woeful caricatures."

The Duryodhana Award takes its name from the mythological villian, Duryodhana, of the Mahabharata. As per the story, he tried to disrobe Draupadi, the wife of the Pandava princes in the Kaurava sabha. It is a different story that she was saved from the travail by Lord Krishna with his supreme divine powers.

The Rakshasa Award is based on the centuries old prevalent notion of the Rakshasa being a symbol of ruthless violence.

As per reports some women, have objected to the use of mythological beings being used for the purpose.

The said functionary defends the use of such symbols as these can be more easily understood by the common people. She laments that only negative aspects of women like crying in distress or being slapped or pushed around are shown in films and advertisements and their positive aspects such as courage and their customs such as "Karva Chauth" (depicting women fasting for the well-being of their husbands) or the "palla" (The custom of women covering their heads in public and in the home) are only rarely shown.

In any case, whatever the effect of the awards, the aim is noble and let us hope the noble results will follow.

What a pity! No Indian film could win the Oscar, but a number of films and advertisements may logically be fit for being awarded the negative the Duryodhana and the Rakshasa awards.

Let us all try to be conscious of and assertive against commodifying of women and hope that the Bollywood films will try to improve themselves and present more worthwhile contents and not just play to the gallery.

Globalisation and Agriculture

A Preview

- ❖ New slogan of modern age
- ❖ A mixed fare
- ❖ Harder competition
- ❖ Wider avenues for growth and marketing
- ❖ Employment position
- ❖ New technology in agriculture
- ❖ Need for change of laws
- ❖ Organic farming, etc.
- ❖ Stocks
- ❖ Fruit and vegetables
- ❖ Need for storage and processing facilities
- ❖ Export
- ❖ Cooperative marketing, etc.

Globalisation is the new slogan in the modern age. Some people condemn globalisation while others are all praise for it. It is a mixed fare which has brought riches to some and misery to others. Countries like Mexico, Malaysia, Indonesia, Thailand and India and Pakistan to some extent have had to get a severe jolt because of globalisation.

Globalisation has thrown a new challenge before all the countries of the world. Now, even the companies in the developing countries have to compete with the powerful giants of the western world.

As a result of it, some companies which could not rise to the occasion have been completely wiped out. Others have suffered heavy losses.

It was believed that globalisation would increase avenues of employment. While such avenues have increased in certain fields like information technology, dramatics, media, services, etc. they have drastically decreased in certain other fields like agriculture, manufacturing, white collared desk jobs, engineering, etc.

As far as agriculture is concerned, now we have new technology like organic farming, genetic engineering and biotechnology; diversification of crops, use of biofertilizers, etc. Besides, now there are wide areas for marketing. But that also means stiffer competition than ever before.

Thus, globalisation is a new challenge to the Indian farmer as much as to the government. In India, there is still shortage of oilseeds and pulses whereas there are huge surplus stocks of wheat and rice. So, it is very necessary to bring about the necessary diversification in the crop system to meet the new challange.

It is also seen that during the season of different types of vegetables, there is a flood of particular kinds of vegatables in the market but a scarcity of these vegetables during the off season.

Sometimes, the market is flooded with potatoes, sometimes onions, sometimes garlic and so on. Then there are no buyers and much of the vegetable goes waste, and the poor farmers suffer. Then during the off-season, or when a particular type of vegetable crop suffers a serious setback due to some climatic or other reasons, there is a hue and cry for a particular type of vegetable, as for instance, it happened with onion in 1998 when the crop in Gujarat failed because of drought, etc.

The prices of onion shot up to ₹ 100/- or more in the market. In such circumstances, only the hoarders and black-marketeers flourish while the man in the street as well as the producer farmer suffers.

To overcome such eventualities not only in the matter of vegetables but also in the matter of different kinds of fruits of which India is the largest producer in the world, it is very important to have a rational fruit and vegetable policy for home consumption and exports abroad of surplus produce.

It is also essential to start processing plants for fruits juice, jam, pickles and tinned vegetables for export. Even in our own country, people should be tried to get habituated to using tinned food items, though it will not be quite easy to change the typical mindset the Indian who prefers to use farm fresh vegetables only.

Proper facilities for cold storage and avoidance of waste should be made available to the farmers at cheap rates so that they can earn handsome amount of money during the off-season.

It will be in the fitness of things if co-operative marketing of farm produce is started which can be of great advantage to the small and marginal farmers in particular. For this, suitable amendments to the Market Committee Act and Agriculture Cooperative Society Act should be brought about.

Globalisation has opened new markets and facilitated imports and exports. This means more efficiency on the part of all concerned.

Agriculture—New Possibilities

A Preview

- ❖ England and India compared.
- ❖ India is an agricultural country
- ❖ Tremendous increase in agricultural production
- ❖ Much depends upon the system—mere production not enough
- ❖ 21st century
- ❖ Population factor
- ❖ Milk production
- ❖ Marginal farmers
- ❖ Populist measures.
- ❖ Electricity should be made available at reasonable rates

Unlike England which has been completely urbanised, India is still a land of villages. India is an agricultural country.

Most of the villagers follow the occupation of agriculture. As such, agriculture is the backbone of Indian economy, great efforts have been made by the government as well as the peasants to streamline the agricultural sector, yet there are several snags in the system.

Though there has been a tremendous increase in the production of agricultural goods, yet, a vast population still is half-fed only. We are living in a strange world that India today is, where even in the period of surpluses and wastage, many hapless people have to starve. Prof. Amartya Sen, world famous Nobel Prize winning economist's findings have come full circle in India.

The celebrated Nobel Laureate says that much depends upon the system. He talks of a particular period when there were a large number of starvation deaths in Africa in spite of availability of a fair amount of food. But in India during that particular period, there were no or fewer starvation deaths in spite of lesser amount of available food. It was because of the system. The democratic system in India made it possible to make the food reach the needy more easily as even a single starvation death in a democratic system could whip up general public anger and displeasure because of the freedom of the press. A similar power was not available to the media in South Africa where there was no democratic set-up at that time.

There is no doubt that India has made an impressive progress in several spheres, particularly industrial and service sectors. In spite of this, agriculture remains the mainstay of the Indian economy. It is still in agriculture that the largest working force of India is employed. It is estimated that about two-thirds of the country's total workforce is still employed in the agricultural sector.

Twenty first century must be considered very crucial for India's agricultural growth. The world is now a small village only as far as the rapid emergence of technological innovations are concerned, particularly in the fields of communication and biotechnology. Genetic engineering is a new phenomenon that can be ignored by any country only at its own peril. Certainly agriculture cannot remain unaffected in such a scenario.

It should be borne in mind that euphoria of bumper crops is just a mirage in certain respects. It is mainly because the country's population is still growing at an alarming rate. The crucial New resources and means have to be discovered to meet the expanding markets for agricultural produces, while at the same time keeping intact and well-managed the existing systems.

It is heartening to note that India is today the largest producer of milk and second largest producer of wheat, rice, fruits and vegetables in the world. Yet, because of India's mammoth population, per capita consumption of quality food products in our country is still well below the optimum qualitative quantity required for a healthy populace. A vast segment of our population still lives below the poverty line and the poor, not to speak of the poorest of the poor, cannot afford to pay the exorbitant rates of fruits, vegetables, pulses, meat, milk and other nutrient foods. Even to afford simple wheat and rice diet is an uphill task for many.

For the purpose of meeting challenges in the 21st century, all the systems—irrigation, genetics, marketing, etc. will have to be brought into full play.

Mere populist measures like free supply of electricity and water to the farmers is not going to solve the problem. What meaning does this measure have when electricity is not available at all or it just suffers from frequent breakdowns ? The farmers will preferably like to be sure of a regular supply of electricity and water at reasonable and afforable rates. Let the authorities pay full attention to this crucial problem.

Forest Fires

A Preview

❖ Importance of forests
❖ National Forest Policy
❖ Loss because of forest fires
❖ Preventive reasons
❖ Preventive measures

Forests are the pride of any country. They are lovable things to all, children in special.The following lines of the famous American poet, Robert Frost, are known to all poetry lovers, and they were most cheristed by Pt. Jawahar Lal Nehru, on whose writing pad they were found written immediately after his death:

"Woods are lovely, dark and deep,
But I have promises to keep,

And miles to go before I sleep,
And miles to go before I sleep."

In India once we had a fairly large area under forest cover. Ideally, about 33 per cent area of a country should be covered by forests. In India this percentage is estimated to be at present about 21 per cent.

Forests are known for wealth and wild animals. The Gir forests in Gujarat in India are famous for lions. In the forests we also have costly medicinal herbs.

It is a pity that in India we have no effective forest fire control policy. Of course, the National Forest Policy was adopted in 1988. But this policy is hardly, if ever, implemented by the states. As per report not many states have constituted Forest Protecton Committees.

The net result of this lackadaisical attitude is that every year forests in Himachal Pradesh, Uttarakhand, Madhya Pradesh and other parts of the country catch fire and there is loss of millions of rupees. Only in Uttarakhand the loss in forests due to fire is estimated to be 8,600 acres in 2016.

According to the the National Forest Policy about one third of land area in India which comes to about 110 million hectares should be under forest cover. At present about 75 million hectares of land in India is officially recorded to be under forest cover but according to the Forest Survery of India it is only 708273 sq.km. which is equal to 21.54 per cent of total geographical area of India.

Keeping in mind the total area of forest land in India, if we consider the area where fire occurs in forests, we shall be astounded to note the extent of these fires. It is said that 14107 fires were reported from forests during the period between November 2018 and February 2019.

These fires covered an area of about 5.7 million hectares which means 1.14 million hectares on average annual basis.

While India loses ₹ 1,176 crore a year to forest fires, a mere ₹ 45-50 crore is allocated per annum under the forest fire prevention and management fund, which also remains unspent. Certainly, this is a huge loss which should be seriously taken note of. According to the estimate of experts about 50 per cent of forest land in India is such that it can catch fire.

This forest fire generally takes place in different parts of the country generally in the summer season due to various reasons.

Forest fires often occur due to the following reasons:

(i) Some people try to occupy a part of forest land. For this purpose they burn the dry or semi-dry undergrowth and carelessly let the fire spread. When the wind helps the fire, it soon becomes uncontrollable and spreads like the proverbial jungle fire and takes the shape of conflagration.

(ii) Some unwary villagers or travellers and tourists throw lighted cigarette butts or smouldering match-sticks on the floor of the forest. The dry leaves catch fire which spreads far and wide reducing the forest growth built up over the years into cinders within minutes.

(iii) Sometimes, some villages or forest dwellers light fire for domestic purposes and leave it unextinguished even after their purpose is fulfilled.

(iv) Another reason for forest fires is the inter-rubbing or friction of dry twigs and branches of trees during the scorching hot summer day. This friction leads to ignition of dry leaves on these twigs and branches. This happens more particularly in the case of cone-shaped trees like the pines. The dry pine needles lying on the floor of the forest act as highly inflammable fuel for forest fires.

These fires destroy the fertility of the land. They destroy precious trees, shrubs and medicinal herbs. With the destruction of trees, birds and wild animals lose their sanctuary and get killed or burnt in fire. The burnt soil is unable to absorb water. Nor is there left the previous thick undergrowth to act as a natural way of soil and water conservation.

This results in shortage of water and acceleration of flash floods in the hilly area and it may affect even the adjoining plains. It can also lead to droughts. Undoubtedly, it leads to soil erosion. As the fertility of the land is affected, new plant growth does not take place quickly or easily.

What are the preventive measures to check forest fires? In 1914, a British Officer, started a standard operating procedure to check forest fires. He issued some instructions. These instructions were later revised in 1940 as more research was done in this matter. But after Independence, all this work was virtually neglected.

One can easily say that first of all, there should be stringent and proper legislation in this regard. Already we have the Indian Forest Act which was passed as far back as 1927. According to this law, any person who owns any protected land or lives near a village, is duty-bound to inform the authorities concerned if he notices any forest fires. In fact, he must even try to extinguish such fire if it occurs on a small scale. In case of failure to do so, he can be fined ₹ 200 or imprisoned for one month or he may have to undergo both kinds of punishment. But, we see, practically the law remains unimplmented.

Still, there can be no gainsaying that villagers and others living near the forests must be involved in the process of fire preventing measures. The help of the village panchayats may be taken. Control rooms and towers should be set up at strategic points. The help of satellite imagery should be taken. As the summer season approaches the fire fighting arrangements should be kept in a state of readiness. In case of any fire report, the fire-fighting engines and competent fire fighters should be despatched immediately through helicopters, if necessary.

A powerful communication network is necessary to monitor all information. Intensive research in the field should be undertaken. All the necessary data should be accumulated and well-preserved and made available when needed. The geographical terrain of the affected areas should be thoroughly studied and kept handy for study and consultation.

The help of the NGO's may also be taken. If the government, the people and the NGOs work in unison and with full sincerity, the forest fires can become a thing of the past, considerably, if not fully.

Wildlife Protection

A Preview

* Act, 1972
* Smuggling
* Elephants, lions, tigers, etc.
* Chiru's wool and shawls
* Reports
* Ancient Indian literature
* Medieval and modern literature
* History
* Bharat, etc.
* Hunting should be banned

While all of us are rightly so eager to manage pollution of all kinds, it is also important for us to help in protecting wildlife. We should abide by the provisions of the Wildlife Protection Act, 1972. It is no secret that a large scale smuggling of wildlife goods is taking place all over the world in spite of requisite laws passed by a majority of countries of the world in this regard.

Elephants' ivory is sold and for that the poor elaphants are killed. Lions are killed for medicinal purposes and so are tigers. White tiger, in particular, has entered the realm of a rare species.

Another well-known rare species is the Chiru known as Tibetan Antelope (Pantholopes Hodgsoni). It is an endangered species. The famous shahtoosh shawls, priced at ₹ 1 lakh or more in the international market are made of the wool of this animal.

As per reports gathered from the press, "As the Tibetan antelope is an endangered species, there is a complete ban on the trade of goods made from the wool of Chiru in about 133 countries. Wool derived from Chiru is smuggled into India from China mostly via Leh and Ladakh especially through Darchule, Rexol and Jaya Nagar routes. The main reason for its smuggling is that artisans are available only in Srinagar to manufacture shawls from this wool. And following manufacturing, these shawls are smuggled to countries like France and the UK where these fetch a very high price."

Under the Wildlife Protection Act, 1972, the minimum imprisonment for violation is of one year. In spite of this, every year, illegal sale of shahtoosh shawls is detected.

We must remember how our ancestors loved wildlife and sought its protection alongwith the protection of trees and forests. There are innumerable references to the wild animals in the ancient books. The Panchtantra stories are about animals. It is said that Shakuntala's son, Bharat after whose name we have named our country "Bharat", used to play with lions. Even in the medieval age, the children of Rajputs like Maharana Jaswant Singh are said to be fond of playing with lions.

In literature, we have the famous poem by William Blake on "Tiger":

> *"Tiger! Tiger! burning bright*
> *In the forest of the might."*

In "The Old Man and The Sea" by the American novelist, Hemingway, these are the dreams of the lions which bring good luck to the hero. Kipling's "Kim" is the story based on the life of wild animals.

In his story on "Puran Dass", the ascetic has friendship with wild animals and it is because of their "sixth sense" that the village is saved, though the saint himself loses his life in the noble cause.

Historically, we cannot forget Ashoka's lions on his piller which is our national emblem. The tiger is appropriately considered our national animal.

Let us all take a pledge to protect wildlife at all costs. It is not only because animals are also living beings like us but also because our future also depends on this planet on the wildlife being safe and protected. Hence hunting of wildlife should be banned with an iron hand.

According to a report, "the centre has asked state governments to include forests and wildlife in the priority sector and come out with a five-year action plan for the protected wildlife areas on the pattern of forest working plans."

As per the report, "protected wildlife areas constitute less than 5 per cent of the country's total geographical area. This will also ensure the much needed coordination between the wildlife and forest staff. The ministry has underlined the need for setting up special courts in the states for the effective implementation of the Wildlife Protection Act. It also proposes to amend the Act to introduce the concept of "community reserves" to recognise and ensure the people's contribution in the conservation of wildlife. A new classification of forests in the shape of special conservation areas will also be introduced to protect isolated grooves of trees."

The newspaper report further points out that "the responsibility of protecting the special conservation areas will be with the Wildlife Department. The Centre has also decided to have the same norms for the resettlement of people living within national parks and sanctuaries outside the protected areas as are applicable in case of those ousted due to the construction of big dams. The oustees will be payed a grant of ₹ 1 lakh per family, besides compensation for the land lost. Taking a serious notice of the fact that officers trained in wildlife management were not being posted in the wildlife wing, the ministry has asked the states to provide details of officials trained at the Wildlife Institute of India."

Science and Human Happiness

A Preview

❖ Science—the greatest boon to man
❖ A result of centuries hard labour
❖ Devices for man's comfort
❖ Electricity
❖ Agriculture, industry, medicine, surgery, education
❖ Health consciousness
❖ Food for all
❖ Destructive role of science
❖ Research goes on
❖ Positive research should be encouraged

There is no doubt that science has been the greatest boon to man so far. But the achievements of science have not come to man as a ripe apple falls in the lap of a man sitting under an apple tree. Science is not just the result of observation and experience. It is, on the other hand, the result of centuries of hard work done by man, even at the risk of his own life or health. For instance, Madame Curie got cancer for experimenting with X-rays emitted by radioactive radium. Burno was burnt alive. Even the great essayist-scientist, the father of Empirical (or experimental) science, Lord Bacon is said to have lost his life while experimenting with the maximum cold the human body can bear.

In any case, we should be thankful to our forefathers who thought so much for us and worked so hard for us to bring out innumerable scientific devices and gadgets for comfort.

Today, man can fly in space. He can fly in the air like birds. He can swim on the surface of the sea like fishes. He can move on the earth at tremendous speed. More recently, he can keep sitting at home and do online-shopping. He can chat and learn a lot on the Internet and also express his own viewpoint through Twitter.

If some outstanding scientific achievements of the twentieth century are to be mentioned, the discovery of electricity must perhaps come at the top. The electricity brings in its train innumerable devices like the fluorescent tube, the bulb, the fan, the desert cooler, the air-conditioner, the geyser, the heater, the electric oven, the washing machine, the mixer, the blower—the list is, indeed, inexhaustible. Even the printing presses, textile and hundreds of other mills and factories and the cinematographs and computers and TV sets and the radio also work with electricity though the battery cells may also be used in some cases.

Today we have inverters and generators which save us from sitting idly in the dark with our work in hand suspended on the breakdown of electricity.

Now, we have fast cars, motorbikes, buses, trucks, trains, aeroplanes, ships, spaceships and what not.

The most notable achievements of science are in the fields of agriculture, industry and medicine and surgery. There was a time when it was believed that a horrible famine was looming large over the Indian horizon. Now, thanks to the Green Revolution brought about by scientific methods, India has become a food surplus nation. Thereafter the White Revolution has made India the largest producer of milk in the world.

In industry, there has been brought about a revolution in the matter of mass production of goods. The calculators, the mobile phones, the ready-made garments, the luxury soaps and detergents, the shampoos, the toothpastes, the TV's, the transistors, the refrigerators, etc. which were once beyond the range of the common man, have now been brought within the range of at least middle classes and even lower middle classes, though we must admit that such things are still beyond the purchasing capacity of the poor, not to speak of the poorest, and the poor in India comprise at least 30 per cent of the population, if not more.

In the fields of medicine and surgery, literally miraculous progress has been done. What are these—the bypass surgery, ballooning, heart and kidney and bone-marrow transplant? They are nothing short of miracles. Today, smallpox stands eradicated from the surface of the earth. All-out efforts are being made to banish polio. Such horrible diseases as malaria, plague, hepatitis—A, B and C, tuberculosis and several others have greatly been controlled. Great efforts are going on to check diseases like AIDS, cancer, heart attack, kidney failure, etc.

Today, the people are greatly health conscious. Longevity has increased in most of the countries. Child mortality has been greatly reduced in number. We have so many health centres, gyms and slimming centres and nursing homes, hosptials and maternity centres. In the field of education and dissemination of knowledge, we have the use of e-mail, e-class-rooms, better schools, new teaching and learning methods, study through CDs and several audio-video methods.

It is a pity that man has also invented and is still inventing new agents and methods of destruction. Horribly dangerous bombs, including nuclear and thermonuclear bombs, missiles, rockets, guns and other armaments have been manufactured and stockpiled by several nations. Then we have biological and chemical weapons which are no less horrible. Unfortunately, man's moral, spiritual and ethical progress has not been in tune with his material progress through science. That is why man is making an abuse and a misuse of this wonderful branch of knowledge that is science. Let him learn some lesson from Dr. Faustus who wanted to learn beyond the proper limit. Any desire beyond the limits of propriety is always dangerous.

Let us hope that man will reform himself and indulge only in positive and constructive research and manufacturing process.

In fact man is still exploring the vast uncharted vistas on the earth and in the sky. He is still trying to probe deeply into the past. Let us hope for the best.

Are We Happier Than Our Forefathers ?
or
Modern Civilization

A Preview

- ❖ A moot point
- ❖ Pure water, food, etc.
- ❖ Simple dress
- ❖ Limited sphere
- ❖ Not many means of communication, entertainment, health, education, art, music, literature
- ❖ Not many scientific devices
- ❖ Prepared a ground for the modern generation
- ❖ Man has lost touch with God and nature
- ❖ Money rules the world
- ❖ All comforts for the rich only
- ❖ Indian culture

It cannot be said categorically in whether we are happier than our forefathers or not.

Our forefathers led a very simple life. They ate simple and natural food devoid of the toxic contents of any fertilizers, pesticides or insecticides. The fruits and vegetables they ate had never been sprayed with highly poisonous substances. The water they drank was free from any debilitating elements and obnoxious metals and minerals which now mar our seas and rivers and canals.

Our forefathers ate and drank simple and natural things, also wore very simple loose clothes. They had never tasted tea, coffee or coca cola. They did not know much about fashions, etc.

Our forefathers were illiterate. They could hardly read or write anything. They had no or very little communication with the world outside their homes, fields or limited spheres of activity. They knew nothing about cinema-houses, theatres, libraries, circuses, exhibitions, museum halls and not much about schools, colleges and universities, not to speak of modern computer centres, dancing halls, auditoriums, stadiums, lecture theatres and the like.

They worked very hard for us and did the spadework for us to emerge in the modern world, though they themselves never had the imagination, like that.

Our forefathers have disappeared from the stage of this world, after providing us with means to create a new world. We have to acknowledge that man has progressed step by step. One step leads to the next, the next to the next and so on. Rome was not built in a day. Similarly, all the inventions, discoveries and explorations of the earth, space and even mind were not made all of a sudden or in a day, month or years. It took them centuries to come into being. They are still going on, particularly in the field of science and their pace has now become tremendous and even mind-boggling. We can now sit in an AC room free from heat. We can drink cool water from a water cooler whenever we like. We can eat delicious fruits, vegetables and canned dishes procured from all parts of the world. We can hear music, see scenery or dance or drama just by pressing a button.

Modern life of hustle and bustle has changed man into an antomaton or a robot. He has virtually lost his sense of proportion and is unable to think in a proper and systematic manner about himself or mankind or about all the creatures on the earth. He has lost touch with God, the Creator, who sustains all. Hence, he has become cruel, ruthless and selfish to the core.

It is an irony of fate that man's own diabolical creations like the nuclear bombs and missiles are haunting to destroy him.

We talk of material comforts. Of course, they are good enough if they do not lead to corresponding or more serious drawbacks or what may be called side-effects.

Now, we have great money and business magnates who live in palatial houses, have fleets of cars and have opulent things of art in their houses. They have no real love for works of art. But, they just believe in displaying their facile sense in this context. Or, even if they have any genuine liking, their wealth turns them into snobs

In the modern age, it is only money which controls agriculture, industry, art, theatre, etc. Good education, health, good houses, etc. are also meant only for the rich people.

Then, who are happier than our forefathers? Of course, only the wealthy few. All others are being ground in the mills of poverty, disease, unemployment, etc. and there seems to be no remedy in the near future.

However, we should have faith in our culture and still hope for the best. We must wish with our cultural heritage. *"Sarve Bhavantu Sukhina"* (may all be happy!).

The Population Explosion

A Preview

❖ One of the biggest problems
❖ India next only to China
❖ People in different areas
❖ Illiteracy, credulousness, superstitions
❖ The poor want more hands
❖ Efficient health measures
❖ Decrease in the rate of child mortality
❖ Politicians' role
❖ Many related problems created regarding health, clothing, housing, education, employment
❖ Measures

The population explosion is one of the biggest problems of India. India has at present the mammoth population of more then 1.25 billion. Even if India has a vast area, yet this population is too large for her.

In population, India is next only to China. But, with the present rate of increase of population, India is poised to outdo China in this matter if not in any other matter.

Most of the reasons for this rapid increase in population are well-known. It is a fact that most of the people in the urban areas have started restricting their families to two or three children. But in the rural areas the people are still not quite aware of the significance and benefits of a small family. Even in the urban areas, the slum-dwellers and other poor people often have no regard for having a small family.

Many people in rural areas the poor people, are illiterate, and by nature very superstitious. They think that a child is the gift from God. So, they welcome it. They cannot understand that a child's coming can be avoided through family planning methods.

There is another reason why the poor people want to have more children. They think that if they have more hands, the family would be able to earn more. They forget to realize that a child does not come only with hands, it has a mouth also. They cannot realize that every man needs so many things like food, clothing, shelter, education, health, employment, etc.

Another important reason for the rapid increase in population is the most efficient health measures available now to vast sections of society. Because of these health measures, the rate of child mortality has greatly dropped. On the other hand, longevity has also increased. The people now live for much longer period. The average life of man has jumped to about 67. This is still short of the over 80 in advanced countries, but it is a big jump up, as far as India is concerned.

Many of the politicians are also responsible for this sorry state of affairs regarding the rapid increase in population. It is because many of them themselves have large families. Thus, they cannot preach the importance of having a small family to others. Moreover, because their eye is always fixed on votes, they do not take any stringent measures to check the rapid growth of population, lest the credulous poor whom they can easily sway with empty promises, should get displeased.

The population explosion creates many allied problems as a natural consequence of it. First of all, there is the problem of food. Fortunately, for the time being, India has solved her food problem, but this problem cannot be claimed to have disappeared for ever.

If we have more people, we need more clothing and houses. This is how the problems of clothing and housing are created. It is almost impossible to provide house to all. At least, the per capita space of accommodation goes on decreasing day by day. Moreover, if we go on building more and more houses on the agricultural land, the area of the latter will go on decreasing.

Then traffic on the roads increases day by day. This leads to pollution and traffic jams.

Prices of essential commodities rise whereby the poor people get most affected. Some of the commodities become scarce in the market for the low supply as compared to demand. The goods whatever there are, are hoarded by the hoarders to create further scarcity. Such unscrupulous elements flourish as they indulge in the black market of such goods.

Some of the other problems are related to education and health. As more and more children arrive in the world, it is very difficult to provide education to all of them. Good education becomes a commodity for the elite only. In schools and colleges, classes get overcrowded and teaching methods, however superb, suffer and even become ineffective. A sort of disparity and inequality is created in the society.

Then all the educated people cannot get jobs. Unemployment increases, as jobs do not increase with the the same ratio as the population. At present our country is groaning under the weight of this massive problem of unemployment, which encumbers not only the white collared people but also the skilled and unskilled workers.

Another problem which population increase has created is the health problems. Hospitals get overcrowded and doctors cannot attend to all the patients properly. Moreover, treatment of even common diseases becomes too costly.

Among the measures which should be adopted to overcome this problem of population increase is the propaganda on a large scale in the newspapers and magazines and over the radio and the TV Population education should be given to children in schools, colleges and other institutions. Volunteers should be sent to rural and slum areas to spread literacy and the message of importance of having a small family. People having small families should be given various incentives and rewards. Let the government and the people, including the NGO's join hands to overcome this problem which has eaten away the tremendous progress India has made since Independence.

Live and Let Live

A Preview

- ❖ Peace vital for man's existence and growth
- ❖ Scriptures' advice to man
- ❖ W.B. Yeats
- ❖ Peaceful treaties and agreements
- ❖ Eras of peace and growth
- ❖ America and Canada
- ❖ India and Pakistan
- ❖ A garden and a forest
- ❖ Gandhiji
- ❖ Transformation of earth into heaven

"Live and let Live" is not only an ideal thought but also a pragmatic point if one were not inclined to accept idealism as a way of life in the modern life.

However, says G.L. Banks,

> *"I live for those who love me,*
> *for those who know me true;*
> *For the heaven that smiles above me,*
> *and awaits my spirit, too;*
> *For the cause that lacks assistance,*
> *for the wrong that needs resistance,*
> *For the future in the distance,*
> *and the good that I can do."*

—G.L. Banks

Those who let others live, alone can live themselves and in peace.

> *"Those who live by the sword,*
> *Shall perish by the sword,"*

Says the Bible.

Thus, peace is vital for man to live on this earth. To quote the Bible (New Testament),

"How beautiful upon the mountains are the feet of him that bringeth good things, that publisheth peace."

In fact, all the scriptures of all religions advise man to live in peace and spread the message of goodwill toward all men on earth. Unfortunately, man does not care to listen to this sound advice. That is why he suffers and makes others suffer untold miseries. In fact, says W.B. Yeats "We are weasels fighting in a ditch."

Unmindful, petty brained little animals fallen in a ditch start quarrelling among themselves for occupying the maximum space in a narrow ditch, not realizing that room there is not unlimited. Similarly men have to live on this earth whose geographical boundaries cannot be extended or stretched, at least not by any means for the present. The most evolved but still narrow-minded man likes to quarrel with his fellow-men over the control of resources of this earth which are limited but can be augmented by joint efforts.

Instead of quarrelling over the sharing of the resources of the earth or controlling the land on earth, men should enter into various treaties and agreements through peaceful and non-violent means with a spirit of goodwill, cooperation and mutual benefit. That process will help man to grow himself more and more and create grounds for the growth of others also because thus an atmosphere for growth and development would be created for all.

It may be argued why Shakespeare could emerge only in the age of Queen Elizabeth of England and in no other age. No other poet and dramatist of his stature had ever before appeared and may not appear again. Why the age of Emperor Augustus in Rome was the Golden Age for literature and arts ? Why in India Kalidas emerged in the age of the Golden period of the Guptas and in no other age? Why Tulsidas lived in the comparatively peaceful period of the Mughals? It is all because these periods were periods of peace and calm and great encouragement to all kinds of literature and art when the atmosphere was created for all to grow and evolve their personality.

The dictum "Live and let live" holds good in international relations. America and Canada have allowed each other to live and let live and both have made tremendous progress. India and Pakistan are neighbours. But they are always at daggers drawn with each other. One neighbour does not believe in the policy of "live and let live". The result is that although these two countries have made some progress, they have not made it to the extent they could. At present, the maximum number of the poorest, blind, handicapped, illiterate and corrupt people lives in these two countries. What a shame ! Had they lived in peace, they would have so far solved all the ticklish problems like population explosion, poverty, unemployment, shortages, corruption, illiteracy, drug taking, trafficking and smuggling, etc.

Even in a family, if the policy of live and let live is adopted, the family makes a notable progress and each member is able to evolve his or her personality effectively and efficiently.

Look at a garden and a forest of dense growth. In the former, the gardener has arranged the plantation of each plant at a reasonable distance, just as an efficient farmer does in a well-planned field. Here, in the garden or the field, each plant gets enough oxygen and light and space to expand and grow. Hence all the plants are green, healthy, leafy and blooming. In a forest of dense growth, the tall trees and plants stunt the growth of tiny plants that are deprived of proper supply of oxygen and light in the air and minerals in the soil. Hence, many plants are seen to be withering or suffering from various ailments and hardly any of them is blooming. The tall plants that curb the growth of other plants, themselves have only slender trunks and no leaves or branches upto several feet above the ground.

It is pitiable that man does not generally believe in equality. Even the equitable distribution of wealth and resources is a myth and often a trick is played using this term, with those who are, unfortunately, at the receiving end. The result is widespread discontent, privation and scarcity even in the era of surplus, prosperity and even profundity. This leads to violent political and social upheavels and even bloody revolutions.

Gandhiji showed the path of peace and the real meaning of the saying,

"Live and let live" through his Civil Disobedience, Passive Resistance, Satyagraha and other passive and non-violent means whose basis was truth.

If we sincerely believe in the policy of live and let live in letter and spirit, the whole world in all its components—family, village, town, city, state, country, international relations, all castes and communities, and races etc. can be transformed into heaven instantaneously, and not a day later.

Some Emerging Science Trends In India

A Preview

- ❖ DNA laboratory
- ❖ Explanation
- ❖ Conversion of polythene into fuel
- ❖ Explanation
- ❖ Novel method of detecting fingerprints
- ❖ Research facilities lacking in India
- ❖ Raman and Bose
- ❖ Hargovind Khorana
- ❖ Chandershekhar
- ❖ Organic Food

A bio-chemical DNA laboratory, the first of its kind in the country has been set up in Chandigarh at the Central Scientific Instruments Organisation (CSIO).

There is scope for a revolution in the electronic sector, as bio-molecular technology in which DNA is used as the base material, is likely to reduce substantially the size of electronic devices, whereas their capability will increase manifold. For instance, it is claimed by one of the scientists concerned that "DNA can hold more information in a cubic centimeter than a trillion CDs".

A great difficulty in India is that the Indian scientific laboratories, except for a few selected ones, are not research oriented. Research work entails vast resources of funds and very hard and long, arduous work and then there is no certainty that the results will be encouraging. Consequently, many of our young scientists have left the shores of India and settled abroad where they are doing wonderfully well. Thus the brain drain continues. The western countries being rich ones can offer better prospects.

Conversion of Polythene Into fuel

Recently, an Indian scientist was successful in converting polythene into fuel. It is said that can be refined further to yield substitutes of even petrol and diesel.

In the USA, the process is commercially used. In Australia too the process has already been discovered.

New Method of Detecting Fingerprints

There is another achievement in the field of science. A Delhi based college teacher and his wife who are said to have developed a novel method of detecting latent fingerprints. The new method, which utilises novel spray formulations based on dyes, is cost-effective and non-hazardous.

It is clear that given the proper atmosphere and facilities to work and do research, Indian scientists are second to none in the world. It was long long ago that Dr. C.V. Raman won the Nobel Prize for his Raman Effect. Dr. Jagdish Bose was another great scientist who worked on plants and demonstrated convincingly that plants were as much living beings as animals. For example, he proved that plants were very sensitive to light and sound. They also loved to hear sweet, melodious music and sounds. They could detect the passing of a cloud over them and the sky. He could not get the Nobel Prize, but his findings were startling. He even devised a machine to detect the sound beats within a plant similar to the one as in human heart.

We have had many scientists since then. Hargobind Khorana and Chandershekhar won the Nobel Prize for their genetic and astronomical theories respectively. Even if they had migrated from India, yet originally they were Indians. Now, we have many great Indian scientists in many fields.

Science has already penetrated with a vengeance in every field of our life. Now, as the people are becoming more and more health conscious, organic foods have started invading the market.

The producers of such foods are coming up in a big way to woo the consumers.

It is clear that in India a sort of revolution is going on at present in the matter of scientific inventions and discoveries.

Terrorism

A Preview

- ❖ Terrorism in India
- ❖ Terrorist attack on America
- ❖ America's action against terrorism
- ❖ India's long sufferings
- ❖ India's action against terrorism
- ❖ POTO and POTA
- ❖ The Punjab and Haryana High court judgement
- ❖ Terrorism and human rights organisations
- ❖ US President's assertion
- ❖ Views of experts

Terrorism has become a serious problem in the modern world. India has particularly been facing this menace for the last many years. Thousands of innocent men, women and children have been killed by the terrorists in our country, particularly in Kashmir.

Unfortunately, the world community has not taken much note of India's sufferings. America felt the heat of terrorism for the first time on September 11, 2001 when the World Trade Centre Towers in New York and the Pentagon were attacked. Thereafter, America declared global war against terrorism and brought down the Taliban government in Afghanistan and that was all. Mainly, the Al-Queda men were targeted. These were the militants who had masterminded the attacks in America. In 2003, the coalition forces headed by America, attacked Iraq to end the regime there, which, they said, was terrorist in essence. But, America virtually remained disregardful of India's problem with terrorism, particularly transborder terrorism from across the border and that particularly in Kashmir.

Later, the Jammu and Kashmir Vidhan Sabha was attacked by the terrorists on October 1, 2001 but fortunately the members of the Legislative Assembly had a narrow escape. The same thing happened when the Indian Parliament was attacked by terrorists on December 13, 2001. Again the members of Parliament and cabinet had a providential escape, but the precious lives of some security men were lost. On May 10, 2002, the terrorists attacked the kins of army men near Jammu, killing more than 30 of them. The government took a serious view of it. Terrorist killings in Kashmir have been regularly going on.

After the December 13 attack on it, India had to take some strong measures. Flights of Pak planes over the Indian space were banned. India recalled her High Commissioner from Pakistan. A number of terrorist organisations in India were banned. Army was deployed on India's borders with Pakistan. After the attack on the army in Jammu, Pakistan High Commissioner in India was asked to leave the country within seven days. India had also forwarded a list of 20 wanted terrorists to Pakistan. India had the information that these terrorists lived in Pakistan and were even being provided all facilities to work against India. But Pakistan refused to hand over any of them to India and later, its High Commissioner even denied that they were in Pakistan.

To fight the menace of terrorism, India had to promulgate the Prevention of Terrorism Ordinance (POTO) which was later passed by the Lok Sabha and it came to be known as Prevention of Terrorist Act (POTA). The Act was challenged in the Punjab and Haryana High Court. But the learned judges declared that the Act was the need of the hour. The court explained in detail.

"The upsurge of terrorist activities, intensification of cross-border terrorism, violence perpetrated by the insurgent groups are in existing reality and a global phenomenon. The modern means of communication and other facilities enable the terrorists to strike and create terror at will. The existing justice delivery system was not equipped to deal with heinous crimes. Thus, there was an imperative need to make provisions for the prevention of and for dealing with terrorist activities and for matters connected therewith. The aims and objectives disclosed at the time of introduction of the Bill and the preamble provide a clear answer and the real rational for the promulgation of the Act by the Parliament."

The learned court also explained:

"The government did not rush. The Act was not promulgated in haste. However, the situation in the country showed no signs of improvement. In fact, the acts of violence were on the increase. The attack on the World Trade Center on the morning of September 11, 2001, bears a testimony to the fears expressed by the protagonists of a law for the prevention of terrorism. The senseless attack on the Indian Parliament could have reinforced the view. Organised acts of terrorism are no longer confined to a particular place or country. The threat is global. And is on the increase. Despite, the fact that America has attacked Afghanistan with the most effective means of destruction. Thus, there was a need for the impugned Act".

It is, indeed, strange that whenever the terrorists attack the innocent people, the human rights organisations keep mum, but when any terrorists are killed such organisations raise a hue and cry. Such a situation prevails not only in India, but also in foreign contries and particularly in the western countries.

In the book : *"Terror and Containment,"* edited by K.P.S. Gill and Ajai Sahni, one of the contributors, Arundhati Ghose, points out that "in almost all western countries human rights at international level are handled as a foregin policy issue rather than an issue which affects all society."

Ms Arundhati Ghose thinks that foregin human rights organisations are a "veritable industry" and have their "pernicious" aspects as far as containment of terrorism is concerned.

It must be said to the credit of various American Presidents that they have often been the global trendsetters, as shown in the examples given below:

It was the first American President George Washington who said, "If you want peace, be prepared for war."

Again, it was the American President, Abraham Lincoln who said, "Democracy is the government of the people, by the people and for the people." Similarly, much can be quoted from the mouth of most of other American Presidents.

Speaking at a function on March 11 to remember and respect those who died on September 11, 2001, President Bush proclaimed: "There will be a day when the organised threat against America, our friends and allies is broken. When the terrorists are disrupted and scattered, many old conflicts will appear in a new light, without the fear and cycle of bitterness that terrorists spread with their violence. We will see then that old and serious disputes can be settled within the bounds of the world beyond the war on terror. With courage and dignity we are building that world together."

This to a great extent woke up the world against terrorism. But, unfortunately, America is still more worried about its own security than the global security.

Mr. I. K. Gujral, a former Prime Minister of India, in an article, cogently points out the foresight of Mr. Martti Ahtisaari, a former

Finnish President, known as a world crusader, when the latter rightly surmised that the September 11, 2001 Al-Qaeda attack would transform the world relations and that is exactly what has happened for instance, Russo-American animosities are over, so much so that Russia has joined NATO, an organisation created to contain her and Sino-American suspicions have diminished.

Mr. Gujral also quotes another authority on world affairs. He is Mr. Gareth Enams, a former Foreign Minister of Australia, who, according to him told the Monesh Asia Institute's Seminar in Italy that 9/11 (the September 11 incident) has generated a "...new sense of vulnerability (caused by) a handful of people willing to commit suicide employing zero primary technology and what would be the impact of a really full-scale attack going chemical, biological or even nuclear.

According to Mr. Gujral, President Gareth also said, "for the first time for many people globalisation moved from abstraction to reality. September 11 made abundantly clear that no country can immunise and isolate itself entirely from external events: grievances bred elsewhere can have catastrophic consequences half a world away... people in developing countries have long had the sense that their future was in the hands of those in other continents, but it came as a shock to the citizens of New York and London and Brussels that decisions directly and immediately affecting their own security can be made in the Hindu Kush."

President Gareth's observations were pithy and to the point when he said,

"... the 9/11 terrorists weren't themselves poor or without influence, but they were supported by millions of people who resent perceived US support for their own corrupt and insensitive regimes. And indifference hitherto to the democratic vacuum which has existed from Morocco to Pakistan (though) 9/11 seem to have made some old problems easier to solve".

India's Foreign Policy

A Preview

- ❖ A vast country
- ❖ Independence after a long struggle
- ❖ Nehru's period
- ❖ Chinese invasion
- ❖ A peace-loving country
- ❖ UN
- ❖ Bush
- ❖ Study of India's foreign policy by a noted diplomat
- ❖ Non-alignment
- ❖ Failure of India's foreign polcy
- ❖ India torn between Russia and America
- ❖ Pakistan and Kashmir
- ❖ Indian Defence Secretary's remarks
- ❖ Foreign policy and defence closely related
- ❖ A noted journalist's observations

India is a very vast country. It is called a subcontinent. In population, it is next only to China. She remained under foreign rule for many centuries. It was after a long struggle and innumerable sacrifices that she at last attained independence in 1947.

It was expected that after attaining independence, India would enjoy a respectable and enviable place in the comity of nations. No doubt, India became a power to reckon with during the period of Jawaharlal Nehru when India's voice was heard with due deference at international fora. But later events showed, particularly China's attack on India in 1962, the hollowness of the policy of peaceful co-existence being followed by India at that time.

As a matter of fact, we, the Indians, have never been imperialists and expansionists. We have always believed in love for all mankind, peace and universal brotherhood.

With the emergence of the UN as a forum of world government, though on a limited scale, it was believed that India's policy would find a greater force in the world. Of course, the UN was founded only two years before India attained Independence and thus, its full effectiveness was still to be tested and Indians, always optimistic, as far as a world forum is concerned, hoped too much of it. This was with such an idea of getting a fair deal from the UN that Jawaharlal Nehru took the Kashmir dispute there, which is unambiguously a creation of Pakistan. And it must not have surprised us when our hopes were belied.

Unfortunately, we have not so far been able to understand that our universalism can be no substitute for true nationalism. In fact we have never been nationalists. Our leaders have always cared more for the welfare of other nations than our own, whereas the Americans, Chinese and others have always been pragmatic nationalists in spite of all their professions of internationalism and universalism.

Just take the case of Mr. Bush, the former President of America, while vowing to fight terrorism on global level after the 11 September happenings in America, had actually behaved in a manner which had furthered only American interests in the world. He had eulogized the dictatorial President Musharraf of Pakistan and virtually allowed him to continue his nefarious designs of promoting, abbetting and helping terrorists in Kashmir against India.

In his book *"India's Foreign Policy and Its Neighbours"* J.N. Dixit has clearly stated that independent India had no clear foreign policy goal. She never had a well-thought-out policy towards its neighbours.

India stuck to the Non-alignment movement and was even proud of being one of its founding fathers. But that was, in fact, not a policy. That only kept India out of power blocs with hardly any other gain. The large number of other members were too small states to be effective.

It has to be admitted that as far as India's foreign policy is concerned, she lacked and, may be, still lacks vision. She never has had any clear political goal or defence strategy. Even though she defeated Pakistan a number of times, she is miles behind in possessing most of the sophisticated defence components.

J.N. Dixit, the veteran having held various diplomatic assignments, lists five areas of India's failure in particular regarding her foreign policy: *(i)* in taking the Kashmir issue to the UN, *(ii)* in not reacting firmly when Pakistan signed a security agreement with the USA in 1954, *(iii)* in not being alert to the Sino-Pak nexus, *(iv)* in letting China take over Tibet without demanding a quid quo pro, and *(v)* in not going ahead with the nuclear programme after China exploded the bomb in 1964.

In the opinion of J.N. Dixit, the main failure of India's foreign policy lies in the lack of the spirit of nationalism. Had India been inspired by this spirit, she "would never have failed in these areas."

As a matter of fact, Indian options have always been torn between leanings towards America and Russia. While India's mind has been with Russia, her heart has been with America. So thinks Mr. Dixit.

No doubt, India has got tremendous help from Russia, but Russia's own downfall has made the world a unipolar one and in such a world, India's woes have increased with Pakistan being such a hostile neighbour and America being still at her back in spite of all the professions to the contrary.

The main difficulty is that India has never been pragmatic in her foreign policy. When in 1948 Indian forces were pushing back Pakistan troops dressed as tribals in Kashmir, India ordered ceasefire and knocked the door of the UN. Had there been any other country, she would have not only recovered the lost territory from the enemy, but also captured the latter's territory to teach her a lesson.

Thus, India's trouble started with the first blunder in Kashmir and this policy of peace has been pulled along by India all through so far. How can India live in peace when wars are forced on her again and again? India unrealistically hoped China to be a permanent friend. All overtures to Pakistan for eternal friendship have failed likewise. Who cares for India? None. Not even a small country like Bangladesh. India must have some introspection and frame a strong and realistic foreign policy.

The other day, the Defence Secretary of India highlighted India's foreign policy in the following words: "We have to link defence purchases with the foreign policy."

Observing that India was suddenly finding itself being thrown up as a "super regional power" because of its economic and military strengths, the Secretary said, "a large number of countries expect us to play a bigger role in the world arena instead of confining ourselves to the region."

He said that besides Russia, India was buying defence equipment from France, South Africa. Israel and Italy. But, India would now insist on transfer of technology whenever it was placing an order for defence purchase with any country.

A retired Lieutenant General and former Director, General Military Training says:

"There was a time in the history of Independent India when public discussion of defence weapons, tactics and strategy was taboo... Suddenly, the public and the media in India have become the powerhouse of defence planning and strategy."

We should remember that foreign policy and defence are closely related in the modern world and the outcry of "coffingate" is a living example of public interest in defence and foreign affairs.

A noted journalist observed in the relevant columns of a famous English daily as under, particularly in the backdrop of deployment of forces on the western borders in an offensive posture and the consequent and continuous stand-off between the armed forces of the two neighbouring countries in the Indian subcontinent.

Since long before 13/12 (December 13) India's policy quite clearly has been first to cooperate with any country which claims it can persuade or pressure Pakistan into stopping terrorism against India. Second, if Pakistan takes steps to control infiltration of terrorists across the Line of Control, India will respond with appropriate steps, Third, if such efforts fail and Indian security is put at serious risk, then India must do all it needs to end the risk, undeterred by threats of a nuclear response by Pakistan. Fourth, while protecting itself India must stick to its commitment not to be the first to use a nuclear weapon. Fifth, in the event of a nuclear response by Pakistan to India's conventional efforts, India must respond in kind, undeterred by possible international reactions.

At present, certainly India is quite a strong country and she must pursue a forceful, vibrant foreign policy.

Non-Government Organisations (NGOs)

A Preview

- Doing good work
- Should be registered
- Various kinds of service to different sections of society
- Voluntary service
- Some NGOs embezzle the funds raised by them or the grant provided by the government
- LCC—a selfless NGO
- Other NGOs—Helpage, SOS, etc.
- Love and mercy natural
- A visually challenged person
- Aman Samuday in Gujarat

There is no denying the fact that NGOs are doing yeomen's work not only in India but also in other parts of the world.

These are voluntary organisations but must be registered to earn credibility and legitimacy. Most of the NGOs raise their own funds on voluntary basis, often through donation from and contributions by willing philanthropists and others through appeals or otherwise, but they also get grant and assistance from government if the genuineness and sincerity of their work and purpose is transparent and is recognized as such.

These organisations do various and all kinds of jobs, often social obligations in public interest, at least apparent, selflessly and as a thankless job or as love's labour in the name of human service.

Thus these organisations fan out in areas of distress like flood, cyclone, drought, earthquake or riot victims and provide free food, legal aid, medicines, blood, etc. They hold blood donation camps, free eye operation camps, free medical check up camps and help the poorest, the forlorn, the neglected individuals in society. They set up orphanages, widow houses, destitute night shelters, old people houses etc.

It is a pity that sometimes certain NGO's are found to be indulging in malpractices. NGOs hold camps, rural reconstruction and development projects, etc. not only through their own resources and volutary donation by members, but they also collect funds from public and take government help. Sometimes, they siphon off the money meant to help others to the advantage of the founding or managing members of the NGOs who had an elitist and royalist lifestyle.

It, must, however, be admitted that many of the NGOs are really doing service by working selflessly. One such organisation is perhaps the Ludhiana Citizens' Council (Regd) (LCC). It was set up in 1984 by a few persons to promote unity among the communities and serve humanity. At present, it helps the poor and the needy. It comes to the rescue of the sick, the infirm and invalids.

In the words of the convener of the NGO (LCC): "Whether it is war time, troubled time or peace time the LCC is always there to help. During terrorism days, we tried to reduce the rift between Sikhs and Hindus by organising joint gurpurabs. We tried to be a bridge between administration and the people. Through our efforts hundreds of people got redressal of their problems."

The secretary general of the NGO explained the work of the organisation being done in the following words:

"It was human misery that prompted the members of the Ludhiana Citizens' Council to formulate a programme whereby the ailing and the distressed persons in society could be given timely help in the form of medicines, free of cost. We got together and founded medical-aid bank. This concept flourished and a team of dedicated volunteers joined. Qualified doctors offered their services. Medical aid even for cancer, TB and the patients with heart ailment is provided. Expensive medicines have been donated by philanthropists."

The chairman of the NGO (LCC) explained that the organisation has decided to do service to the deserving and needy in the field of education also:

"Our resolution for the new term is to adopt two poor villages of Ludhiana district and provide two teachers so that the children there can avail free education. Moreover, we want to build night shelters for the homeless children who sleep on roads and are easy prey to organised gangs. These children have either run away from their homes due to extreme harrowing conditions or have been rendered orphans. These children always live in fear of being molested".

It is surprising why some people are cruel to others or cruel by nature or cruel for the sake of cruelty. As a matter of fact, mercy and love are inherent in man and they come more visibly on the surface particularly at the time of misery or adversity. Actualy man forgets his own misery when he helps others. The famous essayist, Lord Francis Bacon said that men, particularly the chronic bachelors or others who find it hard to spend leisure time, specifically in old age, can spend their time in reaching out to those who need their help. Thus a learned professor of Punjabi who suffered from the Eales "Disease" and totally lost his eyesight which could not be restored even by the best eye surgeons of international repute, joined the vocational and rehabilitation centre for visually challenged and while helping the needy ruralites, forgot his own suffering. This is how he explains his experience:

"Though I was under shock, but when I learnt that Johnson himself was visually challenged, I took heart. Both of us visited villages, identified ruralites with eye diseases and rehabilitated them. I forgot my own suffering by helping others. I felt I had rehabilitated myself well. I returned to teaching Punjabi."

There are several other NGOs like Helpage which are doing great service to the aged people particularly the homeless. SOS helps the orphaned, abandoned children and has schools in several parts of the country. 30 NGOs organised under the banner of *Aman Samuday* have done great work in bringing the two communities together in Gujarat by organising *"Aman Pathiks"* to go out in relief camps in service of people.

Mother Teresa

A Preview

- ❖ One of the greatest persons in history
- ❖ Name, birth, early life
- ❖ In Ireland
- ❖ In Kolkata
- ❖ As Principal
- ❖ Slum dwellers
- ❖ The Sisters of Charity
- ❖ The "Nirmal Hriday"
- ❖ The Brothers of Charity
- ❖ The Nobel Prize
- ❖ The Bharat Ratna
- ❖ Death
- ❖ Sainthood

Among the greatest men and women who have made a mark in the history of mankind, one of the greatest was Mother Teresa, the like of whom is not likely to be found for generations to come.

The real name of Mother Teresa was Agnes Gonxha Bojaxhiu. She was born on August 26, 1910 at Skopje in Yugoslavia in Europe. In 1928 at the age of 18 she left for Ireland, where she joined the Loreto congregation, an organisation engaged in missionary work.

It was there in Ireland that young Agnes learnt that the sisters of Loreto were engaged in missionary work in Bengal in India. She made up her mind to do missionary work to mitigate the sufferings of the needy people and those others in distress and a year later in 1929 she sailed to India for the noble cause.

Agnes taught for some years in the schools of Loreto congregation and finally became the Principal of St. Agnes High School for girls in Kolkata.

There was a large slum area near the school where she taught. She saw the frightful condition of the dwellers from very close quarters. She was deeply moved and her heart cried within herself to do something for the suffering humanity.

In 1948, she got the Indian citizenship. Now, the main vocation of hers was to collect the forlorn and forsaken, homeless human wrecks rotting on the streets, the destitute, the handicapped and others. She brought them with her and for the sake of their survival, she begged from door to door for food, caring not a bit for her personal comfort or social dignity that even any average human being would think of. She considered welfare of others above her own and was ready to make any sacrifice for others.

It was in 1950 that she collected a few sisters and formed the Sisters of Charity. Then it was in 1956 that she formed the famous "Nirmal Hriday" which has become a byword not only among the Indians but also among the common people all over the world.

The 'Nirmal Hriday' was a place donated to her by the Corporation of Kolkata and it became a home for the helpless destitutes, mostly on the verge of starvation and death, and there she made all out efforts to save their lives and provide them succour to whatever extent she could within her meagre means and limited capacity. It is a pity that help from people for such a noble cause instead of being overwhelming, was only in trickles.

She formed the Brothers of Charity in 1963, when Nirmal Hriday, was serving excellently the destitute. Earlier, some leper colonies and dispensaries for the poorest, the loneliest and the lost had also been set up by her. At present many hundred such missionary homes for the needy are being run in all corners of the world, not only in Asia, Europe and America but also in Australia.

Agnes borrowed the word "Teresa" from a little known saint and it was by this name that she came to be known all over the world. Now, she is lovingly called "Mother Teresa".

She won the Nobel Peace Prize in 1979. In 1980, Bharat Ratna, the highest Indian Civilian Award was bestowed on her. For promoting the cause of friendship among the people and for doing great service to the poor and the needy she got the Soviet Land Nehru Award in 1990.

In 1991, this "Angel of Peace" as she was being hailed, fell ill with pneumonia. This led to her prolonged illness and later death by cardiac arrest on September 5, 1997.

She was laid to rest at Mother House in Kolkata. She is destined to go down as one of the greatest personalities in history. She will, indeed, be remembered for all times to come. She had already appointed Sister Nirmala as her successor. The latter is carrying on Mother Teresa's work with equal devotion and diligence.

Mother Teresa has been declared 'Saint Teresa of Calcutta' on September 4, 2016 on the eve of her 19th death anniversary by Pope Francis at Vatican City.

The Use of Narcotics and Tobacco

A Preview

- ❖ Hostels & drug-takers
- ❖ All sections of society affected
- ❖ Young people
- ❖ Western countries
- ❖ Tobacco
- ❖ Nicotine
- ❖ Supreme Court directive
- ❖ Cough syrups
- ❖ Measures
- ❖ Rural and urban areas
- ❖ Old people
- ❖ Even women
- ❖ Hippies
- ❖ NGOs
- ❖ Passive smokers
- ❖ Condition of drug-addicts
- ❖ Golden Triangle & Golden Crescent
- ❖ Drug-de-addiction centres

The consumption of narcotics by the young people has reached alarming proportions. The hostels of both boys and girls are full of drug-takers.

Drug-taking has become common in both rural and urban areas. Previously, the old people whose nerves had got weakened with age used to consume opium, charas or other drugs and that also not universally. Only some of the old men had this pastime. The women's number who used drugs was almost nil.

Now, not only men, but women also consume drugs of all kinds. Moreover, drug-taking has become common among people of all sections of society, from the richest to the poorest. It is no solace to us the Indians, to know that in America and other western countries, even small school going children indulge in the luxury of drug-taking.

This drug taking on a large scale has been imported into India by the hippies and western pop-singers who invaded this land into hordes in the sixties.

Closely related to drug-taking is the consumption of alcohol and tobacco. The Supreme Court of India has prohibited smoking at public places, in offices and in trains and buses. Still the menace goes on more or less.

It is said that the passive smokers suffer as much as the active smokers. Those people who smoke in their houses cause a great disservice to their children.

Like alcohol and drugs of all kinds, tobacco causes great harm to the individual and society. It causes heart and lung disease and can lead to asthma and other diseases.

"No Tobacco Day" was celebrated on 31 May. Prior to this day a week-long programme called "Tobacco Alert" was held to make the people aware of the menace of tobacco consumption.

A memorandum was submitted to the Editor, The Tribune, Chandigarh to "impress upon the government to initiate the strictest measures against tobacco."

As per report published in the newspaper, ...the memorandum says "while the Government of India earns ₹ 6000 crore from tobacco, it spends ₹ 2,70,000 crore on tobacco related diseases. Every day, 2,200 persons die of tobacco."

As the President of an NGO Youth Engaged in Services (YES) Club said regarding the next programme to persuade the vendors of tobacco to change their profession, "The idea is to rope in the government and make the anti-tobacco ban effective. Through the government we can use their means for achieving our end. We are telling the public that they can boldly object to passive smoking as well."

A number of NGOs have undertaken the task of eradicating the menace of tobacco and drugs. More and more NGOs should come forward for this noble cause.

Every school child knows that tobacco contains nicotine which is highly poisonous. So, tobacco is also a kind of highly toxic drug. Other drugs which are commonly used by the drug takers are heroin, smack, charas, bhang, ganja, opium, etc.

Drugs give a kind of momentary hilarity to the takers. Thereafter, he/she has to suffer the pangs of depression, pain and convulsions. The withdrawal symptoms are extremely painful.

Drug-taking is a very harmful habit which when once formed can be got rid of with great difficulty. So, drugs must be avoided in the very first instance. A person in the habit of taking drugs is ready to do anything to purchase a small quantity of drugs which are often very expensive. For instance, a kilogram of heroin is valued at ₹ 1 crore in the international market.

A person who once falls in the habit of drug-taking often in company with the addicts, is ready to beg, borrow or steal. Many poor men waste their hard-earned money on drugs while their families starve. The students in hostels, instead of spending their money on books and other study material waste their parents' money earned with the sweat of their brow.

Drugs are taken not only orally but also injected straight into the blood stream. Some addicts, not being able to get any other drug in the market, start consuming certain cough syrups, and expectorants like Phensedyl, Corex, etc. are drunk in large quantities by drug addicts.

Drug-taking shortens life. Many young people who fall into this bad habit leave this world in the prime of their life. So, it is not only that their families are ruined, but also it is a great national loss.

We have the Golden Triangle and the Golden Crescent countries which produce opium and other drugs in large quantities. India is mainly a transit route. But drug taking is spreading here day by day, particularly among the young people.

Some stringent measures should be taken to overcome this menace. No doubt, a strict Narcotics Act has been passed according to which there is a fine of ₹ 1 lakh and imprisonment for ten or twenty years for the first offence. The Act should be strictly implemented. And still more strict Acts should be passed, if necessary. In some countries there is capital punishment for trafficking in drugs.

De-addiction centres have been opened at some places. More such centres should be opened. One should remember that if a famous film star like Sanjay Dutt can return to normal life by giving up drugs through de-addition therapy and will power, why can't others do so?

Looking After the Disabled
or
War Against Disability

A Preview

- ❖ Red Cross Day
- ❖ Kinds of the Disabled
- ❖ Examples of ailments and disorders
- ❖ Situation in India
- ❖ Solution
- ❖ Measures provided by the government through legislator
- ❖ Implementation of the relevant Act

World Red Cross Day was observed on 8th May. On that day, a camp for the disabled was held at the village Karsan. Even prior to that a year long house-to-house survey was held. Of the 250 disabled children, 60 per cent suffered from locomotive disabilites, 15 per cent from ocular disabilites, 10 per cent from ear, nose and throat troubles, 10 per cent from psychiatric maladies and 5 per cent from other miscellaneous disabilities.

Disabilities such as paralysis of one of more (mostly due to polio), muscular dystrophies, etc. were the kinds of locomotive disorders.

Such disorders as cataracts of all kinds, retinitis pigmentosa, high myopia, etc. were the kinds of ocular disabilities. The examples of psychiatric disorders were autism, schizophrenia, mental retardation, low IQ, etc.

According to an article published in a newspaper, "If not in things to be proud of, we are on top of the world at least in disease and disability. Mother India has over sixty million disabled persons, including over ten million disabled children, the maximum in the global comity of nations, mostly in families a little above or below the poverty line.

While the disabled girl child is utterly neglected to die early, the disabled male child is allowed to languish longer. Hardly 50 per cent of disabled children reach adulthood, and no more than 20 per cent survive to cross the fourth decade of life."

This is, indeed, a pathetic state of affairs and needs serious thought. Taking a cue from the views of the learned writer, we can think of some means to mitigate the misery of the disabled, e.g.,

1. There should be a holistic approach to the problem.

2. A medico-surgical initiative on a large scale should be taken to solve the problem to the maximum extent possible.

3. Arrangements should be made by the government and NGOs for a life-long physiotherapy of the disabled where the disorders cannot be set right perfectly.

4. All kinds of training, including vocational and higher education to the extent possible should be given to the disabled so that they can stand on their own legs.

5. There should be started some confidence-building and rehabilitation measures among the disabled and the handicapped like

   i) Self-employment suited to the person concerned for this, the necessary monetary and other help should be provided.

ii) Where possible or where the person concerned cannot or is not willing to do self-employment, a salaried job should be provided.

6. There should be more reservation for the disabled in the matter of admission to various institutions and getting of jobs than is hitherto available.

7. It must be ensured that the disabled are not given less salary, perks, etc. than others while in some employment.

8. There should be substantial relief to the disabled in the matter of payment of income and other taxes.

9. The people in general should come forward in a big way to donate liberally to the NGOs doing Yeoman's work in the matter of providing relief and succour to the disabled.

It is heartening to note that the government have to some extent risen to the clarion call of providing relief to the disabled.

In 1995, the Equal Opportunities, Protection of Rights and Full Participation Act was passed. The Act came into force from January 1, 1996.

Referring to the steps taken so far to implement the provisions of the Act, the Chief Commissioner, Persons with Disabilities, Government of India said that under the Act a Central Coordination Committee, headed by the Union Minister for Department of Welfare, and a Central Executive Committee, headed by the Secretary, Ministry of Welfare, Government of India, had been constituted to ensure complete implementation of provisions for the disabled under the Act. She said that all states had been asked to appoint independent commissioners to ensure fast implementation of these provisions.

It is mandatory for the government and aided schools to give admission to the disabled for which the government would provide required teaching equipment and teaching staff. She said that special training and refresher courses had been launched and so far five national-level workshops have been organised, where six persons from each state were imparted access audit training.

She, while referring to the steps taken to create more job opportunities for the disabled, said that in the government offices 3 per cent quota had been reserved and so far six states, including Punjab, had achieved this target. She said that to ensure self-employment opportunities soft term subsidised loans were also being provided after giving required vocational training. So far 1450 job categories have been identified, she said."

The US Department of Justice has provided a comprehensive definition of disability which runs as under:

"Any physiological disorder, or condition, cosmetic disfigure-ment or anatomical loss affecting one or more of the following body systems: neurological musculoskeletal, special sense organs (including speech organs), respiratory, cardiovascular, repro-ductives, digestive, genitourinary, lymphatic, skin and endocrine; any mental or psychological disorder such as mental retardation, organic brain syndrome, emotional or mental illness, and specific learning disabilities."

It is to be noted, in particular that in countries like India, the society is not so far attuned to the problems of disabled persons, particularly women and girls. A male disabled person does not face so many problems as a female one. It is a misfortune that the money spent on a disabled girl particularly when there are male children also in the family, is considered a waste of resources and time. The result is that it becomes almost impossible for a handicapped girl to get the benefits of rehabilitation which the modern science has so liberally provided.

As a writer in a famous daily says—"The United Nations Standard Rules on the Equalisation of Opportunties for Persons with Disabilities are important human rights tools for all persons with disabilities. For girls and women, the CEDAW (Convention on the Elimination of All forces of Discrimination Against Women) is another human rights instrument. With the help of these rules; it would be easier for various governments...."

There is no denying that the NGOs should also come forward in a big way for the help of the disabled persons, particulary the disabled girls and women.

What is Death?
or
Are You Not Afraid of Death?
or
Death—the Leveller of the Bravest

A Preview

- ❖ The very idea sends shudders
- ❖ The Buddha and the dead
- ❖ A saint
- ❖ Water in the tank
- ❖ The Mystery of Death
- ❖ Why lament?
- ❖ Doctrine of transmigration
- ❖ Stories about children telling about their past life
- ❖ Science
- ❖ First the mystery of life has to be fully solved

The very idea of death sends shudders through the frames of most of us, although all of us know that we cannot escape it.

The story about the Buddha and a dead child's mother is well-known to most of us. A woman brought her dead child to the Buddha and pleaded with him to bring life into its body. The Buddha said to the woman, "Please go to every house in the neighbourhood and bring me back the name of the head of the family in which nobody has ever died."

After an hour or so the woman came back and told the Buddha that she had not been able to find out any house where there had been no death. Then the Buddha explained to her that since death was unavoidable in the long run, it was futile to lament over it or to avert it when it came.

There is another story. It is about a saint who was sitting in his *ashram* at a little distance from a tank. A woman brought her dead child to the saint and requested him to infuse life into its body. The saint said to the woman, "Please here take this jug full of water and come back after pouring out the contents of the jug into the tank." The woman did as she was asked to do and came back.

Now, the saint asked the woman to go and bring back the same water into the jug as she had a little earlier poured into the tank. The woman said, "My lord! how is it possible? The water in the jug has got so mixed up with the water in the tank that now it is difficult to separate it and get it back."

Then the saint explained, "Just as the water in the jug has got mixed up inseparably with the water in the tank, the soul of your child has inseparably got mixed up with the supersoul, that is the Almighty." The woman understood the point and went away.

The great men have indeed explained to us the inevitability of death in several ways. The main purpose is to keep us free from tension and unnecessary bewailing.

Certainly, a man after committing a most heinous crime, may hide somewhere, but he cannot hide anywhere from death. Death will come when it comes and it will certainly find the way.

If death cannot be averted, why lament over a person's death? Often we lament for the past associations and memories which slowly fade away, as time is a great healer.

Actually, man is more afraid of the supposed or real pangs or agony at the time of death than death itself.

Still, in India, at least, many people, even highly educated among them, have a firm faith in the Doctrine of Re-incarnation, or Transmigration. They believe that after a person's death, his or her soul enters some other body which takes its birth somewhere, and we sometimes hear about stories of little children telling about their previous birth. How far such stories are correct, can be learnt only after a thorough verification of places and persons mentioned by such children.

In India, there is the long custom of prayers and rituals concerned with person's death to enable his or her soul to get salvation. It is said, otherwise the person cannot escape the wheel of 84 lakh rebirths or he or she may turn into a ghost and remain in a state of suspended animation— a state which is believed to be even more painful than the human life.

In any case, the mystery of life is a question which must be considered insoluble. It is because one who is dead can never come back to tell what happens after death.

Science tells us that even the existence of the earth is just an accident. Then life on this planet is an accident. DNA is the basis of life. Consciousness man still does not know much about. The mystery of death cannot be solved until the mystery of life is fully and convincingly solved.

According to Sri Aurobindo, human soul has descended from the supersoul, that is, God. As such it is immortal. It is only the body that dies, as death comes. Death cannot destroy the soul.

Flood Control

A Preview

- ❖ Major part of India overflooded during the rainy season
- ❖ Efforts should be made in advance
- ❖ This does not happen—example
- ❖ China
- ❖ States in India
- ❖ Causes
- ❖ Reckless felling of trees
- ❖ No bunds on rivers
- ❖ Embezzlement of funds
- ❖ Losses
- ❖ Harsh steps necessary
- ❖ Loans etc. to people living in low lying areas

Every year a major part of India has to face the fury of major rivers which get overflooded and cause havoc to both urban and rural areas. This happens particularly during the monsoon period.

It is needless to point out that arrangement for flood control should be taken in advance much before the start of the rainy season. It is because it entails huge earthwork which cannot quickly be disposed of on the onset of the season. But this does not actually happen. Here below, we have a news report which bespeaks amply of the indifference of the authorities in a particular area. The situation is not different in other parts of the country. The report appeared less than a month before the usual start of the monsoon season:

"The monsoon is expected to hit this region in the last week of this month. As per the predictions of the authorities concerned for the current year, it will again be a normal monsoon in the region.

It will be difficult even to do 30 per cent of the work needed to counter the threat of floods in flood-prone areas in the state at this stage, according to official sources. Only a few cosmetic touches can be given to the already existing flood-protection works.

As a lot of earth work is involved in flood-control measures, it is difficult to handle such work once the monsoon sets in.

The sources said till the end of the last month, the state government had not released funds to initiate flood-control measures in the state. The matter was brought to the notice of the government by the authorities concerned."

It is surprising that even more than seventy years after the attainment of Independence, there is no proper and efficient flood control system in our country, whereas countries like China have long managed their rivers. The Hawang Ho once the sorrow of China which had once devoured lakhs of people by crossing and marching away from its banks, is no more a sorrow, but a benign river catering to the needs of the Chinese and very much a partner in their measures for a prosperous future.

In India most often the Ganga and the Yamuna become unmanageable, UP, Bihar and Odisha get submerged. In Odisha, the sea waves also let loose terror as they did a few years ago when the poor small state had to face a huge rise of tides upto the height of several feet due to a sudden supercyclone of unprecedented magnitude. The standing crops were destroyed. Houses, offices, shops, schools, hospitals and other concrete buildings were washed away, not to speak of small huts, boats, electric poles, trees and other such vulnerable things. Even at that time, neither the people nor the government were well equipped to meet the calamity, though afterwards those were provided immense succour from far and wide from all parts of the country and even from abroad.

The Gomti causes havoc in cities like Lucknow. In Assam and adjoining states, the Brahmputra rises to menacing heights.

In Punjab the Sutlej and the Beas expand to dangerous volumes across their bank, submerging vast areas.

The question is why does all this happen? One important reason for this state of affairs is the lack of funds. A large amount of funds are required to build bunds and embankments on the rivers. This is often not done. The problem is not only of funds. Even the funds which are allocated for the purpose are often embezzled. Such is our moral character. Perhaps we hardly have the desire to live and let others live. As in every walk of life in our country which is considered one of the most corrupt countries of the world, funds are embezzled even for such life saving measures. Surprisingly, even in the tarpaulins meant for the Odisha supercyclone victims there was embezzlement of money.

Another important reason for the havoc of floods is the ruthless cutting of forest trees. Thick growth of trees in forests ensures a thick under growth of vegetation and grass which prevents the sudden flow of water during the rainy season and let the large collection of water flow and filter only in trickles by holding back large amounts of water, such that there is very little likelihood of the water taking the shape of a flood to threaten a rural or urban populated area.

Flood water causes havoc not just to human life. It takes a heavy toll of the precious livestock also. Highly valuable fertile land gets eroded. Trees are washed away in water. Woodwork and plastic and other goods from homes and shops and offices are carried away by the swirling currents.

Let the authorities and others concerned wake up. Stringent laws should be passed against the poachers and pilferers of forest wealth. Proper steps should be taken to build bunds on rivers and other water channels. The poor people living in low-lying areas should be persuaded to move to other sides or to raise the platforms of their houses. If need be, necessary financial grant or loan should be proved to them for the purpose.

It is said, "Eternal vigilance is the price of liberty." Likewise we can say, "Eternal vigilance is the price of safety."

Further, large tanks should be built in the catchment area to store the rainy water. This collection of water will not only prevent the floods but also serve the useful purpose of the necessity of water for irrigational and even drinking purposes for men and cattle during the dry season. Some of the tanks can also be used as fish aquariums and thus blue revolution can be made a reality.

A paradoxical situation regarding lack of planning, governance and management appeared in 2002 when a few eastern states like Bihar and Assam were reeling under the fury of uncontrollable floods while the remaining part of almost the whole of India had been transformed into a land of dry, yellow and brown wilting crops on hard, dry, waterless lumps of soil due to a severe drought created by the most spectacular failure of the monsoon in about two decades.

Let, we, the people and Government of India arise to the reality of our destiny still being controlled by God Indra, and chalk out the means to have an efficient system of flood as well drought control to mitigate the misery of all concerned.

Globalisation and Strikes

A Preview

- Newspapers
- Even in advanced countries
- French Revolution
- Prosperity to some, misery to others
- Give the devil his due
- Corruption
- Lethargy should be given up in the interest of national development
- A balanced view
- A particular strike
- Peasants' Revolt in medieval England
- Ostensible reasons
- Irreversible
- Teething troubles
- Schemes for the poor
- Eternal vigilance required
- Laxmi Sehgal

Today, when we open the newspaper in the morning, we read about strikes, more than anything else. Sometimes, the factory workers, sometimes the students, sometimes the teachers, sometimes the doctors, the engineers and even the lawyers are on strike. The shopkeepers, the chemists, the petrol pump dealers, the journalists, the employees of all departments, the bus drivers and the conductors all go on strike for one reason or the other.

The particular strike which had in it the portents of a "gathering storm" as a newspaper reported about it, was held on 11th May, 2000. It was a general strike and was expected to have an impact at all-India level. But, it appeared, it had not been quite successful and even the media did not give it much coverage.

However, the strike mentioned above, was important and a noticeable incident for many reasons and from many angles. For one thing, the strike was near total in several states, mostly ruled by the opposition, like Kerala, Bihar, Tripura, West Bengal and Assam. As per expert estimated, the strike heralded the return of the trade union to the centrestage after a long period of hibernation.

The most significant fact about the said strike was that apart from bank employees, and emloyees of the insurance sector, even the workers and employees of the unorganised sector and the small scale industry and the peasantary, youth and women participated in the strike.

It must be noted that even in a number of advanced and developed countries like England, France and the USA, the workers and trade unions are on the march. One can say they have come out of their hiding and are on the streets.

In the said strike in India, more than 25 million people were reported to have participated. We learn in British history, more than five hundred years ago, there was a Peasants' Revolt in which about one lakh peasants (a very large number at that time) converged on London demanding their rights. Their famous slogan was—

> *"When Adam delved and Eve span,*
> *Who was then the gentleman?"*

Apparently, the Peasants' Revolt failed, as it did not show any immediately palpable results. But the later history of England has proved beyond doubt that it had actually not failed. It was a revolutionary revolt and revolutions never fail; their results can at the most only be postponed or delayed.

We should never forget the French Revolution and the Reign of Terror it brought in its train towards the end of the eighteenth century. Nor can we ignore the great Bolshevik Revolution in Russia.

In India strikes are not powerful enough or matchable to any of the revolutions like the French or Russian Revolutions, still, their significance must not be lost sight of.

The ostensible reasons for strikes or protests are often the steep rise in prices of essential commodities, widespread unemployment, privatisation of banking and insurance, withdrawal or reduction of subsidies etc. But one common point in all this was the privations and difficulties being faced by the common man, particularly the low-income groups as a result of globalisation and privatisation.

It is indeed deplorable that whereas globalisation has brought prosperity to some, it has brought, all-the-same, misery to many. Probably the governments all over the world, (including the one in India) have been too hasty, thoughtless and unfarsighted in properly implementing the idea of one economic world. They haven't much bothered about the interests of the common men, particularly those belonging to the weaker sections of society. Consequently, scenes of protests have already been witnessed in the USA and Thailand. In the latter case, the outgoing chairman of World Trade Organisation was even hit and attacked.

Even if it is argued that globalisation is now irreversible and the teething troubles are bound to be there, our government must take some concrete steps to mitigate the lot of the poor.

At the same time, we must not put all the blame on the government. Even if some people may consider the government a devil (which a popular government may possibly not be), the saying is that "the devil must be given his due."

We must not forget that the government have started several schemes for the poor in the matter of housing, food, health, employment, education, etc. Some poor people are really benefiting from such schemes. Let others also avail themselves of them. There is no doubt that a wide-spread corruption hinders greatly the process of poverty alleviation. It is the duty of all concerned to bring to the notice of the Intelligence and Vigilance authorities all the corrupt elements that are eating into the vitals of our society.

Thus much more alertness and vigilance on the part of the common people is required. Only then the desired money meant for the poor can reach them. Otherwise, Rajiv Gandhi's observation that every rupee meant for the schemes for the poor gets frayed continuously, such that when it reaches the really deserving section of society, only fifteen paise are left of it. Let the government officials also give up their lethargy and work hard for national uplift to help one and all in our country.

It is true that globalisation is a double-edged weapon. It has both plus and minus points.

Globalisation has opened the doors of world trade and now goods can move easily from one part of the world to the other. All kinds of technology is getting easily transferred. The developing countries have gained a lot in the sense that those countries that cannot afford to go in for long and arduous task of research, can get the benefit of such research from developed countries. The developed countries gain in the sense that they can easily sell their products to the entire world and easily find out the takers and those who are ready to pay the maximum price.

India can gain immensely in the field of bio-agriculture in particular. The genetic engineering is something which has to stay.

If we study the scenario carefully we can realize that it is the developed countries that are the greater gainers in this game. It is only they who can manufacture more and more qualitative products in large quantities. Hence the multinational companies with new technology and flushed with funds to flood the market have entered the arena in our country.

According to Laxmi Sehgal, whom Netaji characterized as "the new Jhansi Ki Rani" and who was the left parties' candidate in the presidential election, "The worst thing is we are now allowing foreigners to enslave us economically. The conglomerates are servicing the vested interests of a few rich businessmen and politicians. Today the big companies are spreading their tentacles, tomorrow they will be interfering in every decision-making process of the country. Just like the British rule in India which had its root in the East India Company.

If this is not stopped, our economy will soon be controlled by foreigners. They will be dictating our annual national budget. That will be the ultimate disaster. In the 20th century we were slaves to the British. I hope we don't become economic slaves to the West in the 21st century."

Mobile Technology

A Preview

- ❖ First Telephone Call
- ❖ Bluetooth
- ❖ GSM
- ❖ Mobility
- ❖ AT&T-IMTS
- ❖ 3G Service
- ❖ Portability
- ❖ Advantages

Now-a-day's every individual use the mobile technology. In 1946 first telephone call was made and in 1965 first cordless phone was invented. After that AT&T launched the IMTS in 1971. First commercial call was made in the year 1983.

From the year 1946, mobile technology encountered lot of changes. The invention of the Bluetooth was made in the year 1994 and the first camera image was taken in the year 1997. In the year 2001 first 3G service was launched. These are the important milestones of mobile technology.

Cellular communication uses the mobile technology. In past few years GSM technology improved rapidly. Mobile technology is based on mobility of devices. Such technology is used in various industries like car etc.

Mobile technology is specially used by mobile phones for wireless communication purposes. Transferring of data done through mobile technology by means of voice, text, videos, images etc. Mobile technology provides the portability of devices. Examples of portable devices are: • Laptop • Mobile phones • GPS devices • Tablets. Mobile technology provides the improved services to users and provides the flexibility in work.

Mobile computing allows people to use IT without being tied to a single location. Any business with staff that works away from the office can benefit from using it. Whether you are travelling to meetings, out on sales calls, working from a client's site or from home, mobile devices can help you keep in touch and make the most productive use of your time. You can use a range of devices to stay in touch including laptops, notebooks, personal digital assistants and smartphones. Mobile IT devices can also change the way you do business. New technologies lead to new ways of working and new products and services that can be offered to your customers. Mobile technology is exactly what the name implies—technology that is portable.

The growth and development of mobile technology has had positive effects on society. There are many advantages that are experienced from the implementation and use of mobile technology. Mobile technology is set to take over as the driving force of global commerce. This is because in recent times., mobile technology has blossomed to such an extent that you are able to access all of the market data you require using your mobile phone. With the introduction of 4G technology, mobile technology and smart phones with capabilities of handling video calls, browsing the internet and sharing large files, mobile technology has made it more efficient to conduct business. Mobile technology enables you to get breaking news as and when it happens. By bringing you real time information, mobile technology enables you to make speedy and informed decisions. Mobile technology has played a great role in the education sector by enabling people to access the Internet, even in remote locations using mobile broadband.

Corruption

A Preview

- ❖ Worldwide phenomenon
- ❖ Foreign companies
- ❖ In India
- ❖ CBI, CVC, etc.
- ❖ Scams
- ❖ Our duty
- ❖ A country of scams
- ❖ Only small fry caught
- ❖ Straight punishment recovery
- ❖ The evil nexus
- ❖ A helpless situation
- ❖ A new type of corruption

It is rightly said that corruption is a worldwide phenomenon. It is generally seen that the foreign companies and governments often pay bribes in the interest of their own country. It is condemnable according to the tradition of the Indian culture.

Even if we admit that corruption is a worldwide phenomenon, yet we have to agree that in India probably it has crossed all conceivable limits. Corruption is there right from the peon level to the level of the highest officers. The politicians are probably the most tainted people.

You cannot think of moving a file from one table to another until it has wings of silver attached to it. Every almirah in a government department opens only with a silver key.

There are innumerable scams in our country. One cannot even remember the names of some of them. There is hardly a government or semi-government department where there is no major or minor scam of one or the other kind.

It will be right to say that corrupt public servant is a menace to society as he does not discharge his duties properly. He does not adhere to the rule of law and brings disrepute to the government and society.

Thus we have urea scam, fodder scam, sugar scam, housing scam, recruitment scam, stationery scam, rice scam, land grabbing and encroachment scam, petrol pump scam, telecom scam, coalgate scam, 2G scam, modigate scam and so many others.

No doubt we need some awakened citizens to overcome this menace. Some agencies like the CBI, CVC, etc. are also trying to check this menace. The courts are also doing a lot to punish the culprits. But the success for various reasons is limited. Legal squabbles (which are sometimes unavoidable) also at times hinder the process of corruption management. For instance, the Bofors case had dragged for years.

The most important thing is that the people themselves should show awakening and resistance and vigilance not to give bribe to any employee or other person to get their work done quickly.

The tainted politicians should not be allowed to contest elections. They should be socially boycotted by the people apart from being punished by the courts under the due process of law. Respect for the honest citizens in society should be restored.

Now, we are confronted with the seemingly intractable problem of corruption which has penetrated all parts of public life and is virtually eating into the vitals of our great country.

Take the case of bribe. We should remember that though the law considers both bribe-taking and bribe-giving criminal offences, yet the bribe-givers think that only bribe-takers should be punished.

It is a pity that India has become notorious for being the land of scams and scandals. There are scams galore in India. To make a list of some of them, we can name the following as outstanding examples:

1. The Hawala scam	**2.** The Bofors scam
3. The Urea scam	**4.** The Fodder scam
5. The Sugar scam	**6.** The Recruitment scam
7. The Housing scam	**8.** The Petrol pumps scam
9. The Telecom scam	**10.** The Securities scam
11. The Text-books scam	**12.** 2G spectrum allocation scam
13. Commonwealth Games scam	**14.** Coal Block Scam
15. Augusta-Westland Helicopter Scam	
16. Modigate Scam	

Let us stop the list at the figure comfortable for such things, otherwise we could count many others known and many others unknown.

It is a strange logic that the small fry who offers soft targets, is punished whenever caught, but the bigger sharks go scot free. The corrupt politicians and leaders who have amassed so much wealth disproportionate to their known sources of income, often get no punishment or very little punishment. With the ill-gotten money, they can engage the best lawyers in the country. The latter are pastmasters in finding out loopholes in law and taking full advantage of such loopholes. Thus, they save their clients from punishment. The Vigilance Commissioner has rightly said that until a provision to confiscate the ill-gotten property of culpritis is made, it is impossible to eradicate the menace of corruption from the Indian soil.

Thus, stringent punishments should be given to the corrupt politicians, bureaucrats and others. At present, a powerful nexus is going on between the politicians, bureaucrats and industrialists. The rich industrialists secure bank loans and forget to repay them. They indulge in evasion of excise duty and other taxes on a large in collusion with the powers that be.

The whole social system in India from the top to the bottom has gone corrupt and there is no hope of its coming on the right track. Probably, only God can save this country from the grip of the anaconda of corruption.

A new type of corruption has become the order of the day. It is the white-collar corruption.

Those committing professional, financial and business frauds now hit the headlines more often than known hardened criminals, including those of the underworld. The busting of the country's biggest-every recruitments scam and reports of "kickbacks" in government and public sector procurement, frauds in financial institutions, intellectual property piracy and identity theft are only indicators of the boom in white-collar crime.

Thus, the society and the government have to fight not just one type of corruption, but varied kinds of it. Corruption is a hydra with many heads. When one head is cut, a new head emerges and we have to grapple with this new head. The common man simply feels baffled and helpless.

However, if we have a firm determination, we can certainly overcome this menace rather sooner than later.

Water Management
or
People's War for Water
or
Water and People

A Preview

- Pre-requisite for a national policy
- Green Revolution in Punjab
- Imminent water shortage in Punjab and Haryana
- Malthus's theory
- Main sources of fresh water
- Drought of 1987
- Local variation
- Condition in Haryana
- Water disputes among states
- Satellite mapping
- Rain-water rivulets and drains
- The Makkowal case
- People's efforts
- Water famine will lead to food shortage, starvation and death
- Self-dependence on cooperative basis—only remedy for people

The problem in India (may be in almost every country) is that land features change every few kilometres and, therefore, there can be no uniform or standing national water policy which can be put into practice properly unless it takes into account the elaborate terrestrial conditions of the terrain in its diversity which is too large and whopping. Then we have local variation depending on soil, crops sown and the mode of irrigation. The result is that whereas there may be an acute paucity of water in one area, another one, not quite far away, may be suffering from the acute problem of water logging.

In certain states, as during the Green Revolution in Punjab, the underground water has been tapped to criminal excess, thus lowering the level to an alarming extent.

This local variation can be gauged from the situation prevailing in Punjab and Haryana. In Punjab, whereas in several areas there is scarcity of water, in the districts of Ferozepur and Bhatinda there is the problem of water-logging and water there is brackish and unfit for human consumption.

In Haryana most of southern and central districts have light, loamy soils. Such soils have a higher capacity for water retention. The result is rising water tables, poor drainage, water-logging and high soil salinity. The reverse is the case in the northern districts. In these districts, the soil is heavier. Such a soil cannot retain water for long. The result is falling water tables and soil-compacting.

Unfortunately India's water policy at state, national and international level has all along been defective. India doled out 85 crores of rupees to Pakistan long long ago for the sole utilization of water of the Ravi through what was called the Indus Water Treaty. The present value of 85 crores "donated" to Pakistan by Nehru now comes to billions of rupees. But, India has all along failed to make a proper utilization of the Ravi water, thanks to the water dispute between the Punjab and Haryana mainly and the precious water worth billions, may be trillions of rupees, has flowed down unprofitably through the Ravi Channel into the Arabian Sea.

The water disputes between states such as between Punjab and Haryana and Karnataka and Tamil Nadu, thanks to the lack of foresight of the hind-eyed politicians, have played havoc and caused untold and immense misery to the common people and incurred heavy losses to the country as a whole.

Now, it is possible to have precise data concerning surface and underground water resources, vegetation and soil through satellite mapping and the government and the people can have, through a joint effort, a more comprehensive water policy for the benefit of all.

There are certain steps which can easily be taken. For example—

1. Roof top water can be tapped during the rainy season. The Union Minister for Urban Development, indicated sometime back that the roof-top water harvesting would be incorporated in building by-laws.

2. It is reported that the Human Settlement Technology for the conservation of rainwater has been finalised by the Indian Institute of Technology.

3. The farmers may be asked to change the cropping pattern by giving more emphasis on crops like sunflower which require less water.

4. Many of the tube-wells in certain areas are built in wells which lie at the field level. During the rainy season, often much of the water just goes down the drain. The farmers build temporary walls around the tube-wells to prevent the water from flooding the wells which are sometimes covered. The farmers can be asked to keep the wells uncovered and unwalled during the rainy season to let the rain water flow freely into their wells. This can raise the water table of ground water to some extent.

5. Sometime back, it was suggested by a retired chief engineer from a state that deep bores at certain places should be made into the soil during the rainy season to let the freely-flowing rain water seep into the soil.

6. In areas where water-logging is a problem, channels should be built to carry water to the areas of scarcity. Such channels should preferably be covered to prevent the water from evaporating.

7. In certain areas there are rain water rivulets and drains as "choes" in district Hoshiarpur in Punjab. In the rainy season these rivulets are flooded while otherwise they are dry. Some underground pipes may be built in such areas to gather and carry the rain water to the areas of paucity for drinking and irrigational water. This is what has been done in the Makkowal village in Punjab.

The newspaper report is worth-mentioning in detail:

"A case to the point is Makkowal village, in Bunga block, 30 Km from Hoshiarpur. Before 1984, there was just one well,

100 metres deep, which used to cater to some of the requirements of the villagers. Fetching water was a full-time chore and "water fights" were frequent.

Then a dam was built in 1985 by the Soil and Water Conservation and Waste Land Development Department, Punjab. The water flowing in a perennial choe, near the village, was tapped and taken through the underground pipeline system by gravitational flow and collected in a tank from where it was taken to the fields through a network of conveyance system. "Earlier, there used to be scarcity of drinking water and the area was susceptible to crop failures also. Today, water is in abundance here," says the Chief Conservator of Soils, Punjab.

The dam was so successful that the government replicated it at 30 more places, at a cost of ₹ 6 crore thereby irrigating 6,000 acres. Such dams came to be known as "Makkowal-type" dams.

Report or no report, the important point to be noted is the people's participation alongwith high, responsible officials' innovation and initiative in bringing out new scheme in such matters. Managing the diabolical rivulets by virtually controlling and harnessing them to the people's advantage cannot but be appreciated. Let us hope more such schemes and that all over the country.

There are certain regions in our country where traditional techniques are no longer viable. Such are mostly the coastal zones and arid areas. In such cases, solar and wind energy can be brought into use profitably and inexpensively and that in an extremely convenient way. The method can be used, besides for extraction of ground water, for desalination of water for drinking purposes.

It is succinctly clear that unless the people wake up from their slumber at local level and the government rises to the occasion to take decision and firm steps right from now for arrangement of drinking water for all, keeping in view the alarmingly rising population, the situation is too grim to be visualised quickly. The future stares us in the face. A terrible water famine is imminent and to prevent it from becoming a reality, we, all concerned, shall have to take bold steps.

Alas! even more than seventy years after independence, we have had no national or practicable water policy and we are still overwhelmingly dependent on the monsoon. The food bowls of the country, Punjab and Haryana are heading for changing into deserts within the next three decades and we can ill-afford to ignore this fact. The net result of it is ultimately to be not only river water shortage, but consequential food famine, starvation, hunger—and that for millions!

Healthcare

A Preview

- ❖ Great efforts
- ❖ CAD
- ❖ Shaw
- ❖ Periodontal disease
- ❖ Aroma Therapy
- ❖ Hepatitis–B
- ❖ Diet, etc.—Gandhiji
- ❖ Sivananda
- ❖ Nature care

Great efforts are being made by India at the present moment to bring good health to its citizens.

Two of the most serious diseases which have spread in India are Hepatitis-B and AIDS.

The following points should be noted :

- Hepatitis B causes serious liver disease. 60 per cent of liver diseases and 80 per cent of liver cancer in India is due to Hepatitis B.
- The risk of becoming a carrier is highest in infants.
- The infection is spread through non-sterile medical equipment & syringes, infected blood & body fluids etc.

According to a noted cardiologist, we should change our lifestyle to avoid heart disease.

According to heart experts, we should adopt the lifestyle of a labourer and do intense physical activities during the day. That alone can ensure a sound heart in a sound body and a sound sleep at night. There is no need to take sleeping pills and other drugs. We should also give up drinking, smoking, sedentary habits and reduce the intake of fat and salt. We should avoid diet comprising a high number of calories.

Even Mahatma Gandhi who experimented freely with several health measures advised:

A well regulated diet, water and earth treatment and similar household remedies.

A sound belief in recovery can also lead us to health. Thus, Swami Sivananda says that during illness, detach yourself from the body. Connect the mind with Buddhi and soul and the disease will take to its heels.

Auto-suggestion is a powerful Vedantic tool. Say to yourself: By the grace of God, I am becoming better and better, day by day, in every way.

Whereas people in foreign countries are careful about their teeth, in India, in spite of wide awakening in all fields, including health matters, people are not still quite aware of the serious complications that may arise due to periodontal (gum) disease.

Man is a part of nature and he cannot ignore nature at any stage in his life except only at his own peril.

Even in the matter of health, whatever advance medical science of any category might have made and might make further, he cannot show his back to nature.

Thus, it is highly important for man to follow the system of nature cure to avoid disease and cure diseases whenever they do visit him for any reason.

Nature cure implies an ideal mode of life. The name of God is, of course, the hub round which the nature cure system revolves.

In the modern age, we have several systems of medicines such as—

(i) Allopathy	*(ii)* Homeopathy	*(iii)* Ayurveda
(iv) Unani system	*(v)* Nature Cure	*(vi)* Acupuncture, etc.
(vii) Auto-suggestion		

Another system now becoming popular is the aroma therapy which means cure through smell. The vapours of the natural colours and aroma compounds are made to be inhaled by the patients. It is claimed that through this method several diseases can be cured and many others averted.

AIDS
or
AIDS Has no Cure
or
Observe Prevention to Avert AIDS

A Preview

- Spreading like wild fire
- A report
- Causes
- Not a contagious disease
- Observe precautions
- Measures recommended
- No cure
- An AIDS patient needs love and sympathy
- Several companies engaged in research
- AIDS vaccine
- Prevention, the best remedy

We know that now AIDS is spreading like wild fire throughout the world. India is particularly affected by the disease as there is in India the ever-increasing number of HIV positive cases as is clear from a report also:

"It is well-established that STD (Sexually Transmitted Disease) is a major health problem in India which has been further compounded with the emergence of HIV infection. The "dramatic" increase of HIV positive cases in India has, however, limited modes of transmission and majority of the cases can be attributed to sexual activity, parenteral transmission, through receipt of infected blood and infected needles."

Thus, we know there are the following modes of spreading of AIDS:

1. Promiscuous extra-marital sexual activity without ample precautionary measures such as the use of a condom.

2. Transfusion of HIV positive blood.

3. Use of infected needles usually non-disposable ones.

4. Heredity — when both or either of the parents is infected.

The disease does not spread by shaking hands, sitting close to an infected person, use of same towels and clothes, kissing etc.

Since there is so far no effective remedy for AIDS, adequate precautionary measures are indispensable.

These measures include:

1. Abstention from having sex with anybody other than one's own spouse. If at all one is inclined to have an extra-marital or promiscuous sex, adequate precautionary measures, such as the use of a condom, must be taken.

2. Only sterilized disposable needles should be used for blood test purposes or transfusion of blood.

3. Blood before being transfused, must be tested for HIV positive.

4. If one or both of the spouses are suffering from AIDS or have HIV positive blood, the production of a child should be avoided. Proper family planning measures should be adopted to prevent such a birth.

If a person does suffer from AIDS or has HIV positive blood, we should not hate him or her. We should remember that AIDS is not a contagious disease. Hence we should not desert such a patient but show him or her love and give him/her encouragement to bear the trouble boldly and patiently since we know the disease is a hundred per cent fatal one as the whole immune system of the body is destroyed.

Although several companies are engaged in research and even claim some success, yet at present no worthwhile remedy is there.

Fortunately, more recently, we are in receipt of more encouraging news regarding the manufacture of an AIDS vaccine in the near future which may mitigate the lamentable situation as we find ourselves in at present. Let us hope for the best. Still, it must be remembered. Precaution is the best remedy.

"Youngsters are the most vulnerable group which are falling prey to the acquired immune deficiency syndrome (AIDS) and our aim is to create awareness among them about the deadly stalker and help them make the right decisions," said Dr. Erma W. Manonocurt, Deputy Director (Programmes), UNICEF, sometime ago while participating , in inter-industries symposium on "HIV/AIDS and drugs-free work place : a key to women health and social equity."

"We are concerned that an increasing number of youngsters are falling victim to the deadly disease and there are examples where a large percentage of the youngsters, especially in developing countries, are HIV positive. This is a cause of great concern to not only to any country but our global society as a whole," she added.

Indian Agriculture
or
How to Increase Agricultural Production?
or
Increasing Food Production through Technology

A Preview

- ❖ Introduction : Mechanised farming in some foreign countries
- ❖ Mechanical farming in India
- ❖ India still an agricultural country
- ❖ About the Indian farmers
- ❖ The rich farmers and the small and marginal farmers
- ❖ Suicide by farmers in the cotton
- ❖ Supply of free water and electricity to farmers
- ❖ The role of agricultural industries
- ❖ Green revolution
- ❖ Genetic engineering and seeds
- ❖ About fertilizers, insecticides, bee keeping, fishery, poultry, dairying, horticulture
- ❖ About irrigation
- ❖ Conclusion : Let India remain self-dependent in food production

Whereas countries like America, Canada and Australia have long adopted mechanized farming on a large scale, India has only recently adopted it and that too comparatively on a small-scale only. Of course, in certain states like the Punjab and Haryana, several kinds of agricultural machines and instruments are being used to increase and facilitate production in Uttar Pradesh, Bihar, Odisha and many other states, agricultural activities are, by and large, being carried out on traditional lines only, although a lot of improvement in this respect is certainly discernible in certain other states like Maharashtra, Gujarat, Karnataka etc.

Whereas certain European countries (for example, England) are now fully industrialized with little agricultural land left, India is still, even more than sixty five years after Independence, an agricultural country. In India still about 68% of people live in villages and depend upon agriculture. A major portion of Indian population is still engaged in the occupation of farming. Then there are millions of landless labourers who are also engaged in this occupation.

The difficulty with Indian farming system is that most of the farmers in India are petty land-holders. They are small and marginal farmers. They have very small income from the land they have. Thus they cannot afford expensive machines and instruments like tractors and harvesters for agricultural purposes, although in states like the Punjab, certain rich farmers have huge incomes from farming, the same is not the case with small and poor farmers. The rich farmers do make use of modern machines, but not so the poor ones.

In the cotton belt in Gujarat and Punjab, the condition of small farmers became so miserable towards the end of the nineties that a number of them committed suicide. It so happened that they had got huge loans from banks which they could not repay as their crops failed. They had no safety valves. The Punjab government's scheme to supply free water and electricity, also helped only the rich farmers. The poor farmers had no tubewells of their own. They purchased water from the rich farmers. Strangely enough, the rich farmers sold water to such poor farmers, thus pocketing money when they themselves had got it free from the government.

The difficulty of the poor farmers does not end here only. Most of them are illiterate. They know nothing about the new mechanized methods of farming. There is no doubt that some of our universities like the Punjab Agricultural University and Haryana Agricultural University have played a pivotal role in promoting agriculture in India. The Green Revolution of seventies and eighties was mainly because of the research done by the Punjab Agricultural University, Ludhiana. Many new kinds of seeds of cereals developed at the university brought about the revolution. The new seeds gave plants which produced larger number of grains. Now there have appeared in the world, seeds through genetic engineering which can increase production manifold.

In developed countries, there is not only a revolution in the creation of new kinds of seeds, but also in several other fields. For example, fruits can now be ripened. It is possible that hens should lay more eggs and milch animals should give more milk.

Certain such methods are now being adopted in India also, but still not quite adequately. Now organic and chemical fertilizers can ensure more production than the traditional compost fertilizers. Now soil can be tested to find out the deficiency of a particular element or mineral and the same type of fertilizers can be mixed in the soil. It is possible to spray insecticides with sprayers which work normally and with the help of a helicopter.

In certain parts of our country, still the bullock-cart for tilling the land is in vogue. Farmers in India should be taught about the methods of rotation crops and cash crops to enable them to increase production as well as their income. Besides just raising crops, they can raise bees in hives, fishes in tanks and also resort to poultry dairying or horticulture. In certain areas, flowers for which there is great demand in the market, can be grown.

While in some parts of India there are tubewells in large numbers for irrigational purposes, in some other parts, the old artisan wells, driven by oxen are still in vogue. Many regions in India still depend upon rain for irrigation. In south India, rain water is stored in tanks. Certain areas like those of Rajasthan, Gujarat and Odisha go dry when the rain-god gives the slip. Let us make available abundant amount of money to our farmers to purchase new tools and machines. They should be supplied enough power and diesel also. Surplus food production can enable India to export food and earn precious foreign exchange.

The Future of English in India
or
Can India Progress without English?
or
Should English be Abolished from India?

A Preview

- ❖ Introduction : English an international language
- ❖ Legacy of the British Raj in India
- ❖ English literature
- ❖ Effect on freedom fighters
- ❖ English – a storehouse of scientific and other knowledge
- ❖ India's voice in international affairs
- ❖ The Role of NRIs
- ❖ The advent of the computers
- ❖ People's communication at international level
- ❖ W W W
- ❖ Lingua Franca
- ❖ Communication between people of different states
- ❖ English and national unity
- ❖ Negative points and how to remedy them
- ❖ Court Judgement
- ❖ Craze for English
- ❖ English to stay

No doubt, English is an international language. Having started from a small island known as Britain it has spread in all parts of the world. At present, it is the mother tongue of certain countries like Britain, America, Australia etc. It is written and used in many other countries. It is one of the language of the United Nations, along with French, Spanish, Arabic etc., but most of the work of the august organization is done only in English.

The English ruled over India for about two hundred years. When they introduced English into the school and college curricula, many people opposed it, but some enlightened men like Raja Ram Mohan Roy welcomed this step. English brought the new western culture and knowledge that would suppress the Indian languages and the Indian way of living and thinking. The suspicion was partly correct and partly incorrect.

The study of the English language also introduced the knowledge of English literature to the Indians. Many of our freedom fighters like Jawahar Lal Nehru, Gopal Krishna Gokhle and others were greatly impressed and inspired by the new knowledge.

English is the largest storehouse of scientific, technological, psychological and managerial knowledge in the world. Not to study English simply means to remain devoid of this storehouse when our own scriptures advise us to gather knowledge from all sources. For example, a mantra in one of the Vedas says, "Let noble thoughts come to me from every side." Even Jawaharlal Nehru has said in one of his writings that India progressed only when she did not shut her doors against the influence of the outside world. But all progress came to a standstill when she shut herself in a shell.

At present, India is a voice to reckon with in international affairs. Particularly, after the Pokhran-II and victory in the Kargil conflict, India's voice at the international fora has become very powerful. Moreover, some Non-Resident Indians are doing very well in countries like the USA, Canada etc. An Indian, Ujjal Dosanjh, has become the first Indian to be the Prime Minister of Colombia, a significant state of Canada. Some Indian companies like Ranbaxy, Dr. Reddy's Lab, Reliance Ltd. etc. have become international players.

In such circumstances, it is obvious that a very large number of people in the world have to interact for various purposes and transactions. That is possible only in English. It is the only language which people all over the world know in fairly large numbers. Moreover, now with the advent of the computer, in which field India is at the top in the world, the importance of English has still more increased. No doubt, Hindi and some other Indian languages are now also being used for the purposes of computer but that is only on a limited scale. In any case, communication at international level, more so with the advent of WWW is most conveniently and frequently possible only in English.

India does not need English only for international purposes. Many people regard English the Lingua Franca of India. Although very few people in India speak English, yet it is understood in almost all parts of the country. In India there are 22 official languages. Besides, there are more than one thousand and five hundred other languages. The number of dialects is still more. The people of one region do not understand the language of the other region. Thus a Punjabi cannot understand Tamil or Kannada or Kanarese or Bengali. Similarly a Tamil, or a Bengali cannot understand Punjabi. But English can be understood by many people in all states of India. This understanding of English makes the communication between people of different regions much easier. In this way, English helps in the matter of maintaining natural unity and integration.

Of course, there has long been a hate-English campaign in India. It is argued that the study of English suppresses the study of Hindi and regional languages. This is true to some extent. It is also argued that only the rich can afford to study English which is taught in costly public schools and the poor have to study Hindi and regional languages. There arises the disparity between the rich and the poor instead of narrowing the gap. This is true to a great extent.

The remedy does not lie in abolishing or discontinuing the study of English. A national education policy should be adopted and every child should have an almost equal opportunity to gain the study of English. The constitution envisaged the study of English only for ten years. But then the Prime Minister Jawaharlal Nehru had to promise the southern states that the study of English in India would continue as long as they wanted. The same policy is continuing. Now everybody has a craze for English and English-teaching schools. But Indian languages should also not be ignored.

We must remember Robert D. King's views that "English could never have been chosen by legislative vote as the national language of India", as English was the language of the colonisers. In all All-India Conference resolution (before 1947) Hindustani was preferred. As King points out, "Hindustani for all the problems associated with it (India) symbolized freedom and independence, swaraj. English symbolished precisely the opposite servile weakness, bowed heads before the sahib and the memsahib, the topi. The English language was an icon for all that was wrong in colonial relationship."

However, as said by Anupam Gupta in an article : "English is the new father tongue",

"The icon was placed on high constitutional pedestal last week, (a few years back) when a full bench of the Madras High Court, after a bitterly contested hearing unanimously struck down a Tamil Nadu government order imposing Tamil in place of English as the medium of instruction in primary schools from classes I to V."

Earlier, we had seen that Jawaharlal Nehru had to give an assurance to the southern states regarding the continuance of English till the southern states desired. Now with the judgment of the Madras High Court, we must take it that English is to stay for all times to come.

The Role of the Police

A Preview

- ❖ An important law enforcing agency
- ❖ Law and order and safety
- ❖ Essential for the existence of social fabric and civilization
- ❖ Essential for progress and higher activities
- ❖ Nabs anti-social elements
- ❖ Some policemen themselves culprits
- ❖ No sweeping statements should be made
- ❖ Police Commissions
- ❖ Proper training in law and order system and interaction with people essential
- ❖ Kiran Bedi, etc.
- ❖ London police
- ❖ Our police personnel going abroad to provide training to foreigners
- ❖ National Police Commission (NPC) Report

The police is an imporant law-enforcing agency. It plays such an important role in our life which we hardly care to recognize. Most of us often blame the police for all our law and order and other problems. We hardly try to realize that in spite of all the deficiencies in the police system, most of which are at the individual or personal level and not at the system level, it is the police which is mainly instrumental in maintaining law and order and continuing to establish peace in our social set-up.

The most important thing for our existence and progress is safety which implies law and order. "Without safety," as CEM Joad points out, "those higher activities of mankind which make up civilization could not go on. The inventor could not invent, the scientist find out or the artist make beautiful things." The learned scholar goes on to say, "Hence order and safety although they are not themselves civilization, are things without which civilization would be impossible."

Thus, we can say, the police while maintaining law and order and safety, in fact, helps in the continuity and furtherance of the cause of one civilization.

Joad also says, "If today I have a quarrel with another man, I do not get beaten merely because I am physically weaker and he can knock me down. I go to law, and the law will decide as fairly as it can between the two of us."

However, before going to the law straightaway, we have to lodge an FIR with the police and thus the role of the police becomes crucial. It is the police that first of all nabs the thieves, burglars, murderers, pickpockets and other anti-social elements and produces them to the court which decides the matter according to the law of the land.

Says further Mr. Joad, "Moreover, the law protects me from robbery and violence. Nobody may come and break into my house, steal my goods, or run off with my children. Of course, there are burglars, but they are very rare, and the law punishes them whenever it catches them."

It is true that sometimes policemen are found conniving with the antisocial elements. Sometimes, they are found to be corrupt and they take bribes too. But, the practice may not be as widely wide-spread as it is believed to be. Moreover, even such corrupt cops are punished in the courts of law whenever they are caught or brought to public or legal or judicial exposure by the victims or the public at large.

Hence, it is not proper to make a sweeping statement that all the policemen are corrupt, dishonest and have associations with undesirable sections of society, though some of them may be belonging to this category.

It is very imporant for us to cooperate with the police in nabbing the anti-social elements. Every law and order problem must instantaneously be reported to the police. Whenever a policeman tries to harass an innocent person, the matter must be brought to the notice of the higher authorities.

Since Independence, a number of Police Commissions have recommended police reforms. Let their recommendations be given concrete shape. Further reforms in the police should be brought about. The criminalisation, and politicisation of the police force must be stopped. Proper training should be provided to the police personnel, not only in the matter of bringing to book the anti-social elements but also in the matter of interacting with the people.

Let us have a look at some models such as Kiran Bedi and KPS Gill and stop to paint all policemen as blackguards. Kiran Bedi, the Magasaysay Award winner particularly can inspire not only women and people in general but also all cops in particular who should try to emulate her. As incharge of the Delhi Tihar jail, she had brought several reforms which were appreciated not only by the authorities that be and the public, but also by the prisoners themselves. Many of them were given lessons in yoga and meditation and were changed from hardcore criminals into meek law abiding citizens. Such is her loving, docile touch.

London police is known for its politeness and help and succour which it provides to the helpless and the needy. Let our cops take a leaf out of the London Police. It is heartening to note that great efforts are being made to reform the police system. Our police personnel are even going to foreign lands to provide training to the cops there.

It is surprising that India who claims so many plus points in so many fields has been outmanoeuvered in the matter of police reforms. As per a report, based an survey carried out by an expert, "Pakistan has now clearly stolen a march over India by introducing major reforms in the organisation, structure and working of its police, with a view to fully depoliticising it. Ironically, most of the reforms are based on the recommendations of our own National Police Commission. While we have only allowed the eight excellent reports submitted by the NPC as far back as 1981 to gather dust, Pakistan has quietly gone ahead and freed their policemen from political control by enacting the Pakistan Police Ordinance, 2001."

The Importance of Advertising

A Preview

❖ Importance— business	❖ Companies
❖ Exploitation of consumers	❖ DD
❖ Internet	❖ TV cinema, etc
❖ Lucrative	❖ Competition
❖ Knowledge	❖ Family planning etc.
❖ Jobs	❖ Deceptive advertising
❖ In USA	❖ In some other foreign countries

The sale of everything in the modern world depends upon advertising. The big companies which have enough funds to spare on advertising, have a roaring business. They manufacture and advertise new and new products like biscuits, chocolates etc. to attract children and make a quick and easy buck.

Though strange it may look, both ways the poor nations like India are being exploited by the multinational companies with the sheer might of their advertising capacity.

Take the case of a cold drink. Plain water is taken from India. It is distilled or otherwise treated and a few, probably not very costly ingredients are added to it. The total process might be costing a rupee or a little more, if at all, and the same is sold to the Indians for ₹ 10 or so on the sheer strength of heavy advertising.

So important are considered these advertisements (mostly by the multinational companies) for cars, TVs, fridges, mobile phones, pagers, AC's and other luxury items that even the programmes and serials broadcast by the Doordarshan to somehow pacify the penurious, starving Indians, are abruptly paused again and again for the overall benefit of the sharks who are after all the caterers who feed even the Doordarshan which still running into losses at crores or billions of rupees will otherwise starve, wilt, wither and languish away.

In recent times, Internet has emerged as a very powerful and fast expanding advertising media. According to an author, "Information Technology Act, 2000, has made it imperative for the country to adopt a regime of cyber laws which determine the rights and responsible of parties using the Internet for business or otherwise."

Internet is also sometimes used for pornographic purposes. There have been raids on several cyber cafes. Then, as announced by the Information and Broadcasting Minister, certain preventive steps have been taken to effectively trace out and block the pornographic sites, We, however, note with anguish that the malaise has not been thoroughly overcome and the malady continues, more or less.

Advertisements

Our newspapers and journals are replete with advertisements concering computer programmes and education, different technologies, money-earning methods, exports, marketing, profession, etc.

The world is growing so fast that the things are changing rapidly day by day. But the media of entertainment has grown too faster and has gone so big across the world, that it is difficult to make an exact guess. We have TV, cinema, CD players, DVD players and so on, to get a relief from the so called boredem of the whole day. Among them TV is the most popular way of entertainment in the modern society. Not only the children but also the old persons like it very much. It is because of its having a great range of choice due to the starting of many new channels.

This sector is so lucrative that the channels like Sony TV, Zee TV, Star TV etc. are progressing with leaps and bounds. These channels are earning a lot of money through commercial advertisements. Sometimes, we, the spectators feel that the advertisements are even more interesting than the TV serials or feature films.

Through these TV channels we can feel a stiff competition among different companies in our country. We can judge that the awakening in the beauty business has also come as a boon to the ad industry. Most cosmetics firms spend a fortune on advertising. On the other hand there is sluggish growth of economy on other fronts.

Through these ads, we can judge how bold the modern woman has gone. She is more independent and professional. She has to a great extent come out of the so called grip of man and she is no more a slave to the man-dominated society.

Through these ads we can choose a toilet soap which may give a lathery, soft film of soap to our skin and can make our bath a complete one by killing germs and removing foul smell. If it rashes your skin consult a skin specialist please, as early as possible. This is the advice one should bear in mind. And there ends the responsibility of the soap-manufacturers.

If we are willing to have our teeth shining like gems and we like to puff out aromatic smell through our breath, we have a number ads before the start of a TV serial or even in the break-time. But remember a blind faith never brings good to anyone.

If anyone wants to have a particular invigorating drink but is unable to remember its name, let him just sit by his TV set. Just in a moment he will get confused in deciding which drink can give him more energy or vitamins. But for your kind information none of them has such kind of qualities.

Ads are great things in adding a bit more in your knowledge by conveying to you how you can keep your costly clothes white and spotless in the right manner even without using an ultramarine. You will have to use the prescribed solution with great care. So, through ads one can learn how to be cautious in the important walks of life.

By acting upon the advice given in certain ads, you can learn why in future to take most of the ads as material for amusement and not solid action.

If you are applying any sort of family planning instrument, then you are definitely an educated person. Otherwise you should sit by your TV set to get the most imporant education that would save our country from population explosion and that is, what instruments should be used to stop further addition to our so crowded world here.

Hence ads give us a great knowledge about the world around us. Otherwise, such a great part of knowledge cannot be got under the same roof without extra efforts.

Now, keep smiling wherever you go. It will keep you healthy and there can be a bright chance that anyone watching you in such a jubilant mood may select you as a model for his new product and you may also earn millions like Sachin or Dhoni.

So, to be lucky is to be happy. To be happy is to be smiling. To be smiling is to be luckier and wealthier and that finally means to be healthiest, wealthiest and luckiest. Hence, adore the ads and sing their praises and panegyrics in your heart. But don't curse them if you are still not selected as a model.

According to the reviewer (DS Cheema) of the book "Advertising Law & Ethics" by justice P.B. Sawant and P.K. Bandyopadhyay,

"Advertising is recognised by the courts as a form of 'commercial speech' which does no more than propose a commercial transaction." 'Commercial speech' must be regulated if it is misleading, if it concerns an illegal product or if there is substantial evidence that it is against the interest of the community."

It is also rightly pointed out by the writer that "advertising is accused of encouraging materialism and consumption, of causing us to purchase items for which we have no need, of taking advantage of children.... of using sex to sell, and of generally contributing to the downfall of our social system."

In the USA, a special Federal Trade Commission (FTC) Act was passed in 1914 to regulate 'deceptive advertising.' The learned reviewer says that:

"FTC considers a marketing effort to be deceptive if (*i*) there is a representation, omission, act or practice, that (*ii*) is likely to 'mislead' consumers acting reasonably under the circumstances, and, (*iii*) that representation, omission, or practice is "material".

That was long, long ago. We are, even a century later, far behind America in this matter.

While in India, all kinds of advertisements are being shown over the TV and in cinemahouses and broadcast over the radio, this is not the case in all countries. For instance, MTV Europe can't show beer ads in Norway. Brazil requires that all advertisement shown in their country must have some local content. Australia prohibits all foreign commercials, and direct comparison advertisements are not allowed in Austria.

The Working of the Indian Republic
or
A Challenge to the Indian Republic

A Preview

- Democratic republic
- Short-sighted politicians
- Criminalisation, corruption, etc
- K. Santhanam's review
- T.N. Seshan & Election Commission
- A case
- Frequent change of governments
- Many a crisis
- Westminster model
- Anti-defection law
- Constitution Reforms Commission, etc.
- Much more reforms required
- Supreme Court's orders

India is a republic with a democratic set-up. But almost immediately after Independence, some crafty, greedy and short-sighted leaders injected into the Indian polity the seeds of communalism, discrimination and disintegration that have grown to a gigantic size over the years.

No doubt, apart from other conditions, the electoral system needs to be maintained in a well-oiled and healthy condition so that honest and conscientious leaders take over the reins of the nation.

Unfortunately, at present, the Indian politics is marred by criminalization, corruption, deception, false promises, free flow of black money, intimidation of voters, booth-capturing, high expenses and elegance of transparency and accountability in the system. It was after the Bombay blasts that the NN Vohra

Committee brought to focus the nefarious nexus between criminals and politicians. Now, we have not only the criminals and politicians, but also the high bureaucrats and even industrialists hand in glove with one another to subvert the electoral system and to dupe and loot the poor voter by all means.

The electoral reforms is an important aspect which should be borne in mind while thinking of keeping or bringing the Indian democratic and republican polity on the rails. It was, no doubt, T.N. Seshan, the then Chief Election Commissioner who drew most powerfully the country's attention to the menace of electoral malpractices, and he put in his might to overcome the malaise and remedy it. Later, M.S. Gill continued the process. His successor, J.M. Lyngdoh had not lagged behind in his efforts to achieve success and bring out the true picture to voters' mind. But, unfortunately, the evil, with its multifarious years, has got so mingled with the Indian polity that it practically defies all solution.

Not only immediately after Independence, but later for almost two decades, the people were led by the euphoria of the struggle made by the Indian National Congress in the matter of Independence struggle. Later, the people fact disheartened with the misrule of the Congress and began to look for an alternative party. Still, they had not arrived at any conclusion. Since then governments had often changed not only at the centre but also in states. But every party held out wide-promises which it could not or had no will to fulfil.

Hence, the people were baffled. This means that one important thing which could instil confidence in the people's mind was electoral reforms. The Supreme Court directed the Election Commission in May, 2002 to ensure that the condidates who fight elections to legislative bodies should have their criminal background, if any, brought to the voters' notice. For this, a five point mandatory agenda was released by the Supreme Court for the adherence of the Election Commission.

The Supreme Court reiterated this mandate in March, 2003.

All out efforts are being made by the judiciary and the Election Commission to ensure free and fair elections in India which are the corner stone of democracy and which alone can ensure the survival of democratic republic in India. Let us hope for the best.

The Anti-Defection law in the Tenth Schedule of the Constitution was supposed to prevent defections, but in effect, it has become an enabling law for larger defections, as the Constitution Reforms Commission says, "en bloc defections are permitted".

Thus, much more in the matter of Electoral Reforms needs to be done. Above all, the moral and ethical standard of our elected representatives needs somehow to be raised or they will always be able to find out some loopholes to the great peril of our system.

Safety and Security

A Preview

- ❖ These days—commonly used words
- ❖ National security
- ❖ Social security
- ❖ Nuclear and chemical plants
- ❖ Radiation safety
- ❖ A workshop
- ❖ Discovery of ionised radiation
- ❖ Safety for homes, offices, etc.
- ❖ Law and order
- ❖ Courts
- ❖ National security further explained
- ❖ Nuclear safeguards
- ❖ DRDO kits
- ❖ Jai Jawan, etc.

Safety and security are two common, though allied words, which we often find perpetrated on sheets of newspapers, in books and in common men's day to day conversation these days.

We talk of security of the nation, that is, national security. Sometimes, we get alarmed about it and sometimes we get reassured when we realize that we have grown strong roots of democracy, sovereignty and pride in cultural heritage in our country.

Sometimes, we also talk of social security. Then we talk of the senior citizens, the women and children and also of low-paid workers and unemployed youth. We think of such measures as old age pension, unemployment allowance, pension to widows, orphans, handicapped and poor persons and scholarships and stipends to poor but meritorious students who want to pursue their studies, and so on.

We also talk of safeguards regarding nuclear and chemical plants. Had proper safety measures been taken by Union Carbide, there would have been no Bhopal tragedy. We should also not forget Chernobyl tragedy. We now have the term Radiation Safety also. It means safety measures for the patients, radiologists and others engaged in the task of getting exposed to radioactive matter in the process of such things as X-rays, scanning and administration of radioactive matter to certain patients such as Iodine-131 to Thyrotoxicosis patients or administration of radioactive rays to cancer patients, etc.

A "Radiation Safety Week" was celebrated in a renowned hospital. A workshop for the purpose was organised. The head of the Department of Radiotherapy said on the occasion, while highlighting the purpose of the workshop that "the workshop was aimed at educating the target population of medical professionals about the source and nature of ionising radiations, besides the interaction of these with matter. Professionals will receive guidance on human development and tissue renewal systems, adverse effects of radiation, working practices and safety guidelines, radiological protection of patients and the personnel, awareness regarding radiation accidents, prevention and management."

The workshop was held in collaboration with Baba Farid University of Health Sciences and the Atomic Energy Regulatory Board (AERB). The higher-ups of both these organisations were also present at the workshop. More than fifty eminent physicians and scientists from all over India having specialised in different fields participated in the workshop with fervent zeal and enthusiasm.

It should be borne in mind that the process of ionised radiation was discovered in the late 19th century. The discovery revolutionized diagnosis of several complicated diseases and thus proved a great boon to humanity. But the use of the new technique was soon discovered to be a double-edged weapon which could, if used without requisite safeguards, prove dangerous or at least deleterious to the users, patients or curers of diseases. Even Madame Curie, the discoverer of radium is said to have died of radiation which caused her cancer.

Thus, such workshops should be organised all over the country to make the people aware of the dangers of excessive exposures to X-rays and the health workers who must take all precautions to save themselves from the adverse effect of radiation which results in some malformation in their body in the absence of adequate safety measures.

Safety also means safety for houses, offices, factories, mills, banks, powerhouses, etc. Several new devices, besides intricate locks and locking systems have been devised. There are hidden sophisticated cameras installed at big emporiums, banks and other financial institutions, at airports, railway stations, at offices, houses and other premises of the VVIP's and affluent people to keep an eye on any possible attacks of burglars or robbers and the like. In store-houses and emporiums, such cameras and TV sets catch the pilferers and other anti-social elements.

Safety also means the process of law and order. The law and order system is maintained by the police, internal security forces and several other organisations which helps us in leading a peaceful life. If such a system were not there, there would be anarchy and chaos. There would have been no civilization and culture.

As CEM Joad points out, "In the absence of an efficient law and order system, the artist could not pursue his work of art, a painter could not paint, a scientist could not invent and a musician could not compose a piece of music." We can say that in such a state, a poet could not compose a poem, a writer, say a novelist could not write his book or novel, a teacher could not prepare his lesson for the class and a student could not study. Even a preacher could not preach, a businessman could not trade, a doctor could not treat patients and even a judge could not administer justice, just as we saw that it became an uphill task for the members of judiciary to deliver judgements during the heyday of terrorism in Punjab.

Mr. Joad admits that there are still burglars there but they are caught by the long hands of law and punished by courts of law as fairly as possible. Now, if a man is physically weak, he need not fear since he cannot be beaten as in the past. If anybody tries to bully him, threaten him or cause him any injury, he can go to a court of law that will protect him from the bullies, tyrants or scoundrels.

Of utmost importance is the national security. Fortunately, we have mighty armed forces and no country in its senses dare attack us. We have already inflicted crushing defeats on Pakistan in 1948, 1965, 1971 and 1999.

In was a misfortune that we were defeated by China who stabbed us in the back in 1962. We, however, got wide awake thereafter and started building up our military strength.

Now, India is a nuclear force. She believes in the policy of "No-first-use". But, we have the capacity and capability to deal a death-dealing blow to the enemy who dare attack us with nuclear weapons. DRDO has also developed kits to safeguard against possible adverse effects of nuclear, biological or chemical warfare.

Let us be proud of our kisans, jawans and scientists :

"Jai Jawan, Jai Kisan, Jai Vigyan" is a slogan which Mr. Atal Behari Vajpayee has given us.

It is in our own interest to give attention to law and order and safety measures to protect ourselves from danger. In a press release, the Delhi Police highlighted some of the important precautions which the people should take to make their homes safe ones. The same are adumbrated below:

1. All windows and doors should have strong iron grills. Use of chain latches is recommended. Care should be taken to make the spaces for air conditioners and coolers secure.

2. While going out always put some lights on.

3. Keep a dog, if possible.

4. Anti-burglary gadgets should be installed such that on any forced or clandestine entry—alarm is activated.

5. Chowkidar should be provided with a torch, a whistle and a lathi. He should also be advised to keep in touch with beat patrolling policemen.

6. Strangers like balloon sellers, courier service employees, hawkers etc. should not be allowed entry in the home. Particulars of plumbers, electricians, whitewash masons etc. should be known to you.

7. Before keeping a domestic help get his/her antecedents verified from your nearest police station.

Life has become very precarious these days. Safety measures have to be adopted anywhere and everywhere. One advertisement concerning a safety device for homes and commercial establishments is worth being reproduced :

"Meant for Homes and Commercial Establishments, these Microprocessor controlled systems have sensors that detect forced entry, unwarranted movement, smoke, as well as LPG (gas) leaks. There are panic switches to initiate an alarm or call for help in case of an emergency. Besides local sirens and strobes, the system can be fitted with an auto-dialer, which in the event of an emergency automatically dials out to help message to your phone, mobiles, or to a central monitoring station (CMS)."

Now, when these and other sophisticated safety measures have come into being, a large number of rich people are installing them in their palaces, offices, showrooms, mills and other business places. Such devices are being increasingly installed in banks and other financial institutions, cinemahouses, markets, railway stations, bus stands and other public places. Such devices are still by and large beyond the pocket of the common man. But, then, it is only the moneyed people who need them and they are going over to them more and more every passing moment.

Positive Use of Internet

A Preview

- ❖ Mix of good & evil
- ❖ Beginning
- ❖ Cyber cafes
- ❖ Online info
- ❖ World Wide Web
- ❖ Internet
- ❖ Ocean of library
- ❖ Sharing information

Life is about a mix of good and evil. So is the Internet. For all the good it does us, cyberspace has its dark sides too. Unlike conventional communities though, there are no policemen patrolling the information superhighway, leaving it open to everything from Trojan horses and viruses to cyber stalking, trademark counterfeiting and cyber terrorism.

Computer has brought about revolutionary transformations of knowledge, the way it is being acquired and the means by which it is being inculcated. It all began with World Wide Web which acts as a networking system connected to the server and which helps provide ready-made and fast portal of information. Internet is its practical means for providing information and messages.

Started as an important source of information storage machinery, computer has the wider usability in defense institutions and for its various purposes, but slowly it gained access to other domains of human activities. However, the rapid growth of Internet gave rise to the establishment of Cyber Cafes all over the world.

Internet is the speedy means of communication whereby information can be made available easily, messages can be exchanged and wide and varied spectrum of valuable information can be gathered in a very short span of time. In fact, Internet has become the prime source of information encompassing almost all subjects, entities, nations, establishments, field of inquiries, institutions, industries, domains, persons and places.

In this hi-tech era, Internet has acquired an urgent necessity for people of all walks of life as more and more Cyber Cafes gave way to young and old reaching out for easy access for vital information. As a user friendly means, Internet gained tremendous response from the educated professionals, students and business tycoons. Now it has become possible for an individual to send instant message to anyone living in any part of the world in a jiffy and he can get back the reply within minutes. While sitting in his bed room, a person can have all the incidents, news reports, messages. Internet is useful for all; for academicians, researchers, professionals and students—as study materials, vital statistics, readymade information are easily accessible. Students could study, make notes, fill up the forms which are available online or download them, go through the examination results which are placed online before they get published.

Academicians and researchers need not visit libraries as Internet has become a vast ocean of library on any subject, topic and field of studies. Although some of the websites are payee, most of them are accessible for making research papers done in a very short span of time.

For IT professionals, Internet has become all the more relevant as the latest technology is available online except for new patents. Sending and receiving mails is a part of one's life. And from scientists to the layman, information on all genre of life can be accessed through Internet. Railway information like schedule, ticket availability and departure time, to the information on agriculture, economy, including the budget details of every year is displayed online.

For writers and authors, Internet is a must, particularly for patent document writers who can access all the inventions that have been established. Internet is user-friendly, less expensive and speedy in transferring messages, information and relevant data. In this fast paced world, Internet has become the very part and parcel of human activities. It would not be wrong to say that it has become the lifeline of most of the people.

Waste Management

A Preview

- ❖ Phenomenal increase in population
- ❖ Biomedical waste
- ❖ Example
- ❖ Pollution, etc.
- ❖ Recycling
- ❖ IMA
- ❖ Recent attention
- ❖ Other waste—examples

In the modern world when the population has phenominally increased and human activities are ever on the increase, the corresponding increase in waste is natural. But it is equally important that this waste should be managed properly and as early as possible such that it does not act as a factor for diminishing return in the matter of benefit that we get from various research and services.

Take for instance, the biomedical waste. It was considered necessary to have disposable syringe for all cases of taking blood samples, blood transfusion, inoculation, etc. But the proper disposal of used syringes is a problem. They are thrown haphazardly, and lead to pollution and choking of drains and create other problems. Some unscrupulous elements are also likely to reuse them or recycle them unhygienically for use.

This is only one illustration. There must be hundreds of other wastes like used drug bottles, etc.

It is heartening to note that a lot of attention is now being given to manage waste, particularly biomedical waste, though one should expect much more and better results regarding management of all kinds of waste.

It is heartening to learn that the Indian Medical Association has come forward to make arrangements for the proper disposal of biomedical waste.

The biomedical waste should be segregated into containers/bags and proper attention should be paid to its storage, transportation, treatment and disposal.

Similarly, waste of all kinds should be avoided or managed. The broken pieces of glass, chinaware, plastic, etc. can be used somewhere usefully for decoration or other purposes or properly despatched for disposal by the municipal or other authorities, so that they do not become a nuisance. Similar is the case with polythene bags.

Unemployment

A Preview

- ❖ A baffling problem
- ❖ The reverse gear
- ❖ Skilled, unskilled & educated unemployment
- ❖ Low salaries offered
- ❖ Slackening construction work
- ❖ New rules
- ❖ Galloping population
- ❖ Vocational courses
- ❖ Cabinet decision
- ❖ Technical training

- ❖ Govt. departments and PSUs
- ❖ Computer
- ❖ Contract basis system

- ❖ Unwanted graduates
- ❖ SSI small houses
- ❖ Big homes
- ❖ Rozgar Yojanas
- ❖ Government's dilemma
- ❖ Liberalisation
- ❖ Distance education

There is no denying the fact that unemployment is one of the most baffling problems India is facing today. At present more than three crores (out of a population of 125 crore *i.e.* 3.7 per cent) Indians are unemployed.

On the one hand, India went for industrialisation and mechanization in a big way. It was hoped that the installation of new industrial plants will generate more employment opportunities. Without any foresight people were appointed in government departments and public sector units (PSUs) in such large numbers that in many cases, many of them did not have any work to do. As, with the passage of time, their salaries and perks increased, they became a burden on the government and governing bodies, so much so that the major earnings of all departments and concerns were eaten away by the salaries, allowances and pensions of these employees.

Now, the reverse gear has been applied. The government and the governing bodies are trying hard to find out means to do away most of their employees. This situation has been created more glaringly by the advent of the computer which, at first, was thought by many to create more jobs.

Now, the situation is such that not only the unskilled, but also the skilled and highly educated youths are roaming in the streets in search of jobs. Many of them are unable to find any job. Some of them, who are even able to get some job, find the job far from being creative as they are offered very low salaries and little prospects of promotion or progress.

Now, a new system, as prevailing in the west, called "contract basis system" has been started. According to this system, a post is offered on contract basis for a few years only and thereafter, the contract is renewed or extended, or, as most often is the case, the employee has to fend for himself.

The tragedy is that even in this system on "contract basis", the salary offered is often very low.

For instance, there are reports that the B.Ed. trained teachers are at some places being offered jobs on contract basis at ₹ 6000 per month when the minimum wages for an unskilled worker as fixed by the central government are more than its double.

While in the labour sector much of work such as that of construction projects has slacked, the lack of vision in our educationists is the cause for unemployment among the educated. Though now the scene is quickly changing, in the past many decades, graduates have been churned out by Universities as nuts and bolts from factories.

Another reason for this sorry state of affairs is the dwindling profits of the small scale entrepreneurs. When the businesses of these people are showing a downward trend, they cannot employ more people and have to retrench some of their staff.

As far as the big houses are concerned, they cannot keep more men because they have got latest machines and gadgets each of which can do the work of many men. One single factor responsible for this large scale unemployment is still the scenario of galloping population which though slightly checked, has defied all solutions to a tangible extent.

In order to come over the growing menace of unemployment, the central and state governments have started several schemes. Apart from the Rozgar Yojanas under which liberal loans are given to the youths who want to start their own enterprises, there are other schemes to provide free training to the needy.

For instance, the Bharat Vikas Parishad Charitable Trust, Punjab, has started several new vocational courses for the disabled and for those belonging to economically weaker sections of society under the Direct Central Assistance Scheme of the Ministry of Human Development, New Delhi.

It is, indeed, a fact that most of the government revenue collection in states, as well as at the centre is spent on salaries, perks, pensions and office expenses. Very little and sometimes only a negligible amount is left for development. Actually the various pay commissions have increased employees' salaries excessively. When many more young men are unemployed, the same amount as is paid to one employee could be spent to pay to two or more persons.

Sometime back the Prime Minister of India, said in his opening remarks at the meeting of the Council on Trade and Industry in New Delhi :

"The Cabinet has decided to vigorously pursue labour reforms. Now the report of the National Labour Commission has also been received. I appeal to all major political parties for a consensus on labour reforms, so that we can soon give effect to the consensus through appropriate legislation. Above all, these long-delayed labour reforms will create more employment opportunities, thus fulfilling our shared objective of achieving growth with jobs."

Thus, the main thrust of the government is to "achieve growth with jobs." The objective is certainly noble and it evinces sincerity. The only thing is that the business houses and political parties should join hands with the government in bringing about the much delayed reforms to change the system where the poor people and the workers do not perpetually remain at the receiving end, and the unemployed youth can get employment.

The Prime Minister also advised the business houses to reform themselves to restore people's fading interest in the system. He said:

"Businesses, too must reform themselves. The principle of good corporate governance is the touchstone of your commitment to reforms. Recent reports of accounting scandals elsewhere in the world are beginning to worry a lot of people about the bomb shells hidden in the boom-time economy", he said.

It is clear that the Prime Minister was talking about the Xerox Corp. Accounting scandal had shaken many people's faith in the policy of globalisation and liberalisation, and he hit the nail on the head when he said, that the government could not allow "people's faith in economic liberalisation to be shaken by those who do business with an ethical deficit."

Whereas it was believed that liberalisation would provide more employment opportunities, the reverse has happened.

We must, however, need not be excessively pessimistic. The modern youths are quite awakened. They know that future prospects for them lie only in science subjects and those particularly in such fields as computer science and technology. The only difficulty is that such courses provided by certain institutions are too costly. But when an institution like the Punjab Technical University has started such courses at much cheaper rates through its distance programmes, there is an overwhelming response from the enthusiastic, thirsting students. Here is a report:

"Enrolment for the B.Sc (Computer Science and Technology) programme launched last year by Punjab Technical University (PTU) is likely to touch 4000 as the course has received a tremendous response from students.

Reports received from various study centres of PTU across Punjab indicate that the B.Sc. course is receiving the maximum enquiries from students. The two-year programme has been launched keeping in mind the interests of diploma holders."

We know that now the online campus education is also available. This can facilitate imparting of education regarding new courses which are hoped to enable the degree/diploma holders to get easy employment.

Teachers' Day

A Preview

- ❖ We celebrate several days
- ❖ Children' Day, Fathers' day and Valentine Day
- ❖ Teachers' Day is the birthday of Dr. S. Radhakrishnan
- ❖ Radhakrishnan was an intelligent student
- ❖ He excelled in the academic field, became the VC of Andhra University
- ❖ Every teacher should develop the qualities of an ideal one
- ❖ Teachers earn poor salaries and so, their families suffer
- ❖ A teacher can transform his students into real human-beings
- ❖ On the Teachers' Day, teachers are offered gifts and awards
- ❖ The government should accept valid demands of teachers
- ❖ Teachers should strive to build the careers of their students

We celebrate several days as national and international days to commemorate the memories of important persons and events, or to bring to light a lost cause or to give due importance to a particular section of society.

One popular day, celebrated particularly by the children is the Children's Day which is celebrated on 14th November every year to celebrate the birthday of our first Prime Minister, Pt. Jawaharlal Nehru who was a great lover of children. Another day which the children love to celebrate is the Mother's Day which is celebrated on 14th May every year. On this day, children offer cards, sweets and flowers to their mothers and seek their blessings. Still another day is Father's Day which is celebrated on 18th June. The young people in India have now got awakened to celebrating the Valentine's Day on 14th February every year. There are several other days we love to celebrate such as birthdays, marriage anniversaries and the like at domestic and local levels.

It is in this light that we have to study the celebration of Teacher's Day. This day is celebrated every year on 5th September to commemorate the birth of Dr. Sarvepalli Radhakrishnan, who was born on 5th September, 1888.

It is well-known that like Bertrand Russell and Dr. Zakir Hussain Dr. Radhakrishnan was a great educationist and like the latter, he became the President of India. Like the former, and may be, to a greater degree, he was a great philosopher.

As a philosopher, Dr. Radhakrishnan laid stress on recognition of the spirit. He focussed on the purpose of life, importance of means vis-a-vis ends and service to motherland and humanity at large.

It is as an ideal teacher that most relevantly places Dr. Radhakrishnan to be a role-model before us whose birthday is fit to be celebrated as Teacher's Day simply to say that he was a great and dedicated teacher is not enough. That he inspired his students with his absorption in the duties allotted to him will also not be adequate to describe his greatness.

Dr. Radhakrishnan was a voracious reader and a bibliophile. He was a brilliant student who topped his B.A. and M.A.

examinations. After completing his studies, he became an Assistant Professor of Philosophy in Madras Presidency College and later joined the University of Mysore and then moved to Calcutta University. Still later, he shifted to Oxford, Cambridge and Harvard Universities. Later, he became the Vice-Chancellor of Andhra University. He was a great idealist and loved his students who in turn loved him immensely. He also represented India in the UNESCO as a renowned educationist. It is said that when he left a job at a particular place, a vast sea of students went to see him off at the railway station.

This clearly shows how much the students loved Dr. Radhakrishnan who led a life of simplicity and austerity without falling a prey to materialism which is now haunting our society like a ruthless monster.

All this detail was necessary to explain the importance of the day and the man who is behind it. But all these efforts become worth-while only if we get the necessary inspiration and urge for concrete action from the man concerned. It is not so necessary to highlight the importance of the role of the teacher in society. To say that the teacher is a nation-builder is only a cliche. The point is that every teacher should try to develop in himself the true qualities of an ideal teacher like Dr. Radhakrishnan. A teacher can be a nation-builder in the true sense only if he has the spirit of dedication in him and if he takes his job as a missionary of education.

Teachers' Day is, in reality, a day for introspection for all, including the teachers, and not a day just for celebration. And if on this day, the teachers are offered greeting-cards, flowers, sweets, gifts and presents by their loving students, it is a token of love and respect, if these are offered in right spirit. There is no doubt that students are, by and large, innocent creatures and are only sometimes misled by political leaders and even their money-minded parents. All this has to be changed. Occasional parent-teacher meetings in schools augur well for all concerns.

It is good that on this day functions, seminars and workshops are held in schools and elsewhere and awards are presented to deserving and dedicated teachers on state and national levels. But one sometimes feels peeved to find teachers wearing black badges and celebrating the day as a "black day" when their demands are not met. It will be worthwhile if the government accepts their demands much earlier if they are found genuine.

Let us, as students, take an oath on this day that we shall pay full attention to our teachers and show due regard and respect to them. If we ourselves are teachers, let us resolve to work whole-heartedly with a spirit of dedication to teach, guide and train the future helmsmen of our country who have been given over to us by our nation in our custody to make them great leaders. Let us take real interest in removing darkness from this land by spreading light of literacy, knowledge and education.

Dowry System

A Preview

- ❖ Meaning
- ❖ Ancient line of thought
- ❖ Sacrifices done by girl's parents
- ❖ Girl's sacrifice
- ❖ The Supreme Court
- ❖ No compulsion
- ❖ Vijaynagar empire
- ❖ Demands
- ❖ Taunts, torture, murder, suicide
- ❖ Exemplary punishment
- ❖ Media's role
- ❖ Purpose
- ❖ In medieval times
- ❖ Girls affection for her parents
- ❖ Giving of gifts
- ❖ Common people
- ❖ Materialism
- ❖ Present position
- ❖ Ever-increasing demands
- ❖ Laws
- ❖ People's own efforts

Dowry implies cash, jewellery and household and other goods given to the bride at the time of marriage.

In ancient times, this dowry system was probably started by some people to enable the young boy and girl to start a new household without any inconvenience. It was perhaps believed that when the boy's parents had to do a lot to make their son stand on his own legs in business or some service, there was nothing wrong if the girl's parents also put in their mite to help the young couple to start their journey on the path of the world.

There was nothing wrong with such kind of line of thought so far as it went. Of course, it is as much the duty of the girl's parents to help the couple to start their new home as that of the boy's parents. But in such a line of thought there does not seem to be any element of compulsion or obligation. Here there is a question of doing one's duty only, and the girl's parents could provide the goods and necessities according to their capacity, resources, circumstances and will.

Moreover, it should be noted that the girl's parents rear the girl according to their resources with utmost love and affection. They provide her education and means of good health and life. On all this, they spend a lot. Still, the main question is not that of expenditure, it is to be understood that the girl after her marriage has to live in her in-laws' house and according to the arrangements made by them. Hereafter, she becomes a part of their household as a member of the family. She is supposed to promote their cause as that is also her own home now onwards. She has to adjust and adapt herself according to the atmosphere in the new house.

Keeping all this in mind, why should the girl be a liability on her parents? Why should it be obligatory on their part to provide their girl with so much cash and jewellary and so many items of necessity and luxury when she is going away to become a part of a new family about which she often doesn't know much and the new world is almost entirely shrouded in mystery for her?

This does not mean that the girl or her parents are not or are supposed not to be attached to each other. On the other hand, the parents love their daughters as much as their sons. At least, this is so in homes the members of which are enlightened. There may be some rare families in which there is discrimination against girls. And it is an immensely acknowledged fact that girls go on loving their parents even more than their brothers do all their lives.

When we realize the significance of family love, affection and devotion and the spirit of mutual sacrifice and self-effacement, we cannot ignore the fact that no parents would like to send their daughters empty-handed at the time of their marriage. Instead, they would certainly like to load them with gifts whatever they can reasonably afford and which they think will be useful to the girl and will be liked by her husband and inlaws.

This giving of gifts to their daughters at the time of their marriage is prevalent in all communities and societies even western countries. Even the Supreme Court of India has allowed these gifts at the time of marriage to a certain extent.

As already stated, there was no compulsion in the matter of giving such gifts to their daughters or sons-in-law. It depended on one's own will, pleasure, convenience and resourcefulness, and there was never or hardly ever any resentment on the question of a gift being insignificant or below the expectation of the son-in-law or other members in the family of the in-laws. The father-in-law and the mother-in-law of the bride almost always treated her as their own daughter and nobody ever taunted or rebuked her for bringing less or useless dowry. Nobody ever looked a gift horse in the mouth.

As times passed and the world became more and more materialistic and man's lust for wealth and power and love of luxuries increased, the son's parents and other members of the family began to expect more and more from the girl's side as dowry. In the middle ages, the dowry system started assuming alarming proportions, though still not quite pronouncedly. For instance, in the now defunct Vijayanagar Empire in south India, dowry system is said to be a bane of enormous dimensions.

The most obnoxious thing is that the boy's parents now make hefty demands which are sometimes beyond the resources of the girl's parents. Car, airconditioner, refrigerator, desert cooler, TV set, computer, scooter, and all such and other items besides a big amount of money in cash, lands and jewellery are demanded. The poor girl's parents have to beg for loans or mortgage their houses or sell some property to fufil the demands of the boy's greedy parents and elders.

There is virtually the sale of boys in the market. The girl's merits and high education are all ignored or taken lightly and Mammon-worship plays the major role in this horrid drama.

Even after meeting almost all the demands of the greedy in-laws, the girl has to take note of new demands and meet them expeditiously or else, if her parents are unable or unwilling to play the second fiddle, the poor creature must accept regular taunts and torture from various members of her in-laws' family and be ready to commit suicide or to be burnt alive by the heartless mother-in-law with collaboration or connivance or complicity of some or other members in the family and sometimes even her adorable husband.

How can such greedy people understand the meaning of the rights or empowerment of women unless some stringent laws are passed to give exemplary punishments to the cruel recalcitrants and violators of sacred human rights? Such people make a frontal attack on women's rights and female dignity and should not be let off scot-free in any manner.

No doubt, we have a number of laws both at the state and union levels to deal effectively with the dowry-seekers. But almost daily we hear about dowry deaths and tortures, and these laws either have no teeth or are not properly and universally implemented. Those who have some links at higher levels, can manage to escape all the tentacles of laws and roam freely on the streets even after causing the death of the poor girls who come to their house to become a part and parcel of it.

Of course, law alone cannot solve this problem. Much depends upon the people themselves. It is essential that dowry system should be condemned in school courses and young boys should take a vow that they would never demand dowry. They should try to convince their elders that dowry is only a primitive institution, the main thing now being the girl's merits.

Similarly, the girls should take a vow that they would not marry a dowry seeker at any cost. There should be a far-spread campaign over the TV, on the cinema screen and in the newspapers and magazines against this menace. Seminars and functions should be held to convey to the people the dangers of this system. Such a campaign should not be limited to urban areas only. The youth themselves should go to the rural areas to spread the message against dowry system.

The Role of Newspapers
or
Power (or Freedom) of the Press

A Preview

- ❖ An important role in the life of modern man
- ❖ News, views, etc.
- ❖ Articles, advertisements
- ❖ Poems, stories, etc.
- ❖ Vested interests twist the news
- ❖ Some newspapers work only for money
- ❖ A mighty weapon
- ❖ PPSC Recruitment scam
- ❖ Watergate scandal
- ❖ A veteran journalist's views
- ❖ FDI's entry in the print media

The newspapers play an important role in the life of the modern man. A typical urban man even when in a hurry to prepare for going to an office, has the habit of reading his favourite newspaper at the time of breakfast or even earlier. He may get his breakfast or not but he must get his newspaper.

In the newspaper we read news, views, reviews and previews. The newspapers also carry several kinds of articles and advertisements. We have articles regarding political, social and economic matters, matters concerning children, women, students, the youth in general, sports, cinema, TV, etc. The burning problems of the day are also discussed in newspapers. Then there are editorial comments. There is also a column called "Readers' Column" or "Editors' Mail" which gives views of the readers on various kinds of problems and aspects of life.

In the newspapers we also have poems, stories and reviews of books.

Some newspapers are owned by vested interests who give only biased twist to events. Some newspapers only aim at earning money and publish gory and unpleasant pictures and details of incidents which do a lot of harm to certain individuals and sections of society.

Here is a report depicting the negative side of the journalistic business when it tends to only earn money, forgetting all responsibilities to the sentiments and sensibilities of the society at large and the pursued victims in particular :

"A jounalist when filing a human interest story relies on his own compassionate streak to lend a soft touch to his subject, a touch which will in addition to presenting the facts objectively, also communicate to the readers a sense of compassion and sympathetic understanding. Which is why when Princess Diana was killed in a car crash as she and Dodi tried to shrug off the paparazzi who were chasing them for yet another juicy, meaty, money-spinning photograph, it shook the social conscience of Britain who like vultures were feeding on the sensational tabloid tit-bits. The paparazzi were accused of being cruel, and insensitive. They could never hope to understand the agony of the couple they were chasing, whose privacy they were intruding upon and selling to the collective majority. The same streak of compassion is what prevents newspaper editors from choosing less harsh headlines, toning down their unconfirmed accusations and avoiding giving gory details or photographs of accidents, rapes and murders."

There is, no doubt, that even the mightiest kings and others from royal families and politicians who may not be afraid of anybody are afraid of the newspapers. But this also puts a great responsibility on the newspapers to be always conscious of their duty towards society and individuals that comprise this society. It is the duty of the newspapers to play a positive and not a negative role towards society, country and mankind at large.

Power/Freedom of the Press

The press, the fourth estate, has immense powers, probably not enjoyed by any of the mightiest kings, as already stated.

It was the press that brought to light the Watergate Scandal and was instrumental in ending the corrupt rule of the American President Nixon who had the power to destroy the whole world just by pressing a black button.

It was the press which had told about Americans' oppressive practices against the Vietnamese and it was the press again which hightighted the Bill Clinton-Monica Lewinsky affairs.

In the Punjab, it was the press which became instrumental in highlighting the biggest (PPSC) recruitment scam in the country and in pointing out the possible involvement of some members of the judiciary in this crime.

We must appreciate the views of a redoubtable journalist, the President of the Editors' Guild of India :

"I am all for free flow of news and views. I do not subscribe to the concept of pre-censorship or curbs. The Indian Press has been quite liberal and forward looking in accommodating varied viewpoints, howsoever unpalatable. We have also been practising the concept of freedom of the Press objectively and without being selective."

The concept of pre-censorship holds ground when the press becomes irresponsible and partial and when it speaks in a voice detrimental to the national interests, as for instance, when it incites communal riots, or takes sides with the vested interests ignoring the interests of the common man or the victims.

The learned journalist, however, admits that there is some problem, indeed :

"Herein lies the real problem. The newspaper industry has been totally commercialised and it, understandably, follows cut throat practices of most business establishments.

Nothing wrong in running newspapers professionally and as a fair business proposition. The danger lies in allowing them to be playthings of foreign money and vested interests in the name of freedom of the Press."

The editor was commenting in a powerful article on the allowing of the government the entry of the Foreign Direct Investment (FDI) in the print media.

The learned journalist in his reaction to the FDIs entry in the print media said :

"Information has to be free. Views can be varied. What can be disquieting is an attempt to control the thought process through foreign money. He who pays the piper calls the tune. Herein lies the danger to free swadeshi thinking from the grassroots upward."

Education : A Fundamental Right

A Preview

- ❖ Beginning
- ❖ Objective
- ❖ Scope
- ❖ Benefits for Children

- ❖ Free and Compulsory Education
- ❖ Millenium Development Goal
- ❖ Past Achievements
- ❖ Future Projections

The Right of Children to Free and Compulsory Education Act came into force in the country on April 1, 2010. With this, India joined a select group of a few nations where education is a fundamental right. Making elementary education an entitlement for the children in the 6-14 years age group, the Act will directly benefit close to one crore children who do not go to school at present. Nearly 92 lakh children, who had either dropped out of schools or never been to any educational institution, will now get elementary education as it will be binding on the part of the local authorities and the State governments to ensure that all children in the 6-14 years age group get schooling.

As per the Act, private educational institutions should reserve 25 per cent seats for children from the weaker sections of society. The Centre and the States have agreed to share the financial burden in the ratio of 55:45, while the Finance Commission has given ₹ 25,000 crore to the States for implementing the Act.

The school management committee or the local authority will identify the dropouts or out-of-school children aged above six and admit them in classes appropriate to their age after giving some special training.

As per the Act, the schools need to have minimum facilities such as adequate teachers, playground and infrastructure. The State Governments or the local authorities will determine the neighbourhood schools by undertaking school mapping.

The coming into effect of the Right of Children to Free and Compulsory Education (RTE) Act, 2009 marks a historic moment for the children of India. This Act serves as a building block to ensure that every child has right to guaranteed quality elementary education. The state with the help of families and communities, has a legal obligation to fulfil this duty. Few countries in the world have such a national provision to ensure both free and child-centered, child-friendly education to help all children develop their fullest potential. There are an estimated nine million children and young people between the ages of six and 14 out of school. Without India, the world cannot reach the Millennium Development Goal of having every child complete primary school.

The gains in India's education system over the past few decades have been tremendous, reaching close to universal enrolment in Grade I.

The RTE Act provides a ripe platform to reach the unreached, with specific provisions for disadvantaged groups, such as child labourers, migrant children, children with special needs, or those who have a "disadvantage owing to social, cultural, economical, geographical, linguistic, gender or such other factor". In view of reducing disparities, private schools must admit at least 25 per cent of children belonging to these groups.

With RTE, India can emerge as a global leader in achieving the Millennium Development Goal of ensuring that all children complete their primary schooling. It is a challenge, but the resources and political will fuelling progress on RTE, not an impossible task. The world is watching India as it positions itself to take its rightful leadership role in education on the global stage. Millions of children will benefit from this initiative ensuring quality education with equity.

RTE will propel this great nation to even higher heights of prosperity and productivity, by guaranteeing all children their right to a quality education and a brighter future.

Poverty is A Curse

A Preview

- ❖ Reports
- ❖ Johnson
- ❖ Depoverization
- ❖ Tagore
- ❖ Fault—society, govt. etc.
- ❖ Self respect
- ❖ Population
- ❖ Literary figures
- ❖ Byron
- ❖ Responsibilities
- ❖ Sometimes meets death
- ❖ Low quality of life

We sometimes gloat over the tremendous progress India has made in several fields. There is no doubt that now India has turned from a food deficit state into a food surplus state. India has a strong industrial base. India has large resources of foreign exchange. India is the largest producer of milk in the world.

In spite of this, the poor people's lot is miserable. The fact is that most of the national wealth is just in a few hands. The real prosperity has gone only to the industrial and business rich at the top who get loans of crores of rupees from banks and forget to repay the capital as well as the interest.

A vast population of India still sleeps on the pavements. The poor have to go without food even. There is no proper arrangement for drinking water, sewerage, healthcare, education, employment and housing for the poor. A number of schemes in various fields have, no doubt, been started. But red-tapism and corruption torpedo even the well-intentioned schemes.

Although the percentage of the poor is decreasing, yet their total number is increasing. It is because of the rapid increase in population which is one of the most crucial factors in the matter of perpetuity of poverty in India.

It is to be noted that many people in India, particularly the poor low income illiterate people do not believe in the population control system and family welfare programmes being pursued at national level. They think that the more members they have in the family, the more hands and earning capacity they have. They forget that each pair of hands brings a mouth and a stomach to feed also. They should be given education and taught to limit their families.

A man shrouded in a life of poverty, cannot show his real worth. As Dr. Samuel Johnson has said in his "Vanity of Human wishes",

"Slow rises worth by poverty depressed"

We know that so many great literary figures like Goldsmith, Charles Lamb, John Keats, Bronte sisters, etc., though famous in the history of English literature, could not reach the pinnacle of glory, at least not in their life, mainly because of poverty. And when any of them got success in their own life, it was on a limited scale and not as grand as it would have been had they been rich.

Unfortunately, poverty dehumanizes a man and drives him to the thoughts of bondage and slavery. Such a man cannot appreciate or understand the real value of freedom.

Lord Byron has said in his famous poem, "The Prisoner of Chillon"

"My very chains and I grew friends,
For much a long communion tends
To make us what we are.
Even I Heaved my relief with a sigh."

—The Prisoner of Chillon

The Indian Nobel Laureate, Rabindranath Tagore, says in his "Reminiscences", while comparing the lives of two birds— "The tame bird" and "the free bird" :

"The tame bird was in a cage, the free bird was in the forest.
They met when the time came, it was a decree of fate.
The free bird cries, O my love, let us fly, to the wood.'
The cage bird whispers, 'come hither, let us both live in the cage.'
Says the free bird,
'Among bars, where is there room to spread one's wings.'
'Alas ! cries the cage bird,'
I should not know where to sit perched in the cage."

Thus, a man dehumanized by poverty cries to find out excuses to remain a slave even when he is freed from bondage. Freedom demands shouldering of responsibilities and a dehumanised person who has been demoralised and frustrated beyond the proper limit finds it an uphill task to take up the challenge of responsibilities and thus loses the chance of all progress and growth in life.

In this respect, the fault lies also with the society and politicians and governments also all across the world. We daily read about suicides by workers, petty shopkeepers and farmers due to poverty.

Sometimes, even a brilliant man who has been ignored by all concerned, can feel the burden of life too heavy and feel frustrated and longing to meet death.

Thus, even while helping the poor, care should be taken that the step is not taken in a way that hurts their sense of self-respect.

Poverty is mainly responsible for the low quality of life most of the Indians are enjoying at present.

www.ingramcontent.com/pod-product-compliance
Lightning Source LLC
Chambersburg PA
CBHW051813150726

47998CB00001B/128